# What's the Matter
# with Today's
# Experimental Music?

**Contemporary Music Studies**

A series of books edited by Nigel Osborne, University of Edinburgh, UK

This book is part of a series. The publisher will accept continuation orders which may be cancelled at any time and which provide for automatic billing and shipping of each title in the series upon publication. Please write for details.

# What's the Matter with Today's Experimental Music?

## Organized Sound Too Rarely Heard

By

**Leigh Landy**

*University of Amsterdam, The Netherlands*

**harwood academic publishers**
chur • reading • paris • philadelphia • tokyo • melbourne

**Harwood Academic Publishers**

Post Office Box 90
Reading, Berkshire RG1 8JL
United Kingdom

58, rue Lhomond
75005 Paris
France

5301 Tacony Street, Drawer 330
Philadelphia, Pennsylvania 19137
United States of America

3-14-9, Okubo
Shinjuku-ku, Tokyo 169
Japan

Private Bag 8
Camberwell, Victoria 3124
Australia


**Library of Congress Cataloging-in-Publication Data**

Landy, Leigh, 1951–
    What's the matter with today's experimental music? : organized
sound too rarely heard/Leigh Landy.
        p.   cm. — (Contemporary music studies ; v. 4)
    Includes bibliographical references and index.
    ISBN 3–7186–5168–8
    1. Avant-garde (Music)  2. Music—20th century—History and
criticism.  I. Title.  II. Series.
ML197.L26   1991
780'.9'04—dc20                                                91–19226
                                                                    CIP
                                                                    MN

# Contents

v

# Introduction to the Series

The rapid expansion and diversification of contemporary music is explored in this international series of books for contemporary musicians. Leading experts and practitioners present composition today in all aspects—its techniques, aesthetics and technology, and its relationships with other disciplines and currents of thought—as well as using the series to communicate actual musical materials.

The series also features monographs on significant twentieth-century composers not extensively documented in the existing literature.

NIGEL OSBORNE

# Preface

The text before you concerns the lot of the music of sounds (and not just notes), more generally known today as experimental music. This lot, as demonstrated throughout the entire book, has been a peculiar one, if not downright disappointing. One can state simply that music is probably the most isolated of the modern arts. Recently there has been no growth in musical experimentation, but instead there has been a negative trend. Its propagation has also known better times. As something is clearly the matter, and as there has been so much added to our musical language and alphabet through experimentation, this book intends to look into the unhappy state of our art.

The subject of the following text is, therefore, to inspect and evaluate what is happening to musical experimentation, where things might have gone wrong and what might be done. Several chapters or parts thereof have appeared as separate articles during the last eight years and have been modified as needed. More than half of the chapters have been written specifically for this publication. Nonexperimental contemporary music is treated superficially in the following pages (neither lengthy examples nor analyses will be found here) as the author has assumed that music based upon craftsmanship above innovation has always been and will always be a large, but not necessarily important, part of our musical landscape. Perhaps this sector of music performance practice receives more public attention than experimental music (as has been the case throughout most periods); nevertheless, it is the progressive composer who most often enters our music history books. Thus the work of our musical pioneers of the last forty years is of relevance here.

Dividing his time between composition, musicology and music dramaturgy in audio-visual contexts, the author has attempted to design this book so that it could be of interest to all involved in modern music in one way or another, including those "just" appreciating this music. Readers whose knowledge of contemporary music is elementary are encouraged to read the current text after having read a survey book of music after 1950. Terms like *musique concrète* are not defined as this survey knowledge has been assumed (although essential terms like "experimental music" will be presented in the first chapter). In several cases it will be discovered that we are lacking a complete terminology for today's experimental music. Some suggestions are provided to better this situation.

This book's aim is to incite more composers, musicians and musicologists to get this music out into the world and to stimulate the creation of new experimental works. However, to achieve this, the availability of a better terminology and aesthetics of experimental music will be necessary, as well as better treatment of this music in our schools, on our radios, in our newspapers and specialized journals and in our concert halls. The current text makes several suggestions along these lines.

The following introduction will attempt to delineate the field of discussion. Then the next four chapters will concentrate on extra-musical subjects of relevance before a status report is given on experimental music's (lack of) development in recent years in Part 3. A brief survey of contemporary music today bridges these first three parts to the book's conclusion, an optimistic attempt to sketch experimental music's potential in the future. After the conclusion, Part 6 provides ten descriptions of experimental compositions illustrating a number of points brought forth in the first five parts of the book.

In the chapters that follow, no heroes are sought, nor are there enemies to be criticized. The book's concern is to focus upon the general movement of music's trends and the seeming dissolution of the great decades of adventure, the 1950s and

1960s, which to the author at least seem rather distant at the moment.

The author would like to thank both Christiane ten Hoopen and Christian Martin Schmidt in Amsterdam for their critical advice after having read the book's first draft. Furthermore, he would like to acknowledge the friendly advice given by Simon Emmerson and Stephen Montague in London, as well as Tom Constanten and especially Peter Frank in California during the various editing phases.

Leigh Landy

**Acknowledgements:** For permission for use of copyright material, both literary and musical, acknowledgement is made to the following:

Chapter I: Shuko Mizuno - *Tone* for piano solo
  (c) 1970 Ongaku No Tomo Sha Corp., Tokyo.
  Robert Moran - *Four Visions*
  (c) 1964 Universal Edition Ltd., London.
Chapter IV: quotations Theo Loevendie
  by permission of Donemus, Amsterdam.
Chapter VI: John Cage - *Concert for Piano and Orchestra*
  (c) 1960 Henmar Press Inc., New York
  John Cage - *Variations IV*
  (c) 1963 Henmar Press Inc., New York.
Chapter X: reuse of my article
  by permission of Swets & Zeitlinger bv (Interface), Lisse, Netherlands.
Chapter XVIa: György Ligeti - *Ten Pieces for Wind Quintet*
  by permission of the publishers B. Schott's Söhne, Mainz.
Chapter XVIb: Luciano Berio - *Sequenza III*
  (c) 1968 Universal Edition Ltd., London.
Chapter XVIc: Elliot Carter - *Concerto for Orchestra*
  (c) 1969 Associated Music Publishers, Inc., New York.
  International Copyright Secured. Used by permission.
Chapter XVId: Iannis Xenakis - Formalized Music (*Nomos* α)
  by permission of Indiana University Press, Bloomington.
Chapter XVIe: Steve Reich - *Piano Phase*
  (c) 1980 Universal Edition Ltd., London.

Cover design: Iannis Xenakis' graphic model of the Philips Pavilion made in collaboration with Le Corbusier for the 1958 Brussels World's Fair. It was in this building that Edgard Varèse's 'Poème électronique' was first heard. The drawing is based on a similar graphic image which is the foundation for one of Xenakis' early major works, *Metastasis* (1955) — each line represents a glissando. The composer writes, 'If glissandi are long and sufficiently interlaced, we obtain sonic spaces of continuous evolution'.

# Part 1 – Introduction

*In the following chapter experimental music will be defined and two of this book's main "characters" – the parameter and the composer John Cage – will be introduced.*

# I. What it's all about

## 1. EXPERIMENTAL MUSIC DEFINED [1]

The term experimental music is often used today. Surprisingly the frequency of its use has not had any effect in unifying the term's meanings. In general there are four distinct views of what experimental music might be. It is the final view which will serve as our definition.

A) The 1970s have become known as a time of "post-modernism" in several of the arts; the term avant-garde therefore has become a cliché as its literal meaning can hardly be used for describing contemporary art. The problem was, and is still, that the modern public has been presented with so much innovation, especially in the 50s and 60s that one might say that almost all art today is avant-garde due to the relatively small amount of appreciation, or conversely, that there is no new avant-garde art as there is really nothing new under the sun any more.

Whatever the reason may be, avant-garde used as a synonym for that which is innovative and difficult to appreciate due to newness had to be labeled differently. Much music has been grouped together as "new music", "contemporary music" and so on, but these terms are often used as well for all art music of the 20th century.

Experimental music became synonymous with avant-gardism to many as most "before its time" art is by nature experimental. The "Grove" Dictionary (entry by Paul Griffiths) and texts of Robert Fink and Herbert Eimert (all listed in the bibliography), the latter seeing this new notion as a modish cliché, all tended to merge the avant-garde with the experimental. The problem here is that most writers who choose the synonym approach do not define innovation, avant-gardism, or what they call "advanced techniques".

B) In the late 1950s and early 1960s when the sonological field was growing quickly, two of its foremost composers and writers, Pierre Schaeffer in France and Lejaren Hiller in the U.S. defined experimental music as pertaining to music made in the laboratory, that is in the *musique concrète*, electronic and/or computer music studios. This is a very narrow definition of the term which only relates to applied electronic technology.

C) Simultaneously another composer-writer, John Cage, came to a totally dissimilar conclusion as to what he saw experimental music to be. To him an experimental action is one in which the outcome cannot be foreseen. In other words, as is typical of Cage, one can speak of the various ways of infiltrating purposelessness into music. Cage calls it indeterminacy; others, including Boulez and Stockhausen, who limited their purposelessness to small nuances of choice, called it aleatory.

This definition, or version of the experiment has been accepted by many prominent writers including Michael Nyman, Wim Mertens, to an extent Konrad Boehmer, and especially Joaquim M. Benitez as is discussed in his article, *Avant-garde or Experimental? Classifying Contemporary Music*. Benitez claims that "classical avant-gardists" (e.g., Pierre Boulez and Karlheinz Stockhausen) are traditionalists in that they create works of art, whereas composers of the Cage school could hardly speak of making musical works when their outcomes are unknown. Citing Earle Brown he points out that an experimental performance is composed rather than that a composition is performed. The goal is spontaneity and to an extent the loosening of fixed musical boundaries. In citing a manuscript of Susumu Shōno, Benitez presents an interesting four-level division of experimental music-making. The experiment or the indeterminacy takes place:

i. Between the composer and the score (i.e., one uses random-choice operations during the composition process),

ii. Between score and performer (i.e., the score is indeterminate and demands choice and response by the musician during a performance). This can be manifested in three ways: first, the macro-structure of a piece exists, and the performer fills in the micro-structure elements – this is sometimes called the parameter-freer approach (see *illustration I/1*); second, the micro-level is completely written out, but macro-level decisions are left free, as in the *Available Forms* works of Brown (see part 6, chapter XVIf); thirdly, the performer is to react to a graphic image (see *illustration I/2*) or to a prose text (see also chapter VI) in which both macro- and micro-decisions must be made,

    iii. Between performer and sound recording (through electronic modification), and

    iv. Between sound recording and listener, the least common (e.g., the record of *HPSCHD* of Cage and Hiller supplies a unique dynamics chart for each listener to mix a personal stereo version during the duration of the recording).

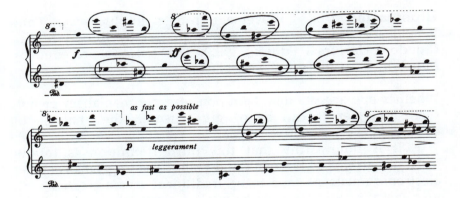

**Illustration I/1:** An example of a score in which one parameter (in this case the duration of the piano notes – encircled ones signify unperiodically played "phrases") is left open to the interpreter: *Tone* for piano by Shuko Mizuno (Tokyo: Ongaku no Tomo-Sha, 1970).

**Illustration I/2:** A movement from a graphic score, *Four Visions* for flute, harp and string quartet by Robert Moran (London: Universal Edition, 1963). This score is preceded by Moran's instructions to the six players.

Whether one accepts this definition of experimentalism or not, these four levels can be of great use in the analysis of contemporary innovative music.

It is noteworthy that this third definition is totally dissimilar to that of Schaeffer and Hiller. The Cageians consider electronic music on tape to be traditional music created with new instruments. The experimental in electronic music is only present before realizing a tape. After a tape has been mounted, a work of art is born which is, according to this group, no longer experimental.

In a sense it is a shame that Cage and Nyman have chosen the term, experimental music for these composition and performance procedures. The reason for this discontent is twofold: firstly, any good definition of *experiment*[2] shows that purposelessness is by no means an experimental goal. The word is misused a bit perhaps. Secondly, the acceptance of the term for Cageian techniques has led to isolating indeterminate works from other innovative forms of composition.

One wonders whether a more natural coupling to other musical developments through the use of another name might have been more useful. It is this coupling which leads to the fourth definition, the one we will use in the remainder of this book.

D) *Experimental music is music in which the innovative*[3] *component (not in the sense of newness found in any artistic work, but instead substantial innovation as clearly intended by a composer) of any aspect of a given piece takes priority above the more general technical craftsmanship expected of any art work.* Innovation has always been present throughout music history, yet in this century many composers have chosen to focus specifically on the new, often rejecting accepted values and sometimes ignoring or compromising themselves in terms of accepted levels of generally known techniques. Of all the writers encountered in the preparation of this text, it was only Paul Griffiths (1981)[4] who chose this path. As avant-gardism was always to a greater or lesser extent experimental, this definition comes closest to the first of the above three. The laboratory or indeterminacy compositions can mostly be included in this wider category of experimental music. As it is a question of weighing innovation against renewal that is important here, one can indeed find some electroacoustic works which are substantially less experimental than others; to a lesser extent this may also be said of a few aleatoric pieces.

It is inevitable in further refining the definition that criteria will have to be developed to examine the experimental of a given work.[5] This will not only concern the most recently composed music, for as said the presence of innovation is a constant factor in music history. Still, one sees a large growth of experimentation beginning around the time of the first surge of electricity and a second, much larger surge after the Second World War. Therefore it is primarily music composed after 1950 that falls into this category.

## 2. COMP(EXP. ♪) ≅ $f_t(\sum_i$ "PARAMETERS"($\sim$))

( = *The composition of experimental music is approximately equal to the function [in time] of a sum of as many sound parameters as you choose,* or, there is more than just one new dimension in recent experimental music.) [6]

In the early 1950s music's *Wiederaufbau* included several developments which demonstrated a great deal of inventiveness as well as creativity. Several of these developments parallel similar activities in the "hard" sciences (as well as in the arts as has always been the case). As in the sciences where one became more acquainted with various minutely small and extremely large worldly phenomena, composers searched to expand their own dimensions.

Take for example the element of musical pitch. In early music history, a typical musical scale contained four or five pitches; modality and tonality utilize a scale of seven tones; in the 20th century, Arnold Schönberg's dodecaphonic music gave equality to all twelve tones within the musical octave; at the same time the Czech theorist composer Alois Haba and many others even divided the smallest interval on the piano into yet smaller pieces, creating micro-tonal music of up to some forty-three tones/octave. With the first experiments in the electronic music studios in the 1950s, C–D–E (do–re–mi) were replaced by pitch described in terms of its physical characteristic (cycles/second or hertz). C might be called 256 Hz; its upper neighbor no longer needs to be C-sharp, which is many hertz higher, but instead 256.1 Hz or even 256.01 Hz which are both "playable" on many electronic instruments. In other words the pitch domain has grown from a handful of tones as basis to a universe of infinite possibilities.

Also the realms of time (rhythm, tempo), dynamics and even timbre have undergone this form of expansion. And in fact there are many other musical dimensions that have been looked into, as will be shown below. Early avant-gardists were certainly aware of this potential, but lacking apparatus to make such expansion feasible, most early 20th-century composers limited themselves to dreams and manifestos.

Although parametric research is not the only form of experimentation within recent music, it has been singled out for this introduction due to its relative importance in most experimental music along with its link to music tradition (studies of melody, rhythm, harmony, and so on) and to assist in delineating our field of interest. It will also be often referred to in the following chapters.

### a. The Parameter

Traditionally the word parameter, which evolved in the latter half of the 18th century and can be found in Diderot's encyclopedia (Paris, 1756), knows two main connotations, one mathematical and one derived from statistics. In general the first connotation boils down to: characteristics of a variable which make it possible to describe and/or compare mathematical functions and/or systems. In statistics one speaks of "parametric values" which characterize the properties of a probability distribution.

The term found its first application in music in the 1940s in various texts of the (music) theorist, Joseph Schillinger. He saw the arts as one continuum containing a system of unlimited parameters. Each art was said to possess two parametric components: general ones (time, space) and specific ones ("qualities"). Although the later use of musical parameters is implied but not stated here, Schillinger's thesis remains idealistic and a bit vague.

In the late 1940s and early 1950s, the information and acoustics theorist, Werner Meyer-Eppler began his long study of potential music parameters independent of Schillinger (see Meyer-Eppler, Christoph von Blumröder 1982a). Essentially he sought – given the arrival of electronic music studios – a new form of musical description, a description which allows a sound to be broken down into its basic components according to the laws of physics. He supported his ideas citing the new objectivity in music derived from Schönberg's and Anton Webern's methods of interval manipulation and a drive to precision derived from applications of modern technology. Meyer-Eppler is seen to be one of the father figures of German electronic and serial music. His focus on musical parameters was fundamental to his theory.

Many have defined the term parameter in music. Josef Häusler's definition will suffice for this discussion: *Musical parameters are all sound or compositional components which can be isolated and ordered* (1969).

In the Middle Ages, Guillaume de Machaut composed isorhythmic motets which called for a melody of length "X" to be repeated as well as a rhythmic phrase of length "Y". The fact that "X" and "Y" could be of different lengths meant that there was a certain autonomy of pitch and duration. Schönberg's twelve-tone music, formulated in the early 20s, was based upon a row of intervals which was to be permuted and combined in various manners without specification of compositional method for any other sound component. Olivier Messiaen's short piano study, *Mode de valeurs et d'intensités,* dating from 1949, specified for each pitch its own unique length, dynamic level and attack (e.g. accented notes). In this case four parameters were fused into a single new one.

Furthermore, recent physics research has helped the musician describe sound color by way of spectral graphs. This sort of research has led composers and musicologists to investigate new orderings. Luciano Berio is known for his experiments with potential sounds of various instruments in his series of *Sequenze.* Robert Erickson has written a monograph (1975) in which timbral types are defined. Schaeffer is well known for the search for order in his *objets sonores* and *objets musicaux* which he employed in his works of musique concrète. The Canadian, R. Murray Schafer calls for the description and ordering of all sounds in his *Tuning of the World*.

Information science has influenced music significantly. Today one uses the computer to produce, manipulate and record sound. Hiller (1959) has been making computer-assisted and computer-generated music since the late 50s. His programs, which employ "main parameters" and "parametric priorities", after being run, result in encoded musical information. (In fact several terms from mathematics have entered into the musical language since the 50s: stochastics, algorithms, groups, sets, aleatory, and many others.) Clarence Barlow (1980) tries to "formalize" his compositions as the computer studies esoteric parameters including melodic curve, metric and harmonic field-dynamic, chord density and several others.

Now that the extent of the potential of musical parameters has been briefly sketched, it will be shown that three major experimental composers of our time have all dealt with the concept of musical parameters in very different manners.

## b. 3 Parameter-users: Cage, Xenakis and Stockhausen

– *John Cage:* Cage was the first of the three to discover more than one potential application of isolating sound components. One historic example will demonstrate how he works. In 1951 the *Music of Changes* for solo piano was composed, one of the first two pieces in which Cage utilized chance operations. twenty-eight charts were constructed: for sounds, durations, tempi, dynamics (including accents and the like) and "superpositions". Each chart contained sixty-four positions corresponding to the sixty-four possible *I Ching* hexagrams. The *I Ching*, the famed ancient Chinese Taoist "Book of Changes", assisted in determining how many of the sixty-four positions a given pitch (including silence, "sound aggregates", "sound constellations" and indefinite [noise] sounds), dynamic, length and tempo would have. It determined the lengths of the four movements as well. Once the graphs were made (Cage: 1961, 57-59), the *I Ching* was used to fill in the entire score, each **"sound characteristic"** (Cage's term for parameter) separately. In this way Cage isolated each sound dimension in his composition to an extent that he could not possibly know what the piece was to become until he had completed it!

– *Iannis Xenakis:* As Cage works with enormous compositional as well as performance freedom, Xenakis calls for mathematical rigidity. In his well-known book, *Formalized Music*, Xenakis attempted to create a universe of sound based on numbers (as did many Greeks, not to mention Pythagoras). He is the only composer who uses the word parameter only in the statistical sense (Xenakis: 103-105). Nevertheless, this connotation is less relevant here.

One learns that each of his pieces is dependent on a branch of mathematics, be it calculus, group or set theory, probabilities or whatever. What holds these works together is his personal technique: decisions are made inside- and outside-(musical) time. The outside-time operations form the mathematical foundation of a work. Potential "paths" or "chains" (orderings) are generated in terms of their own **"vector spaces"** (Xenakis' term for parameter: 23) and later projected onto the musical inside-time graph also known as the score.

Xenakis takes for granted that pitch, dynamics ("intensities"), tempi ("speeds") and durations ("instants") are to be treated separately. He also uses scales for timbre, sound density (many "grains" or "clouds" of sound can create a high "sound energy") as well as a scale for (dis)order (see illustration in part 6, chapter XVId). Outside-time functions can apply new parameters which essentially consist of the fusing of two or more of the above-mentioned ones. This of course does not change the definition of parameter as the new parameter is also isolated and ordered.

– *Karlheinz Stockhausen:*   Stockhausen is without question the most difficult of the three here. The simple reason for this difficulty is that this composer has done nothing else than theorize about and apply parameters in his work since the early 50s. In the six volumes of his writings one discovers very unusual proposals for musical parameters: the continuum between rational compositional approaches and intuitive ones, a parameter which couples physical movement (dance) to specific performed sounds, one formally handling the physical placement of sounds within a given space, another defining all world music as one large gamut (Stockhausen: 1978,  468-476) and, above all, several scales for anything that has to do with musical form. His works entitled *Punkte*, *Momente* a n d *Gruppen* all illustrate one of his proposed time entities which in turn may be used to help generate compositions.

Stockhausen believes in an implicit cohesion of all musical outings. In this way his entire music theory formulates continua which eventually can lead to a sound being related to a work in the same manner as a work can be related to a series of works. Therefore an element that has always been seen to be small (micro) can suddenly take a position of magnitude (macro) on a new scale (for example the isolated note, earlier the smallest entity of a composition, can also be seen as a totality comprising the complex sum of pulses). One again thinks of the sciences, for example biology, in which the nucleus was earlier seen to be one of the smallest possible entities and now is studied as a large body which is composed of many elements. In Stockhausen's case, there is no end to the potential of **"serializing"** (Stockhausen's most used term for parameter) musical components. The following list is therefore a *capita selecta* of the parameters used by the above-mentioned composers.

## c. Isolated Parameters in Recent Compositions
– *Parameters of Primary Importance:*
  – **Pitch:** (see page 6).
  – **Duration:** Other than medieval Gregorian Chant, in which tempo and rhythm were to have been freely interpreted, as related in many a folk tale, Western music has always had its rhythms notated in various systems, of which the best known is the current system with its quarter, half and whole notes. Rhythm can be isolated. It can also be further refined and articulated in seconds (analogous to pitch's hertz). In this case the additive rhythmic relationships of traditionally notated music remain possible, but are no longer mandatory.
      <– – **Tempo:** The second time parameter. Anton Webern was one of the first to add frequent tempo changes in his works, which more or less took the beat out of his music. When scores use time notation, tempo and durations are fused into one single parameter.
  – **Dynamics:** Amplitude, earlier always notated in *p* and *f*, can be measured on its own continuous scale of decibels (db). This is of particular interest in electronic and computer music.
  – ++ **Timbre:** Sound color is in effect the combination of pitch, amplitude and, of course, time. Those mountainous graphs, often used to make record covers look modern, which show a fundamental tone and all of its overtones expressed in three dimensions with amplitude and time, describe timbre in minute detail. Schönberg was the first to call for timbre as a special entity. He formalized the concept of an occasionally applied *Klangfarbenmelodien* in which color and melody played an equal role. Since the early 1950s timbre has perhaps been the sound parameter receiving the most attention by composers. Through the endless new timbral possibilities of our electronic instruments and the drive to attain new colors in compositions (e.g. in the works of Luciano Berio and György Ligeti), this parameter has reached maturity. Stockhausen again is not satisfied with only one timbral parameter; in his article, *...wie die Zeit vergeht* (Stockhausen: 1963, 99-139), half a dozen new parameters for sound color are proposed which he applied in his work *Gruppen* among others.

**– ++ Sound Types:** Sound material has become quite important since the birth of *musique concrète* and electronic music in which the note has become a (small) subset of all sounds which may be used in a musical context. These sounds may also be ordered.

**– Space:** This is the second of two new parameters, along with *sound types* (as well as its brother, *timbre*), which have caught on to such a great extent that they can be seen to be of relatively great importance. Spatial music is by no means new. The San Marco in Venice was built with responsorial music in mind. In the early 20th century Charles Ives dreamt of music to be played on various mountain tops and he, alas, never completed his *Universe Symphony*. Nevertheless, the isolation and organization of sound in space had to wait until the last couple of decades for its liberation. Stockhausen has constantly been interested in this parameter. His article, *Musik im Raum* (Stockhausen: 1963, 152-175) is one of the most important treatments of the subject. Cage has dealt with sound-spaces for a long time. For example Cage has been known to create works in which the performance can take place at any given location on Manhattan Island (or wherever). Chance determines where, when and for how long one plays or simply experiences the sounds of that locale. Xenakis, one of the architects (along with Le Corbusier) of the Philips pavilion at the 1958 Brussels World Fair in which Edgard Varèse's *Poème électronique* was performed on hundreds of loudspeakers, has dealt with sound in space in many ways. His *Polytope* works mathematically combine sound and laser projections spatially. Finally the composer John Chowning has created computer generated sounds that literally move around a circle in a quadraphonic environment (see also chapter IX).

**– *Parameters of Secondary Importance:***

**– Density:** Cage lets the *I Ching* determine the number of notes per unit time. Xenakis never works without considering the parameter of sound density. Stockhausen discusses this parameter as well (Stockhausen: 1978, 360-401). In the 60s, György Ligeti turned density music into an art form. Certainly music has always known great changes of note density in time. These composers recognized this element as a parameter.

**<– – Simultaneity:** Also known as *harmony*, this parameter considers which pitches (or noises) are to be played at the same time and is thus a combination of pitch and density. Earlier the rules of modal and tonal music were sufficient for determining (acceptable) counterpoint and harmony. Today what appears on the vertical and horizontal axes may be ordered. The fact that chords may be given values and used parametrically is of relevance here. Variations on this theme can be found by Mauricio Kagel ("cluster widths" for very dense simultaneities), Henri Pousseur ("polyphonic densities" and "harmonic fields") and Cage ("superpositions").

    – **(Dis)Order:** Xenakis' parameter considers "changes" (Cage's term) in the listener's perception from totally recognizable to totally anarchistic sequences of musical events.

    **<– – Energy:** Xenakis' special parameter for the combination of density + order.

    – **Freedom:** This term is an unhappy one, but will be used as a heading for a number of potential parameters and is of course the heart of the Cage collection as categorized by Benitez above. Stockhausen also adds his own continua: some refer to notation, the others to form (see below). Xenakis, the formalizer is obviously not at all interested in these parameters.

    – **Compositional Bearing:** Only Stockhausen has ordered the way one may compose a given work, beginning with fully rationalized (objective) works and ending with fully intuitive works (automatic composition?, composed after meditation). There are, of course, other points between these extremes.

    – **Form:** Xenakis' outside-time phase and Cage's forms determined by random outcomes are analogous to a number of innovations formulated by Stockhausen, many of which go far beyond the scope of this chapter (e.g. see Stockhausen: 1963, 222-258 and 1964, 130-134). A few examples: a scale ranging from determined form (precise notation) through combined form to "open form" (in which the player determines the order of score fragments during performance), a scale which deals with various techniques of musical collage and a number of other scales based on morphological relationships.

    **<– – "Formel":** A super-term dating from the late 1970s unique to Stockhausen. In this case the first five parameters are molded into a new one which contains the potential of generating short phrases as well as the opera, *Licht* which, when completed, will last an entire week. Von Blumröder defines this parameter as follows: "a characteristic framework employing a clearly articulated melodic row consisting of frequency, dynamic, duration, timbre and tempo information; (the *Formel*) generates the macro-form of the work as well as containing all internal musical details of the same work." (1982b, 185)

One can thus speak of the theoretical and practical liberation of the isolated sound (and its elements) as well as of the largest form. With his article, *Kriterien* (Stockhausen: 1971, 222-229), the integration of anything "micro" with anything "macro" has become reality.

   Given the breadth and quantity of the (in point of fact incomplete) list of parameters above, one can easily conclude that this form of treating sound and morphological aspects one at a time is playing an enormous role in experimental music. In fact the scale of parametric applications serves as an important focus in this book's discussion of the question: what has happened to experimental music in the last decade?

## 3. JOHN CAGE:  MUSIC AS A WAY OF LIFE

Before entering the inner chapters of this book, a few words must be written in dedication to this composer.[7] For it was Cage who, analogous to the subject of the parameter in terms of music's content, was responsible, be it directly or indirectly, for a majority of music's innovations in terms of the choice of sounds, new methods of notation, performance-practice, structure/form concepts, composition techniques and even in terms of our ways of listening over the last three and a half decades. As stated in the preface, no heroes are sought in this book; nevertheless, John Cage will occasionally be called upon to illustrate a great number of experimental points of departure, philosophical bases and practical developments in which he participated. Please take note that the majority of these illustrations could easily have been taken from other sources.

   Ignoring for the moment his unhappy definition presented above, Cage's importance to the entire evolution of experimental music is threefold: through his works' challenge and content, through his lectures and texts about his music as well as about his several eclectic interests which in turn indirectly concern his music, and through his chosen lifestyle, a translation of both the above. Every subject in the table of contents, with the possible exception of fusion-music, has been dealt with in one way or another by the composer-inventor Cage. Perhaps ironically his experiments have been so radical that few works written after 1951, the year in which he first applied chance operations which would become the foundation of all his future works, there are very few specific compositions which have entered the repertoire of frequently performed experimental pieces. As Cage leaves a great deal of decision-making to his performer(s), his musicality (see e.g. chapter VII) is not to be easily found at the surface of his works. In this sense he will be shown to be problematic in terms of a number of this book's most important suggestions. Nevertheless, he is the rare exception in the 1980s, consistently continuing to search for the innovative in his compositions, and remains an inspiration to many within and even outside of the provinces of experimental music and arts.

1) This definition section is the original English version of part of the following article: *Das Studium der experimentellen Musik an der Universität Amsterdam: Befreiung oder Isolierung der neuen Musik?* in *Musik und Bildung* 10/Okt. 1985: 693-694, 703.

2) Webster: "Any action or process undertaken to discover something not yet known or to demonstrate something known."

3) Webster: "Something newly introduced; new method, custom, device, etc.; change in the way of doing things."
Mild experimentation, for example creating something new with old materials, can also lead to mildly innovative compositions. Such works belong to one of the several "neo-" categories discussed throughout the current work; yet this subject is not at the heart of the current study. It is foreground experimentation which we will deal with throughout the book.

4) Alas Griffiths does not define his term, he simply illustrates it by discussing individual scores and composition techniques!

5) There is no single formula which can tie together all aspects of current music-experimentalism. This book, which does not have the pretense of completeness, has been written using a simple, empirical approach of delineation through as large a diversity of relevant subjects and examples as possible.

6) This section has appeared in another form under the same title in *Avant Garde* No. 0: 27-39.

7) A composer portrait will not be given here. The three Cage books listed in the bibliography as well as the books listed under Daniel Charles and Richard Kostelanetz offer sufficient information to those interested.

# Part 2 – Four extra-musical subjects of relevance

The following four chapters concern technological, socio-economical and culture-political influences on our society that are unquestionably of great importance to all who make any kind of music today. These chapters will all speak both of music in general as well as of experimental music specifically. Music's evolution has always been a reflection of the combination of social and musical influences. In the 20th century the amount of change to music's content has been greater than during the rest of the millennium. These changes will first be related to the non-musical subjects of greatest relevance; in part 3 the music, itself will be the focus. One specific aspect of today's technology, the application of the media is perhaps the most significant influence on today's music and is therefore the subject of chapter II.

# II. The media/1

## 1. MEDIA

> "Can one really distinguish between the mass media as instruments of information and entertainment, and as agents of manipulation and indoctrination?" **Herbert Marcuse**

In this hardly-dated remark lies the heart of the challenge posed by the media.[1] Although Marcuse was obviously referring to all of the mass media – specifically to television, radio and newspapers and other news periodicals – most likely a direct analogy can be found in the two forms most pertinent to music: radio and recordings.

On the one hand, these branches of technology can be applied to powerful effect, especially when harnessed to creativity. On the other hand, they are far more often associated with mass appeal, with the consumer society, with certain types of "packaging" ("The Best of ..."), with profit, with propaganda – in short, with industry and politics. This polarity of quality versus quantity can be exemplified by looking at the destinies of the relatively unknown video works realized by various contemporary artists at one end, as opposed to the daily doses of television serials and game shows made for every living-room and kitchen. It is not that the artist is faced with the choice of one or the other; rather, the artist should find the combination best serving his or her qualitative needs, needs not necessarily determined by the various media industries, but instead needs based on formulated (experimental) artistic criteria.

With little effort and imagination, the magnitude of the media's effect on culture as a whole is obvious. One or more forms are present not only in public showplaces such as galleries and concert halls, but also in the home. Artists who do not allow one or more media a central place in their work must be aware of the risk of remaining relatively anonymous.[2]

## 2. MUSIC AND MEDIA

Before we look into the potential of the media within experimental music, a few pages must be given to more general music and media issues, as the media of the masses generate problems which cannot be ignored by those involved in any branch of today's music.

How can one relate Marcuse's statement to music in terms of media? To begin, think of the most radical change to music-making of the last eighty years: musical works can now be easily distributed worldwide. It is a well-known fact that in most Western societies folk music – true local folk (indigenous) music – has slowly but surely been disappearing from daily life. What, then, has replaced folk music in the West?

The only music that is universally accessible these days is the music presented by the media. The repertoires of programs for broadcasting or recording often consist of compositions with commercial potential. Taking into account the amount of sound components turned on daily, one can only conclude that the influence of the media on the "average" listener is overwhelming.

This influence is often based on fashion, be it in terms of musical content (being "in") or in terms of apparatus. The latter, as has been pointed out by many social critics led by Marcuse, often seems to receive the most attention. What does a stereo installation look like? Has the noise level really been reduced to 1/100th the potential of human perception? Etc.

It is not important here to delve more deeply into the problem of the newness of machinery; the only relevant questions for today's musician are whether and how we can use these (new) machines, and whether we are capable of designing other apparatus for our goals.

What then has been the lot of live performance? How many European teenagers go regularly to concerts (one of the few ways of seeing music performed live)? How many have never been at all? It is understandable that, with known recording artists predominating in musical performance, with the coming of the relatively "easy" life of our century, **participation** by the untrained in musical activity – i.e., dancing, singing or playing along with local musicians – has waned. New forms of music and dance centers such as the discothèque have evolved. In these centers, various media – and *not* live musicians – play the central role.

Concert activity has become somewhat less prevalent and participatory music has clearly diminished. This leads to a most extreme and somewhat painful influence of the media, namely, the decrease of active (public/live) *music-making* in general. Today's media-music is listen-to music and most often passive; at home *"music-taking"* is what it boils down to. Music-taking can be interpreted in two senses. Firstly, in the sense of the mentioned drop of live-music performance and appreciation. It also refers to the prominence of passive above active listening. In other words background music (see below) is currently more available and "used" than foreground music. The television "play-back shows" where young people dance and imitate pop numbers without producing a single sound demonstrate how far passivity in music-making can regress.

The media have affected the content of music in another way. As most musicians are bound to the media, and as most radio programs are based on pre-recorded material, the professional aim of most musicians today is to be recorded as often as possible. One might call this "media envy".

A recording is a registration but also a way of **perfecting** through technology. Music interpretation has always called for striving for high-level craftsmanship, although one would need several definitions for describing the various high levels of performance technique in classical, folk and improvised musics. The perfection called for here is flawless music-making, whatever that may be. A path to perfection leads along a studied multichannel technique of montage, repeated performance, and often a final splice-down eliminating all faults. This implies that one of the primary bases of music – spontaneity – is being partially replaced by extreme rigidity (that music is played through a machine does not necessarily mean that musicians should play like one, should they?), an element known only to some premodern Western classical music. It also implies that one can be presented with a recording of a given improvisation which has been made permanent as "the piece" in the mind of many a listener. Is this really the musician's intention? Furthermore, a number of potential amateur musicians have been known to be scared away from performance as unattainable, given their "inferior" ability, being constantly confronted with high-quality flawless recordings. This, in turn, increases today's musical passivity.[3]

Let us return to the question of fashion. A cursory glance at music history shows that dynamic continuity, historically and culturally, has been one of music's strongest points; why, then, must today's music change with every little technological invention? Why must a vogue last but a couple of years, and why must old music (e.g., older than five years) be put prematurely to the grave (only to be resurrected as "golden oldies")? This is the result of a mass consumption market freely applying "Friedman economics" (i.e. market-driven capitalism) a great deal of the time while discarding most folk musics as not commercially viable and placing esoteric new music on the shelf of "low promotion". Recent international research projects executed by musicologists in collaboration with sociologists, evaluating and suggesting how we can put this unhappy situation into a potentially better, more balanced perspective, are quite useful, although probably arriving too late to reharmonize the coexistence of popular, folk and contemporary genres.

Notice must be given to the radio's potential "brainwashing" effect – not in the sense of manipulation, but rather that of allowing "listeners" to "tune out", yet another form of passivity in music. How many people turn on the radio for "company" and then do not listen to the music at all? Some use the steady beat of disco music or the soft, synthetically-produced sounds of "easy listening" (Muzak/musical wallpaper – one wonders whether this is what Erik Satie was looking for in his *Musique d'ameublement*?) to accompany their household chores. Is this the Western equivalent of Indonesian farmers creating a complicated rhythm to optimize pounding rice? The disco beat sometimes comes dangerously close to twice the heartbeat. Muzak is often used to stimulate the purchase of merchandise or the desire to eat. What in heaven's name are we allowing the media do to us?

Now let's finally get to our subject of experimental music and the media.

## 3. EXPERIMENTAL MUSIC AND THE MEDIA

In our world of new music we do suffer from dependence and related illnesses of the media, but fortunately to a much smaller extent than in a realm like pop music. This is primarily due to new music not exhibiting a great deal of commercial potential; therefore this music has not been promoted as much as other musics by various public relations agencies. Nevertheless, the allure of media propagation entices almost all involved in contemporary music. Let's look at experimental music and the media, first in terms of the media (radio and recording industries) and then from the point of view of the musician.

Radio in most countries has been relatively "unkind" to new music and its musicians. (Although it must be said that Germany exemplifies one of the few exceptions.) This has two consequences. First, many people who are "regular" radio listeners do not get enough exposure to this music, which influences potential concert going and acquisition of recorded material. Second, as indicated above, since radio and television have helped cut down concert practice in many societies, the lack of attention paid to modern music by various radio stations can have a lethal effect on its dissemination.

One would expect the information media – radio, television and newspapers – to be reasonably supportive of their contemporary culture. This might be seen as a form of nationalism – support your artists. This support should lead to the coexistence of traditional and experimental cultural development, creating a broad artistic basis in a society. However, since most of our radio organizations have decided to provide the public with music they consider to be appropriate for the masses, relatively unknown experimental music is one of the first sorts to be dropped. Of course it is the musician who is called the guilty party for creating music with no potential mass appeal. But as music-making is a process that develops by way of feedback, less music reaching broadcast means less feedback, creating a large communication gap.[4] In the urban United States the picture is not so gloomy, due to the great number of radio stations. There is often something new to hear. But the programs that are offered can often seem unstructured, incoherent to the "uneducated listener", because regional collaboration among network broadcasters - where "competing" stations broadcasting contemporary music could collectively plan what sorts of music are to be scheduled and how they can best be introduced - seems to be relatively rare. (The announcements on the radio tend, alas, to be either too general and non-informative or, conversely, much too sophisticated for the untrained listener.) In The Netherlands, a country with some 250 active new music composers, there are but five national radio stations plus a few local ones, of which only one is on the air twenty-four hours a day. One national and one local station broadcast classical music at a total of ca. sixteen hours/day, including some eight hours of 20th-century music a week[5] (mainly during work hours or late in the evening, often focusing on the [neo]classics). How can a composer expect to have his or her music made known with so few available possibilities?

Very few broadcasters throughout the world have reasonable budgets for radio recordings or air live performances of contemporary music. European radio does provide various opportunities for specific performers and composers to broadcast concertized pieces, studio recordings, or radiophonic works. It would be hard to support oneself, however, as an experimental musician making only radio recordings of contemporary music. In any event this network of opportunities has given new music the bit of reputation it has today on the continent. In the United States most private radio stations offer little attention to contemporary music. The public stations that pay such attention usually do so on such tiny budgets that they are grateful whenever a composer or musician provides them with a pre-recorded tape. It does seem, however, that contemporary musicians and composers are beginning to "infiltrate" the broadcasting world. If the ensuing agitation achieves concrete results, we may yet see some growth in new music propagation. Of course one assumes that most composers have taken the radio into account in their compositions, in the sense that for them the radio is an acceptable concert stage along with, or even instead of, the concert hall.

The recording industry's influence has been as stimulating to new music (through the potential of recording) as suppressing (through selectivity and promotion of that which gets recorded). The lack of promotion is understandable, for there seems to be hardly any tangible reason in our market-oriented economy for record distributors to push most experimental music recordings; an interested public supposedly knows which labels specialize in new music, and knows as well where to find them. In this sense the dearth of new works on many major recording labels has not hurt experimental music very much. On the other hand, the record and tape industry has kept up in terms of recording quality and technological development (noise reduction, multichannel and digital recordings, video and compact disks) so that the stringent demands of, for example, electroacoustic music composers making stereo (as opposed to quadraphonic) works which do get recorded can normally be met. It might be added that the number of recent compositions of about twenty, forty or sixty minutes' duration seems to reflect the influence that the record and the CD have had on contemporary composition.

The basis of this "media envy" is probably to be found in the goal of many composers and performers that new music should be heard by as many listeners as possible, as this form of recognition might be the best road to "success". Success, of course, is what you make of it. One hypothesis of the present text is that most contemporary musicians should be happy when there is a specific public, a "community", be it local or international, interested in their music. Such a community *can* be created through live music without the help or even the use of the media. Nevertheless, when a medium is found useful or necessary, the subject of quality versus quantity should then arise with regard to the public as well. Shouldn't we be more satisfied with a small active public, than with yearning and fighting for the "big gig" – at which one mostly reaches a less-interested large audience?

The other side of the story is that regardless of new music's current non-mass appeal, new musicians are often the pioneers of various technological developments. For example modern synthesizer pop music flourishes thanks to thirty-five years of electronic music composition and research. Multichannel tape techniques were first sought out by composers, and only then by the recording industry.

Therefore there seems to be reason for hope. Musicians have the unique opportunity of concentrating on the constructive uses of media as described by Marcuse. Our needs are specific, but within reach, as long as we do not allow "consumerism" or "media envy" to overwhelm us. The small record or CD label, for example, is becoming enormously viable for non-commercial musicians; new releases, although they receive little or no publicity, do seem to find their way to an appreciative section of the public. As composers and musicians put more and more on paper or floppy disk and on tape or record; as they learn what constraints exist in the broadcasting world (e.g., live performances set aside in favor of fancy packaged programs); for the experimental musician who is not primarily struggling to obtain a mass audience (which probably does not exist), there is unquestionably an excellent opportunity to explore, develop and apply the media creatively.

1) *Media,* a word with many contemporary ramifications, is used here as an abbreviation of "communications media"; and not in the sense of, say, string quartets and electroacoustic music, as two among the musical media (see Landy: 1982). The audio-visual media are the subject of chapter X.

2) See also page 27 concerning the "musical community". The question here is whether the artist can be satisfied with a (much) smaller public.

3) In Jacques Attali's book , *Noise* (*Bruits* in the original 1977 French edition), the subject of the relationship between the perfect recording and modern society is treated at length. His unusual, but very strong thesis is that the politics of a society is a translation of and in a sense dependent upon what takes place in that society's music and performance practice.

4) A second source of potential growth of experimental music appreciation should be our schools: see chapter VI.

5) Many European countries including Holland have cable radio which means that there are more international and sometimes local stations offered and therefore more broadcasts and choice of new music works. This is only true for the listener, but not for the composer – neighboring German radio has little room for the 250 Dutch composers with the few hours they can give to experimental pieces, given the thousands of composers in their own country. Cable radio aids appreciation, but has not yet been of importance to the composer or to contemporary performers.

The ratio sixteen hours a day : eight hours a week is, alas, a fairly accurate translation of the ratio of Western art music listeners overall vs. those interested in recent works. Of course composers the likes of Philip Glass and fellow minimalists have attracted more listeners through their fusions with popular musics (see also chapter XIV), but this statistic remains painfully symptomatic of new music's isolation.

# III.   Technology

"Music is the combination of
numbers and drama."
**Pythagoras**

## 1. DOES THE ART OF SOUND = APPLICATIONS OF SCIENTIFIC KNOWLEDGE?

The media, whose roles in music should now be clear, are just a
small part of today's technology. What kind of influence might
technology as a more general phenomenon have on our
music?

If technology can be defined as the application of scientific
knowledge under specific circumstances, then clearly any
technology particular to one culture can be reflected in its
music. The reflection is one of the, in the opinion of the current
writer, two predominant factors in the making of music.[1]
History (and geography) bear this out, chronicling technological
development: the relatively sophisticated design and tunings of
Chinese instruments in the 7th century BC; the many scientific
theories of music throughout the ages; mathematical
composition techniques used in the 20th century; and the entire
world using electricity in one form or another – to name just a
few obvious cases.

Nonetheless, these examples fall far short in representing
the presence of technology in music. Western science has led
people to think of technology as an off-shoot of the "hard" (or
provable) sciences. In fact, this theory embraces only a small
portion of the body of knowledge of one cultural group. Musical
technology belonging within the tradition of one group is

31

passed on throughout the generations as in instrument design (e.g. Indonesian gamelan instrument construction) or as general musical knowledge; in instrumental performance practice; in the aesthetics and theory of music; in the creation, development and application of its genres and forms (as in ballads and sonatas); in the use and function of specific musical scales and their frequencies; in tonality (especially in 19th century works); and in the presentation and use of music as a socio-technological phenomenon.

Analogous to today's ever-growing technological presence, it is becoming increasingly common for the composer to turn to the sciences to supplement his or her compositional model, and increasingly common to find successful application of a given technology in music-theoretical works. Iannis Xenakis is a fine example of someone dedicated to such applications as can be discovered in his entire œuvre.[2] These applications nevertheless raise certain questions: what can be the justification for using technology as a compositional tool? Where can one define the boundary between using technology, and being bound by it? Which aspects of technology are applicable to the making of music, and in what way? Obviously, there are no simple answers, given the diversity in technology and the appreciation of music, and the constant changes within these. It is believed nevertheless that each individual musician should be able to defend his or her own uses of technology.

Therefore, the hypothesis of this chapter is that technology in the sense used here is not only a necessary element, but one that has accompanied music through cultural changes over the ages. It should be an integral part of the training of a Western musician to investigate the multiplicity of relationships between technology and music. The physical sciences (tunings and scales, instruments, acoustics, electricity, and so on) should be taught, as should the less tangible, more abstract theoretical science (macro- and micro-form, aesthetics, musical tension, etc.). Furthermore, two problems must be examined most carefully: to what extent are various forms of technology (e.g. potential uses of the computer in composition) applicable to music? Also, how can one avoid becoming enslaved to its use (as was alluded to in the media chapter and as will be discussed in chapter XIII in terms of our new digital instruments)? In other words, are we able to keep technology in its right perspective vis-à-vis music?

## 2. TECHNOLOGY INSIDE MUSIC

John Cage once pointed out that he was not very happy with the twelve-tone discovery in music: "When we changed over to the twelve-tone system we just took the pitches of the previous music as though we were moving into a furnished apartment and had not time to even take the pictures off the wall."

His metaphor, regardless of whether you agree with him or not, does not so much concern the haste implied, but instead the questions that constantly crop up regarding the development of compositional methods. An artist who is determined consciously to utilize an aspect of a given technology must bear two things in mind: the significance of the methodological elements that are to be superimposed onto an artistic field, and the translation of the technological tool into an aesthetic. In other words: (i) why use the technique, (ii) do you understand the technique, and (iii) what can you expect of the technique? (All three questions actually reach the heart of experimentation in general.) Rarely is there an adequate answer given to the third question as Cage implies in his remark. He is interested in arguments in favor in its system rather than discussing its invention. One of the beliefs at the foundation of the current text is that the answers to these questions are fundamental to those consciously applying technology in their music, yet these answers are too often left unformulated.

Let us take a hypothetical example: a composer who discovers beauty in the flashing lights of a machine, perhaps a mainframe computer. He or she thinks that there might be something artistic in using these seemingly random flashing lights, perhaps as triggers to produce sounds. Later, as the creation is presented to the public, many viewers are impressed by the novelty of the piece. Yet, after the initial impression of novelty, the haphazardness goes on, leading to nothing in particular. The work is unique for its presentation of a familiar machine transplanted into a concert context – and nothing more. As far as our three questions are concerned: the "what" has been taken care of; the "why" is somewhat vague and the artistic nucleus – the value, form, communicative nature, the character – inadequately thought out. This lack of aesthetic defense, of definition typifies many "art-for-art's-sake" (i.e. you get what you see – no *raison d'être* is offered; perhaps this light and sound show may be seen as an "experiment for experiment's sake") creations of our time. A single (technological) thought is unfortunately often simply not sufficient, especially in terms of the questions at hand. Had the artist then fully investigated and exploited the potential of sound/light in this context, perhaps the creation would have conveyed an aesthetic attitude. Otherwise the project were better forgotten.

Obviously one is asking a great deal of a composer to expect answers to these three questions. Technological development during our century necessitates this kind of enquiry:[3] points that were taken for granted earlier must be re-examined in the light of progress and change. Granted, the question of aesthetics remains most difficult to approach, but it is primarily artistic insight that is applied in defense of an idea. This insight is the goal here.

## 3.  WHAT DOES THIS TECHNOLOGY SOUND LIKE?

This is of course a rhetorical question. We have now encountered sufficient diverse subject areas in which the technological automatically or (un)consciously has been applied to music-making to know that almost anything from the nature of a sound to the analysis of musical form to (electronic) instrument construction to parametric thinking to aesthetics has at least one foot in technology. So, the obvious answer to technology's sound, namely that of the synthesizers heard day and night on the radio and television, on the street, in elevators and so on, is but just one small portion of technology's share of the art of sound.

The three questions – why, the comprehension of and what the expected result is of technological application – are of greatest importance here. Also the questions cited in reference to the media are equally relevant: can we form (experimental) criteria when applying our technology to music while finding an ideal combination of Marcuse's opposites quality and quantity given our own special needs? Each question should be posed each time we make music for each sort of technological application mentioned above. In this way a *dramaturgy* of contemporary music will be born.[4] Only our young musicians' awareness of the content and the power of technology through education will lead to the formulation of criteria for technological application. What it sounds like is, and that is the moral to our story, but the last in a series of relevant questions of soul-searching when it comes to composition, performance and even appreciation.

## 4.  ADDENDUM (*Food for Thought*)

### – Technology Outside Music: One Approach

> "Technology is the nature of modern man; it is our environment and our horizon."
> **Octavio Paz**

Referring to our definition of technology, we see that stress has been given to its belonging to a specific cultural group; therefore it varies from culture to culture. Social critics, among them the so-called "Alternative Technologists" (among others, David Dickson and Murray Bookchin, the latter known for his term, "post-scarcity" society [see bibliography]) have spent the last twenty or so years trying to relate today's technology to the problems of population growth, especially in cities, to the environment, to utilities and to creativity. Although their theories for decentralization (also to be found in Cage's texts) go beyond the scope of the current chapter, a few of their suggestions are worthy of mention in relation to music today, for it is in such thoughts that a possible link between the technological and the local might be found.

First and foremost, these social critics work together to present a program which includes the potential for regional – and not a (singular) worldwide – technologies. This is the conscious avoidance of cultural unification while still reaping certain profits from common technological breakthroughs. Their philosophy calls for the confrontation of design versus use, both correlated to our diverse ecologies. It also takes into account that "communities" of common interest still exist, be they regional or, as suggested at the end of the media discussion with regard to experimental music's public, spread out internationally. They pride themselves on an anti-large principle and clearly have no subscriptions to R. Buckminster Fuller's "Global Village". Their words bring us "back to nature", not just to the mountains and the deserts, but to the awareness of the nature found by looking out of any window today. Might today's composer be able to apply current technology in new works while finding a musical translation of that window view?

Furthermore, these social critics all believe that the reduction of toil through mechanization in this century should go hand in hand with an increase of creativity. This creativity in turn should in general reflect our technology as well as our local values. In other words, these social critics are not particularly happy with passivity in music-making and the decline of participation referred to in connection with the media. The plea for regionalism in production is not contradicted by man's worldwide travels and his not being restricted to or by his own culture. Local values, assimilation and acculturation are all subjects of chapter IV.

1) The other aspect, the application of local cultural values, will be the subject of the following chapter. Take note that these two elements are not mutually exclusive and are also not only to be seen as singly of interest, but instead in combination. These two chapters are a précis of the much larger treatise, "At a Fork on the Way".
2) See, for example, his description of a "Metamusic" incorporating the entirety of mathematics in music composition in his *Formalized Music*. Then listen to his compositions. The combination of numbers and musicianship is Xenakis' strength.
3) A typical example is the (almost bacterial) MIDI growth in today's music; see chapter XIII.
4) Granted, these answers, when only applied to technological questions, will not tell the entire story (and happily so) of our relation to music. Personal and general cultural values can also be subjected to these questions; see chapter IV.

# IV. Local music

## 1. THE LOCAL IN MUSIC

The local in music is what comes naturally. It could be derived from the nature that includes plants, animals and minerals, but more importantly it comes from the individual human or our collective cultural natures. It is what has stimulated the creation of modal ballads in England as well as pentatonic mourning songs in Thailand. Given the monumental growth of new technology in our daily lives, the "local" has even has led "naturally" to many of today's non-Third-World musicians to composing electronic music.

Examples of the local in music include folk music and a large amount of nationalism in music historically, in which composers turned to the musical sounds of their own cultures as foundations for their own works. Béla Bartók's well-known *Fourth String Quartet* provides us with an excellent example of a piece which was born of the combination of the local with mild experimentation in timbre and form. In this work Hungarian modality and rhythm are combined with Bartók's then current research for new colors and structures. Furthermore, several contemporary experimental composers have attempted to make people aware of various sonic aspects of their environment: this may also be seen as a variant of the local in music.

It must be noted that not all genres of music may be considered essentially representative of the local in music: this element is more abstract than that of musical technology. In essence, it boils down to how any individual makes music given his or her socio-cultural circumstances and traditions.

Today the concept of the local, though still present, has become somewhat vague. The local currently means that anyone, anywhere, can make any kind of music due to its universal availability (think of the presence of "exotic" fruits at any vegetable store, "exotic" music at almost every record store). The increase of this universal consumerism raises a vital question: to what extent can we borrow musically from other cultures before cultural boundaries are dissolved, before traditions are no longer evolved but simply superseded?

## 2. ACCULTURATION

Throughout its history, one of the most dynamic aspects of music has been its diversity. Music has always reflected the diversity of the cultures of the world's peoples, as can be seen in the variety of traditional local musics.

If we define "regionalism" as the making of music based on the traditions and customs of a local area – thus including all folk music – the terms "nationalism" and "internationalism" are self-explanatory. Composers participating in regional schools, at the same time coexisting with composers of more universal vision, have insured the integrity of local music; classical music has evolved through this coexistence, parallel to the evolution of folk music and not endangering it.

In our 20th century, however, the equilibrium has been severely disturbed. Technological developments have diluted many intercultural differences. Richard Wagner's dream of the creation of a sort of universal music for all peoples could not be achieved in his lifetime – for a start, it was not possible to hear his music as universally as that of, for instance, Madonna today. Scanning the globe musically can be too much of a good thing; it might be said that Madonna's music exemplifies that which has become only too universal at the cost of a great deal of regional music. The dramatic phenomenon of acculturation, combined with the media discussion, illustrate this tendency, a tendency which has its parallels in contemporary composition.

The slow, steady flow of acculturation among the migrant races throughout history used to be what made the world go round: it could be found in the influence of one culture's music upon that of its neighbors. It was also found in the creation of what is known as traditional "American music", which other than music of the American Indians, is a sum of its multiple cultural sources (jazz will be cited as an example below). Since the coming of the time that we can circle the globe in minutes instead of in months, can purchase many of the same products and transmit live radio broadcasts worldwide, acculturation has begun to subjugate the integrity of almost every culture. Thus, acculturation does not now solely concern neighbors, but almost all peoples – at least those who live in the presence of electricity and/or radio. In today's music it has become the rule rather than the exception: in Flanders country and western tunes are known to be sung; there are blues singers in Taiwan. At least the Americans sing primarily Afro- and Anglo-American music. This massive acculturation has arisen from an overt attempt to create an international, profitable music market in which the media play no small role.

Acculturation stimulated and accelerated by the media has certainly been highly responsible for the widening gulf between musical regionalism and internationalism. Of course there has been no sign that the powers behind the international media are dissatisfied with their achievements. Therefore, it is up to the musicians and the public either to redress this imbalance or to accept the annihilation of the "weak", including many of the regional genres of music today. The concept of the "musical community" (see below) is an alternative. It is somewhat missing in most forms of music-making today, but may turn out to be one of the saving graces in experimental music's future as will be discussed shortly. First, an instance of dynamism within local music performance will be presented.

## 3.  A POTENTIAL OASIS IN THE LAND OF UNIVERSAL MUSIC: JAZZ

"The value of jazz in our Western society seems to lie in the opportunity it presents for improvisation and the non-hierarchical set-up in which people work, which means that the jazz composer is closely involved with the actual performance; in most cases he writes for particular people, each with their own skills and susceptibilities, and not for an anonymous bunch of instrumentalists. This means that there is a remarkable amount of individual freedom for the musicians, especially those in small groups."

This is a quotation from the Dutch composer-musician Theo Loevendie (1977). Individual freedom and insight into the overall situation can be considered good guidelines for improvisation. This is music where the model has been historically and culturally established; its development and realization is in the improvisation itself.

Loevendie does not limit this vision to jazz as we know it. He also points out:

"...listening to Ottoman classical music in Turkey: ensembles of up to twenty musicians in which everybody plays the same thing and yet something else because they add their own embellishments and move into another octave for a while; in short, unity coupled with a certain freedom for the individual. A

> fascinating effect, but it is practically lost on records."

The earliest jazz performances were not too dissimilar to the Turkish way of music-making. When the recording industry and music impresarios came into the picture, things took a big turn for the profitable. Fortunately, this did not reduce musical interest in jazz as strongly as it did in other forms of popular music-making. The multiplicity of jazz roots and performance practices as Loevendie describes them were too deep to be disentangled from the music.

Jazz is a marvelous example of musical acculturation. Not only was jazz the musical crossroads in the New Orleans jazz days, it was also a music with multi-Black components. Many facets of the music of the West Indies are of African origin, but by the time the West Indian influence had taken a hold on jazz, the music of the West Indies had evolved a character distinctly different to that of its African ancestral counterparts. Modern jazz improvisation is therefore the sum of all these parts flavored by the culture of its musicians. There is an opportunity for everyone to "add his own little something" (identity), as happens in Ottoman classical performance, as well as in group drumming in Ghana for example.

Jazz is based on feeling. In this respect, the education of young jazz musicians should lead more towards performance experience than to theory and technique. Each player's feeling can thus always be found in his/her approach to improvising. Although transience in jazz can certainly modify a player's feeling, the improvisation model is strictly dictated. With the possible exception of free jazz – the name defines the nature – players adhere to the model. As long as each player's input is not biased towards commercialism in the first place, this music will survive the more temporary modes, continuing to enrich in style as it spreads and merges with other musics; further enrichment comes as it is played by new musicians whose feelings differ from those of each preceding generation. Jazz is a relatively young musical genre. In the same way that folk music is what might be called an organic creation of all peoples, so can jazz be naturally added to and molded into the musics of many cultures; it contributes adaptability to the rhythms and individualities of the people of these cultures.

> "Act spontaneously, but be, by
> study and reflection, the kind of
> person who can trust himself to
> be spontaneous."      **Coleridge**

## 4. THE MUSICAL COMMUNITY

In all cultures, music is present. Most human beings make one
sort of music or another, at least they used to. For almost
everyone the most natural sort of music until this century was
the singing or playing of folk tunes (or in the case of middle
European cultures, popular aires), tunes familiar to the region
of the musicians. When groups assembled to play, their music
was always a form of communication among the performers
themselves and between performers and listeners, all giving
and getting what they had come for.

Today, sadly enough, man can live an entire lifetime
hearing every imaginable kind of music – but rarely seeing it
performed on stage or on the street. We should re-stimulate
our need for live music, music made for the people within
their own cultural contexts.

With this in mind, today's experimental musician should
be able to reach a point where a player "X" from society "Y1" can
interpret a piece of music of the composer "Z" from society "Y2"
in a way that communicates it to an audience in society "Y3".
Granted, this last point is less relevant to folk music which is by
definition a music for one folk (although others may
nevertheless like to hear it); still, it is unquestionably quite
apropos to those who subscribe to the idea of the musical
community, be it local or spread out geographically. The
primary aim of the present chapter is the introduction of this
tale of "X", "Y's" and "Z".

Regional cultural boundaries should be redefined and
recognized, so that people can rediscover some sort of collective
identity. As one listens to young Dutch musicians singing
words in English (the language of most pop music) one might
wonder whom they are trying to identify with. What exactly *is*
Dutch music – or music from any society – for that matter? We

must be able to examine this carefully before anything can be done to save music from potential worldwide uniformity.

## 5. WHEN COMPOSING: TURN BOTH WAYS

"The idea is to feed, furnish and let the space speak for itself."
**Antonin Artaud**

If today's musicians would only take the trouble to examine exactly what space Artaud might have been referring to, we might equally become better acquainted with Cage's world as a[n omnipresent] concert hall. Our complete ignorance of our own cultural values, values which might lead us to being able to apply the local in our music consciously, has been responsible for the decline in "regionalism" in all its facets in a great deal of music-making today. The nature seen out of everyman's window should not be ignored, for by doing this we tend to be led towards a Global Village. Technically our satellites have aided in the Global Village's creation, but technical advance does not necessarily have to be synonymous with diminishing variety of cultural values around the globe.

"Introduce a *qualitative* change in technical continuity; namely production toward the satisfaction of freely developing individual needs."
**Marcuse** (23)

If musicians could look the same questions in the face in terms of their personal and cultural values which must be confronted in the case of music and technological application, new combinations of the local in its senses used here with the technological could lead to a better musical milieu.[1] Assimilation of values can and should not be stopped. Our blind acceptance of values of commercial origin on the other hand, which turns acculturation in submission, should be avoided.

What the combination of the local and the technological looks and sounds like is not to be fully described. First and foremost it is as diverse as man and secondly, elements such as aesthetics derived through tradition can not always be completely quantified. The study of semiotics in music, the search for universal and local sound-signifiers, may help us understand these problems better. That these problems be talked about openly is the goal of these last two chapters.

1) Of course it might be difficult to differentiate for example typical S. Italian from W. Canadian rhythmic parameters in contemporary compositions. The point today's composer should deal with is what is being formalized in today's music and how it sounds that is of relevance here.

Idealistically speaking, though, it might be of interest to investigate whether and how (local) technology may serve the examination and preservation of local elements in today's music as well as the application thereof.

# V. Music and politics

## 1. PREAMBLE

To conclude part 2 a few words will follow concerning the most (overly-) discussed and one of the least understood subjects of "music and ..." of this century. Anyone who ever talks about music sooner or later tackles the subject of the politics of music. In fact the word subject (singular) is incorrect. One of the problems in most treatments of music and politics is that people forget to discuss one music-political subject at a time. The following section is a simple attempt to categorize these subjects (derived from Landy: 1981) after which a few typical music-political examples in contemporary music will be placed under the microscope. Obviously the last three chapters were all of a political nature and could have been included here as well. Their special importance was the reason for their separate treatment.

## 2. MUSIC AND POLITICS "SYSTEMATIZED"

The following three general categories will be presented one at a time:

1) Politics in terms of society and its music, the most tangible category. This concerns the place of music in society, the role of the economics of "Music, Inc.": that is, state and private support of composers, musicians, publications, recordings, author's and performance rights as well as of the propagation of musical activities including live performances (and the cost of being present there) and the media. It is the reflection of a society's politics in its musical milieus.

2) Politics within music-making. Here one refers to the interrelationships of composers and interpreters in terms of political processes. For example, how democratic is (orchestral) improvisation after all?

3) The politics of the composer in terms of his or her intention and of music's content. Can a piece of music really be communist through its composition techniques, or is it a culture which imposes a certain symbolism to the piece? And what about Muzak? Furthermore, the point which is probably least spoken about and which interests the current writer the most is the composer's intention, his or her dramaturgy. In other words, in a pluralistic world, what do musicians try to reach with their music? The composer's choice of a theory/aesthetics is a political decision even when one has no specific politics in mind. For, as Cage might say, those who do not discuss such subjects have taken on an apolitical political standpoint (silence is a sort of sound, no opinion is an opinion).

Let's elaborate on these three points.

1) What is the place of music in society? Earlier, tradition provided us with the answer. Today politics often plays the main role. At the nucleus of politics is control. Control limits, as can be illustrated in any history book. Only anarchism, governmentless politics, or better said government from below, the politics of the idealists most rich in fantasy, offers unboundedness. Only here is control disbanded. (See the writings of John Cage on this. Of course Cage does compose, a seemingly contradictory way of avoiding control.) Needless to say there is no known completely anarchist society at present. Our big cities are anarchistic (perhaps a bit chaotic) least of all, so comments along these lines are more visionary and wishful than relevant to the current situation. As long as our First-World societies are not looking in a Marxist or anarchist or whatever direction, applying political philosophies alien to those societies' music is at best synthetic.

To the musician in our Western culture earning money and promoting music are as important as the making of music itself. This refers to the word which interests (almost) everyone, "success". What kinds of success are we actually looking for? Add to this question the fact that most discussions of music and politics, at least in terms of new music, seem to concentrate on leftist politics. Are fame and fortune a form of leftist politics or is success simply getting music performed? Wasn't it Karl Marx's aim to wipe out poverty, level income and create devotion to a more socialized world? His ideal was not one in which the great musician gained enormous popularity through fattening his bank accounts. Furthermore, in the alternative leftist, anarchist society, the musician is theoretically anonymous, "just" an integral part of society due to music's universality. Success therefore perhaps contradicts itself in this case.

Knowing press releases pertaining to Muzak's products, following the imperialistic growth of the Top 40, reading the somewhat puzzling theories of Hanns Eisler concerning music for the *masses*, one wonders who they are? Masses tend to be created, they *are* not.

Politics, Inc. and Music, Inc. create these masses. They define the economies of music-making throughout most of the world and highly influence music's creation and disposition. The heart of almost any discussion of music and politics must be centered around questions like: what are the economical circumstances and the atmosphere surrounding composition and music interpretation? What are the chances for a work's propagation? What kind of criteria are involved in choice of repertoire? These questions are equally relevant to the powers that be (state, industry, media, educators) as to the musicians themselves. Even the public should participate in such discussions as musical offerings as well as the cost thereof are at the heart of such questions.

It is feared that the only way for seeking change in terms of a society is to change the politics and not necessarily the music. The call for better subsidy distribution, free photocopying and the like is evolutionary within our system. The composers who will fight for these things are therefore seeking evolutionary change. Whether these changes have an effect on the dispersion of a quickly changing art world is nevertheless highly uncertain. Every musician is constantly involved in this form of music and politics and should, given a somewhat unstable world economy, prepare for a period of continued belt tightening, something that can either lead to the industrial nations' need (as in the 30s) of more musical nationalism and pride in relatively hard times or to a large-scale cut-back for the "black-sheep of the bourgeoisie" (this term is from Gregory Sandow), the experimental artist.

2) Concerning the politics of music-making, one must be extremely careful in making judgments. It all boils down to the place of music in the various societies (see 1). The interrelationships between musicians are dependent on this. Therefore, all-encompassing remarks on musicians and politics are most difficult.

Hierarchical questions belong to this second category as well: examples can be found in the relationship between composer and musician, conductor and musician and among musicians themselves. These subjects are often spoken about in periodicals concerning new music and need not be elaborated here. Still as far as discussions of problems of experimental music's problems are concerned the subjects of the first category are more prominent than these hierarchical questions here.

Let's exemplify the politics of music-making through the subject of improvisation. African improvisation might be seen to be illustrative of what may be called democratic music performance. This performance practice reflects the politics of the music in African society. It is a music of participation – by master musicians, ordinary musicians, dancers and even the public itself, all of whom are necessary and integral to performance. Surely the master musician plays the most virtuoso role, but all others are necessary for a piece to sound complete. This communal participation is different than the projecting of the same values on orchestra players who are requested to improvise a work although they were trained for something else and quite frankly prefer that something else as well.

Again, if we want to change the politics, possibly leading to educating improvising orchestras, the work must first be done in the political world, then in the musical one. That the same orchestra players want more say in choosing what they play is more their sort of democracy – still, they will generally not receive it, as orchestras are slaves to subsidies given by institutions who generally want to know that they are making a "good investment". When a democratized orchestra calls for programs which do not reflect the subsidy-giver's view of what is expected, then the life-line (salary) of those players is in danger. In other words, it must be reiterated that the politics of the societies in which the orchestras exist must be taken into account before one talks about democratizing the orchestras themselves.

Hierarchical relationships among interpreters and composers are often taken for granted although some composers are trying actively to narrow this distance (see further chapter VI). As long as this is the case, decisions made within category 1 will of course continue to reign supreme. Relevant to the question of hierarchy are subjects such as authoritarian personalities, rebellious attitudes and the like which in turn can be most influential in terms of musical interaction. Democracy begins through social agreement and continues through its constant reinforcement. In this sense democracy among musicians may be exemplary as in both the African cases as well as in situations where composers and musicians consciously explore democratic ways of musician cooperation. Clearly this can reflect a society's politics; sometimes it demonstrates exemplary social conduct.

3) Why does one compose? For whom does one compose? What are the factors that might go into one's style of composing? Might social factors affect the way of composing? More importantly, what is one trying to communicate in his or her compositions? Are the (formal) theories used in a composition and/or the aesthetics involved in any way translatable into a "dramaturgy" of that work in which music's abstraction can be verbalized? These are the most pertinent questions of this third category, questions any and every individual composer with any political sensitivity should consistently deal with.

Yet, what does political music sound like? György Ligeti once recounted the history of a royal Rumanian hymn, written by a commissioned Austrian composer, which he knew from childhood. Later as the somewhat reactionary Rumanian government was replaced by a socialist one, this hymn was banned. However, by some evolutionary process, the music still continued to exist with another text as an Albanian fighting song! This music is currently the Albanian national anthem (Ligeti: 45). In other words, a text can obviously inject a political vision into music, as can a familiar political melody (both occasionally made propagandistic by a society's "awareness education"), but not necessarily the sounds themselves. The way in which African drumming ensembles work is a political process, the sounds they create are a reflection thereof, but are in themselves not specifically political. They can only be related to their makers and the society to which they belong.

In summary, it is suggested that musicians of all sorts express their feelings on the subject of politics and music in its various forms, for if society itself does not provide an awareness education in these politics, then stimulation from the artistic provinces might be useful. Visionaries are necessary in society as Jean-Paul Sartre pointed out on so many occasions in claiming that the future, whatever form it may take on, will need its workers as well as its intellectual groups as man, a thinking and working being, needs both to survive. Today the experimental composers belong to this group of pioneers, music philosophers who carry the weight of tradition while trying to search for ways towards understanding as well as investigating music's potential roads in the future.

With this in mind, it is hoped that one can and will speak more specifically on music-political issues of all three categories, issues which are not independent of the musical subject areas of parts 3 and 4 of this book. One of these issues is the subject of idealism known to many of today's composers, including the present writer, a part of this pioneering attitude, but one that knows its dangers.

## 3.   IDEALISM/1: SERIAL MUSIC = ALL NOTES ARE CREATED EQUAL?

What is democratic about music? What is the composer's equivalent to Western Europe's social-democratic parties?

One of the most curious, yet unfortunately undocumented anecdotes that one comes across in which composers and music sociologists speak of democratizing music concerns serial music. In the Darmstadt 50s, it was occasionally suggested that one of serial music's bases was to be found in the equality of each pitch within the octave. This restructuring of diatonic thinking into chromatic thinking was therefore a form of primitive musical Marxism. (Do note that octaves were not taken into consideration in the Schönberg system. In other words if a b-flat is called for, any octave b-flat may be used.) If this were the case, then Stockhausen's quantification of all musical parameters would inevitably lead us to rigid musical Marxism. Marxism, of course, was created on the basis that man, being more intelligent than other animals, might be able to be willing to help his poor brothers economically. It is therefore unlikely that inanimate major scales have the same thoughts for their poor brothers, including the tritone.

In most cases of atonal serial music, at least so far, the listener has had a great deal of difficulty finding the aural key which is related to identifiable structural units in a serial work. If one were to assume that music appreciation generally has something to do with one or more describable entities that the listener can "hold onto", and in the case of the learned listener, identify (such as the two themes in a typical sonata movement), the liberation of the twelve or ninety-six or whatever number of tones has not yet found a musical language which includes such perceivable structural units. (Webern's *Variations for Orchestra*, Op. 30 with its almost ever-present and most often perceivable four-note groups is a noteworthy example of an exception.) In other words, the fantasy that serial composition might democratize music is an idealistic thought with a very shaky foundation.

A better example of democratizing music can be found in the discussion of improvising African musicians and orchestral repertoire committees above. But then again, we are far away from serial-like topics and the "E pluribus unum" visions of individual composers. Of course the improvisation example concerns the potential equality of musicians, serialism concerns the "equality" of sounds.

The choice of "democratizing" music is perhaps an odd one. Western European social democracy is a comfortable halfway house between Milton Friedman (e.g. Darwinian laissez-faire) capitalism and Marxist-Leninism. It would be difficult to imagine that there exists a musical equivalent to this combination which is not rooted in purely economic questions.

## 4.   IDEALISM/2 VERSUS REALISM: COMMUNIST EXPERIMENTAL MUSIC?

> "Paul Dessau war erst Kommunist und dann Komponist."
> The **Minister of Culture** of the former G.D.R. at a Dessau memorial concert in E. Berlin – 1979

The two "isms", communism and realism, have not been named here with respect to what is known as socialist realism, but instead are to be seen in the light of the questions: what is the daily realism of the communist musician in a communist country[1] as well as in a non-communist country?

It is hard to say whether the cultural minister of the former GDR was correct in appraising the priorities in the life of Paul Dessau who had then just passed away. It is certain, however, that two things play a major role in the world of composition in these countries: 1) extremists the likes of Cage, Xenakis and Stockhausen who push the boundaries of traditional music in terms of kilometers as opposed to centimeters have not traditionally been received with open arms, and 2) as suggested above, the inclusion of communist texts and a socialist dramaturgy in one's compositions is most useful. With this in mind, experimental music as we have defined it, is essentially absent in the communist countries, with the exception of electroacoustic music which is tolerated in several of these countries as well as some innovative performance activities in Poland, the most tolerant of the Eastern bloc nations. In other words, the reality of the East is that experimentalism with a small "e" can get through the sluices of those nations' selection committees when its padding is familiar, a difficult and most challenging foundation on which to build.

Still, Eastern European philosophers, such as the East German, Wolfgang Heise, have articulated where the experimentation might take place within such cultures. Heise is known to have described the theater in socialist society as "a laboratory for social imagination". When these laboratories organize the possibility to stretch socialist imaginations through "glasnost", more music of experimentation will be made possible in these nations.

In our Western world, the case is quite different. Attempts to make socialist music have not reflected our capitalist realism in the slightest. Luigi Nono's goal in his experimental work, *La Fabbrica Illuminata* which calls, among other things, for industrial sounds to be placed in a musical context and performed in factories to stimulate workers' interest in contemporary music, has, with all due respects, not really been attained. He kept up excellent contacts in the Eastern European world as a communist sympathizer; still, collaborations in his later years with the most virtuoso, not to mention expensive, solo artists, ensembles and orchestras, somehow clash with the basic premise. His "coming out" and accepting his armchair-communist sympathies was a most noble and courageous, not to mention honest gesture.

How much influence has Hans Werner Henze had on the revolution of the proletariat by writing operas for houses the likes of Venice and Vienna? These are not quite the best known "laboratories for social imagination" at least in most peoples' opinions. Anti-bourgeois slogans have more effect in daily protest demonstrations than at the highly subsidized, often arrogant opera house. If we choose for the above-mentioned "masses" in Western – or Eastern – countries, don't we have to write "communist pop music" (a genre awaiting its definition)? By the way: have the composers with communist leanings *ever* had any influence on the consciousness of our farmers and workers who generally prefer to listen to lighter genres of music?

Perhaps the answer might be "yes" when small-scale socialist music experiments such as Cornelius Cardew's Scratch Orchestra (see for example Cardew: 1972) are taken into consideration. The choice for a primarily amateur ensemble collectively composing is an intimate affair in which the hierarchy of creation is temporarily broken. The dozens of people who worked together in the Scratch project can most likely attest to a rethinking of what is possible for *everyone* given modern music's potential.

Yet one wonders why this sort of social experiment ended with this one ensemble? It has often been said that this music is of greater interest to its performers than to the listener. If this is indeed the case, so what? Scratch Music was music of participation, of collaboration, music for a group of musicians of all levels. Why didn't the Scratch idea extend to the overly dynamic America of the late 60s, or equally curiously, why is Christian Wolff's socialist-influenced playing together music so difficult in general (to the extent that few musicians seem to be able to feel they have successfully interpreted his works - see also part 6, chapter XVIg)? It all boils down to two points similar to those mentioned above: 1) the circumstances of Western performance as well as Western daily life are in shocking contrast to the ideals of those who try to create new communal performance practices, and 2) without that text of proletarian struggle, the message can only reach a restricted audience, be it those participating in a Scratch context or those who are well informed about a certain work or composer's reputation.

Experimental music in communism can exist. The reality on both sides of the rusty iron curtain simply has made it relatively impossible so far.

## 5.   IDEALISM/3: THE BEST CONDUCTOR IS NO CONDUCTOR AT ALL?

Anarchism is a word which knows two very distinct significations: one political – or better said anti-gorvernmental (the title of this section is a paraphrase of an anti-government quotation taken from Henry David Thoreau) – and one more general, meaning disorder. There are many who consider aleatoric music in which chance plays a role in a work's composition and/or performance and even free jazz improvisations as belonging to both – no rules, no leader – but this is of course is a naïve over-simplification.

Anarchist music, in the sense of anti-government, is anti-hierarchical music, anti-podium music, even anti-[art]work music. There is no room for the soloist genius or the great (wo)man. It's more like what Cage calls: "letting circumstances decide" and "music (not composition)" being a possession of no one or, better said, of all.

In a recent article (Landy: 1989) regarding Cage's vision of (musical) anarchism, the spontaneous/the natural were found to be more important to an anarchist (experimental) music than the pure search for the new. Models are created and dynamically molded in group participatory context. This resembles ancient music-making in economically poorer countries on the one hand and the idealistic views of the alternative technologists referred to in chapter III on the other hand.

Admittedly there is little anarchy in the anti-government from above sense to be expected in the near future. Those who attempt to "compose" anarchist music[2] (a contradiction in terms if you think about it) are all trying to help us experience another way. This is idealism pur sang, one trying to derail established values if only the slightest bit, idealism which fascinates many in the same sense a good piece of fictional adventure does – it takes you to a place you would love to visit, perhaps live in, which simply does not (yet?) exist as long as the global top forty village is next door.

## 6. THE POLITICS OF EXPERIMENTAL MUSIC

It is hoped that it has now been demonstrated that the non-musical elements – in fact all these elements have been political – in this part 2 are highly relevant to the central question of this book, what is the matter with experimental music, perhaps equally important as the questions of content which now follow.

One could summarize: with a clear realization of what the subjects of politics and music are, realization of which subjects are important to whom, and how solutions for mutual development can best be sought; with the often forgotten questions of possible combinations of potential uses of (new) technology as well as local values in experimental music, including the potential application and development of today's media; there is a basis for a wide discussion of what can be done for experimental music's further evolution, its economic foundation and its distribution.

This is in fact 50% of the challenge to today's experimental musician. If these questions are ignored, any solution found for issues of (musical) content will remain relatively anonymous. The experimental musicians and their partners in the worlds of musicology, music journalism, concert programming, subsidies, publishing, recording, radio-TV and rights organizations should team up to find new roads towards positive strategies for all involved in today's experimental music instead of falling into the traditional Darwinian trap of large-scale competition (or is this simply human nature?), jealousy and professional hatred. It is in fact in this last sentence that the author's idealism is showing for the second time (the first being the addendum of chapter III), for this is the most Marxist plea one can make for experimental music's survival ... but still we have not yet touched upon the question of what's happening in the music itself.

1)   This part of the chapter was written before the great events that took place in Eastern Europe in 1990. The author has chosen to leave it "as-is" as its thesis is its primary objective. All questions concerning the lack of popularity of these governments and their *Nomenclatura* will be skipped here.

2) If Edgard Varèse was right about music being organized sound, then really disorganized music is not music. Furthermore with the advances being made in chaos science (see for example Ilya Prigogine and Isabelle Stengers <u>Order Out of Chaos</u>) it seems likely that a purely anarchistic music in the sense of chaos can not exist. Therefore anarchism must be found on the human/musician level and, yet again, not at the sound level.

# Part 3 – Status report: advances within experimental music

In parts 3 and 4, experimental music will be discussed from the point of view of music's content, especially in terms of parametric discoveries as well as specific technological issues including audio-visual applications and electroacoustic developments.

For some reason or another, there are fewer subscribing to experimental music these days than say fifteen years ago: composers, musicians and listeners as well. The economic background has already been looked into. Problems in composition techniques, education and a general lack of communication between composer and musician as well as between composer and listener are those of importance in part 3.

# VI. New notation and instrument practice

## 1. SUMMARY AND A HYPOTHESIS

The hypothesis of this chapter is, despite comments made in chapter I concerning the definition of the subject at hand, that avant-gardism as we know it is *extremely* present in a great deal of today's music. What is ahead of its time is the challenge arising from various sorts of new notation and instrument techniques for contemporary musicians. In other words, the public may be tolerant of new varieties of sound materials and performance situations, but the musician is too often unable or unwilling to grasp two of the most essential breakthroughs in post-World War II music, namely the active sharing of the creative process of music-making and extending traditional instrumental practice. In the following pages these problems will be approached, first by delineating the area of concern, then by inspecting two pages of works by John Cage as an illustration of the notational challenge mentioned above, and finally by accusing the world of music education of acute stubbornness.

## 2. AVANT-GARDISM VERSUS EXPERIMENTAL MUSIC

No, we are not going to start again with something which has already been settled in the first chapter. This time the question is whether avant-gardism might exist within the provinces of experimental music. As the reader already may have guessed, it is the opinion here that avant-gardism refers to the musician and not to the public.

Luigi Nono once commented about how long he expected one form of experimentation, chance operations, to be of relevance (Nono: 45): "It will be valid as long as it is used as a means of widening our empirical experience, as a means of exploring possibilities". This comment is quite apropos today, for throughout recent times the listener's empirical experience has in fact been widened to many sonorous borderlines. Again, this is not the question here. What is important is how many musicians have experienced equally extreme boundaries in their own performances and/or whether they are interested in such types of exploration at all.

## 3.  THE MUSICIAN AS CO-COMPOSER

In this section the users-group and types of music will be specified.

**a.  Whom it may concern:** The answer to this question is actually quite simple. In the first place this chapter concerns those musicians who are open to specializing in or incorporating contemporary music into their repertoires. But in fact the problem involves anyone at all who participates in new music in one way or another. The composer is partially responsible for stimulating interest and assisting in preparing performances in which new notations are involved. The music educator (see section 6 below) is responsible for systematizing notation advances and incorporating them in the development of a performer's contemporary techniques. The people of the concert and media world should have an interest in new music's being presented in the best way possible. And finally the listener certainly is in no position to enjoy music if a performer or an orchestra is playing with a grimace resembling a migraine headache. These are whom it may concern.

**b.  What it may concern:** We are concerned with new notation including pieces which have been classified as open form works. (Our concern also includes extended instrumental techniques – see section 5 below.) We are therefore concerned with improvisation as well and this will be our starting point.

*Improvisation:* In an article by the ethnomusicologist Bruno Nettl one of the universals of music, improvisation, is discussed. He tries to place it within the world of all music compositions. His hypothesis is that: "the juxtaposing of composition and improvisation as fundamentally different processes is false, [...] the two are part of the same idea" (Nettl: 6). This notion is particularly interesting given the fact that many composers have sought more of musicians today than just *interpretation*, often their sole métier of years past. Interpretation has been supplemented by *improvisation* therefore broadening the performer's horizon to include participation in the creative process of composition in all its aspects. In section 3C, some composers' justifications will be mentioned. Of course, Nettl is correct when he adds in this same article that this sharing the act of composition is an international phenomenon and that it has also played an occasional role in the history of European music. (For example, Liszt, as well as various Baroque instrumentalists "improvised" using what today might be seen to be partial score information.) What is of relevance to experimental music is the extent of improvisation and the new definitions of its models (i.e., that which is notated).

*Notation:* The composer-theorist Erhard Karkoschka has classified contemporary notation into four distinct groups (Karkoschka: 1966): *Präzise Notation* (precise, sometimes called result notation which includes traditionally notated scores as well as post-scriptive precise notations used by ethnomusicologists and some electronic composers. To be precise many symbols have been added to the standard 19th-century set. Other than the occasional too-virtuosic piece in which the performer must make choices, this is the only type of notation that is not under investigation here), *Rahmennotation* ("framework" or reaction notation: in this case the notation resembles traditional notation, but one or more elements have been freed. For example Morton Feldman's taking the stems away from his notes in several of his pieces opened up the parameter of rhythm. His multi-voiced works in which the rhythm is not precisely notated are said to be written in "race-course" notation [Behrman: 60]), *Hinweisende Notation* ("reference" notation: this type of notation is the halfway house between "framework" and graphic notation; it also includes prose scores. There are musical references given, such as notes, time scale, and/or loudness scale, but the notation takes on a semi-abstract form calling for more creative additions by the performer[s] than the first two categories. This notation has often been employed by the likes of Sylvano Bussotti and John Cage), and *Musikalische Graphik* (abstract graphic or action notation). Karkoschka continues by isolating electronic music notations, but in fact with the exception of live-electronic situations in which any one of the above might be used, most electronic music notation is precise, be it often including exotic variants to traditional notational symbols. The only addition to the above worthy of mention is notation for non-musical performance aspects. For example Mauricio Kagel's personal notation often calls for a great deal of visual theatrical effects. Others have attempted to define audio-visual notations. These are of relevance to this discussion when a good deal of interpretation or even co-composition is requested of the musician. Cage's old sampler, the book *Notations* (Cage: 1969) is a great "*Reader's Digest* version*" of these four categories.

*Open form:* This "do-it-yourself" notion has been present in several art forms for about a century. When Pierre Boulez applied aleatoric processes to his works allowing certain procedural decisions to be made during performances, it was not in the shadow of of earlier indeterminate Cage works, but following the likes of Stéphane Mallarmé and James Joyce. Earle Brown's version which he calls "mobile form" is obviously influenced by Alexander Calder (see part 6, chapter XVIf).

Great treatises have been written on the subject of open form, not the least of which being Konrad Boehmer's *Zur Theorie der offenen Form* (Boehmer: 1967). Furthermore, in a recent article on open form in music, Christian Wolff looks at three new second generation works (Wolff: 1987). He separates two types of open form: those pieces primarily involving *sophisticated and flexible modes of control* and those involving *liberation: individual and possibly social*. His examples show Nono as belonging to the former category and Pauline Oliveros and himself as belonging to the latter. Interestingly enough, Umberto Eco predicted this split in his *Opera aperta* written in 1962. The link between both of Wolff's variants can be found in Marxist dialectic thinking. Eco discusses this in his chapter entitled "Form as Engagement".

The two Cage pages to be discussed below will elegantly combine all of the what's it may concern.

**c. The concerns of those concerned:** "Form can only be invented; material can only be discovered" (Haubenstock Ramati: 41).

What have composers and musicologists as well as musicians and music educators written about these subjects? In reverse order, one might summarize: musicians and music educators: next to nothing as may be expected – yet specialized technical discussions might be of great value; musicologists: too little - the likes of the productive author/composer Thomas de Lio (see below), who has analyzed works of the entire Cage school as well as of Robert Ashley and others, are exceptions; and the composers: a great deal, be it mainly in the form of informal manifestoes.[1]

In an article focusing on the novelty of some recent forms of notation, the current writer discussed the inevitability of breakthroughs in instrumentation, notation, form, and sound sources as a reflection of socio-economic cultural changes in our highly technological Western society (Landy: 1983, 13). It is in this sense that both of Wolff's elements, control: a reflection of new technical (im-)possibilities and social liberation: e.g., anarchist, Zen, and other anti-authoritarian movements of the 60s, have been reflected in new music-making. In this chapter's conclusion (7) the question will be posed concerning the extent of time dependence of all such musical activities.

How have the composers presented these ideas? Most of the relevant texts date from the era of the greatest concentration of creative notational development. The following is a brief selection of relevant statements concerning form, material, and control from a number of composers. One of the most prolific spokesmen, Cage, will "speak" later on.

i. Earle Brown speaks of many composers' striving for the "liberation of (sound) objects" (Brown, citing William Seitz: 1966, 58). As materials are liberated, the time dimension must also be treated in new ways. Morton Feldman, more form- than material-minded, is known to have claimed that "process itself might be the Zeitgeist of our age" (De Lio: 1981b, 528). Adding one and one, new music can be achieved in which its "sounds ... (are) unfolding in time" (De Lio: 1983, 478), in which "time relationships (are) discovered *over* time" (and not *through* time: the difference between process as form generator and classical form applications – De Lio: 1983, 479). According to

David Behrman, in the early Feldman parameter-freed works, "the player must ask himself what sort of pitches (or rhythms) are most appropriate – in effect, what sort of music it is that he is playing" (Behrman: 63). Umberto Eco, while referring to similar Henri Pousseur compositions, speaks of the "art work in motion" (Eco: 42) which is achieved through a sort of compositional pluralism in which control in all its senses has been redefined. These ways of thinking and the vision of a dynamic art work (the permanent work in progress) are at the heart of the subject of the current chapter.

ii. Dieter Schnebel and Christian Wolff represent the more politically oriented. Returning to the concept of process in new music, Schnebel has said: "I believe that cultural processes influence compositional processes in many ways, and that new music is often a direct reflection of social situations" (e.g. his *Visible Music* series, Pauli: 14). He also finds music to be open to new influences derived from our mass consumer society. (Musical) "materials ... are approaching those of our daily lives to an extent" (e.g. Cage's *Theater Piece*, Pauli: 19). In his above-mentioned 1987 article, Wolff is careful about the subject of notation in open works: "Open can suggest possibilities, multiplicity, heterogeneity, change. It can imply open to participation ... At any rate, open comes down to how it sounds, hence also to how it's played, more or less regardless of how it's scored" (Wolff: 134). It all boils down to spontaneity, true for any improvisation, according to this composer. Wolff's reaction to the liberated sound object: "Sounds are autonomous because we think them so, and that gives them content: their autonomy is what they signify. Content, then, guarantees the openness of form, its dialectical character" (Wolff: 135).

Between Brown, Feldman, Schnebel and Wolff all sounds and ordering procedures are potentially applicable to composition as long as the musical idea (in the Schönbergian sense) is aesthetically substantial. But what about the notation? Kagel has been known to call for a music notation that is able to "grasp all sound dimensions" (Pauli: 86). He finds that when one inspects a new score, "the optical impression is the basis for the (primary) comprehension (of a work)" (Pauli: 88). But, as Cornelius Cardew warns, "a musical notation that looks beautiful is not [necessarily – LL] a beautiful notation, because it is not the function of notation to look beautiful" (Cardew: 1972, 29). He is of course attacking those graphic composers who were equally if not more interested in having their scores put on exhibit than in having them performed. Cardew is therefore against notation for its own sake. What he expected of his notation was the solution to the eternal question of interpretation. "In my pieces there is no intention separate from the notation; the intention is that the player should respond to the notation. He should not interpret in a particular way (e.g. how he imagines the composer intended) but should be engaged in the act of interpretation" (Cardew: 27).

Returning to Wolff's music, as Thomas de Lio points out, it is rarely the case that when one of his works is repeated, patterns are produced which are recognizably similar. Wolff does not consider this problematic: "People sometimes ask, why don't you just specify what you want and be done with it? I do! Actions are specified..." (De Lio: 1981b, 200; orig. Mainstream Records MS5015: 2). Behrman, when discussing Wolff's music speaks of the conduct of games. "The complexities of this notation (*Duet II*) are directed less at an arrangement of sounds resulting from performers' actions than at the conditions under which their actions are to be produced. (It addresses itself to the player's mind as well as his fingers)" (Behrman: 1965, 73). The game includes false starts and disguised cues, reminding him of the Indian improvisation technique known as *Laratgheth* (Behrman: 1965, 67, cf. Nettl). Thus improvisation, social collaboration, and new notation are combined in Wolff's music. Comprehension of the composer's ideas leads to mental virtuosity's joining hands with its instrumental/manual equivalent. This is exactly what all these composers are looking for. Surprisingly many find Wolff's music among the most difficult of those whom it may concern, but he is also one of the best documented composers in the sense of the present discussion. Perhaps Wolff's personal combination of both types of openness and his thirty-five years of experimental perseverance might be the reasons why.

## 4. TWO OF CAGE'S PAGES

The challenge of new notation will now be illustrated by a page taken from two of John Cage's works, *Concert for Piano and Orchestra (1957/58)* and *Variations IV (1963)* - both scores are published by C. F. Peters (New York).

**a. "Concert" (Page 1):**[2] Actually it is page 53 of the (optional) solo piano part (see below). Each (optional) part, be it the solo piano part, or any of the orchestra voices or even the conductor's part (also optional), is written in a new notation, in open form. Here is Cage's introduction to this "solo" piano part: *Each page is one system for a single pianist to be played with or without any or all parts written for orchestra instruments. The whole is to be taken as a body of material presentable at any point between minimum (nothing played) and maximum (everything played), both horizontally and vertically: a program made within a determined length of time (to be altered by a conductor, when there is one) may involve any reading, i.e., any sequence of parts or parts thereof.* This introduction is followed by a clear description of each and every "rehearsal number". Here follows three examples of these rehearsal numbers on our first Cage page: <u>A:</u> *Following the perimeter, from any note on it, play in opposite directions on the proportion given. Here and elsewhere, the absence of any kind means freedom for the performer in that regard.* <u>BB:</u> *Notes are single sounds. Lines are duration (D), frequency (F), overtone structure (S), amplitude (A), and occurrence (succession) (O). Proximity to these, measured by dropping perpendiculars from notes to lines gives, respectively, longest, lowest, simplest, loudest, and earliest.* <u>BK:</u> *Like "A", but with noises. Of those notated play only that number given. I=interior piano construction. A=auxiliary noises. O=outer piano construction. The position of the note vertically gives its loudness (high = fff) (low = ppp) (amplitude free).*

At first glance one can identify all of Karkoschka's non-precise notations on this one page. As pages may be ordered in any (random) order, Cage also employs open form. This implies that the triangle, *BW,* which is completed on page 54, does not have to be seen as a single element as page 54 does not have to follow page 53 (or be played at all). Rehearsal numbers *A* and *B* are "Rahmen" notations, as well as the notation in the middle of the page which began on page 52. Rehearsal number *BK* is "hinweisend" and *BB, BV,* and *BW* are all graphic.

Each musical parameter must be reckoned with in all of these fragments. In *A* pitch is clear, their ordering less so; in *B* and *BK* more choice is involved; in *BB, BV,* and *BW* Cage's indeterminate notation reaches an extreme (these look like outcomes of the transparents included in his *Variations* works). Rhythm/time distribution, timbre, note density, and dynamics all generate similar scales of freedom. Should the pianist write out his or her own part? Obviously this is not Cage's goal as the sought spontaneity and differentiation between performances would then be lost. However, writing out a score for this page as a rehearsal exercise should be mandatory in any music student's training.

The independence of parts, the optional conductor's part (who can only manipulate the general flow of time), the flexible instrumentation (including none) all reflect Cage's anarchistic view of music-making. The anonymity of the score, its indeterminacy is clearly Zen-derived. The use of I Ching chance operations is an Eastern reaction to Western technical advance. (Ironically these days Cage does use computer print-outs of I Ching outcomes.) Yet, despite this anonymity and the great unknowns of the score, it is clearly Cageian. Pauline Oliveros once wrote of his similarly notated, stellar chart-based *Atlas Eclipticalis:* "The notation ... is as accurate and precise as conventional music notation, yet the performer has a new kind of freedom. The results guarantee a performance with details indeterministic, yet faithful to the overall character of the piece, as if viewing the stars and their relationships from every different position in space" (Oliveros: 204).

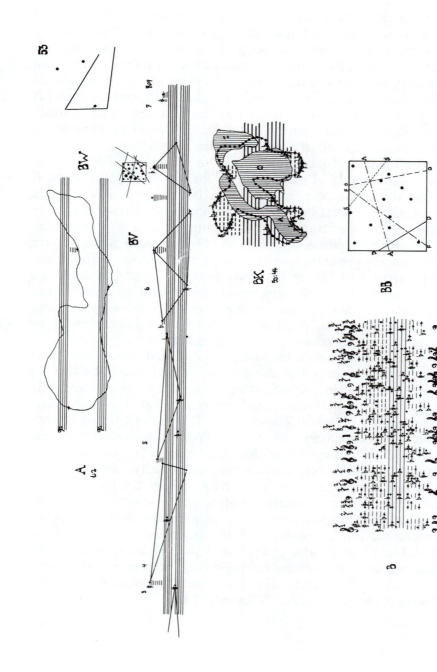

Sadly enough personal experiences of performance results have been less pleasant than one might hope. Some performers who have not taken the trouble to "enter" the piece end up freely improvising, mostly poorly. As several classical musicians only know of Cage's undeserved reputation of being a nihilist joker, a composer of scores any fool can play, they end up adding silly dramatic effects to their uninteresting improvisations. When the likes of a David Tudor is playing the solo piano part, his exemplary total command of the piece, its notation and its form potential, represents the eye of the storm of amateurism, lack of interest and seriousness. In short, most players do not possess the tools needed to make this piece accessible to themselves as players and to the listeners who are saddened by the musicians' failure to (independently) mix into the potentially fascinating indeterminate ensemble with all its notational challenges known as the orchestra.

**b. ...with "Variations" (Page 2):**[3] "Cage's *Variations IV* is the most ... anarchist work around" (Charles: 107). This work, "for any number of players, any sounds or combination of sounds produced by any means, with or without other activities" serves as an example of a prose/graphic score in which all sorts of spatial electroacoustic possibilities are open. Enclosed in the score is a transparent sheet filled with dots and circles to be cut out and used along with the prose instructions. The score's text reads as follows:

> **Material not provided: a plan or map of the area used for performance, and optionally a copy of it on transparent material.**
> **Material provided: seven points and two circles on a transparent sheet. (Cut so that there are nine pieces, each with 1 notation.)**
> **Place one of the circles anywhere on the plan. Let the other circle and the points fall on the plan or outside it. Taking the placed circle as center, produce lines from it to each of the points. (Straight lines.) The second circle is only operative when one of the lines so produced (one or more) intersects or is tangent to it.**
> **Make as many readings of the material as desired (before or during the performance.)**

**A. Theater Space (auditorium with doors)**
**1. One floor**
**2. With balcony or balconies**
**Sound(s) to be produced at any point on the lines outside**
**the theater space (extend lines where necessary), Open**
**door(s) pertaining to a given point. (Sound production**
**may be understood as simply opening doors.)**
**Intersection of second circle = sound in total theater**
**space (public address system) or at any specific point on**
**the produced line within the space. Two or more points**
**may be taken as a sound in movement. (Open pertinent**
**doors.) Movement is also indicated by using transparent**
**map in addition. A single notation will then give two**
**points in space. Several of these may be associated with**
**one sound.**
**B. Building with one or more floors.**
**When necessary open windows instead of doors.**
**C. Apartment or suite.**
**The performance can be in reference to one or any**
**number of rooms. (The meaning of "outside" may**
**change.)**
**D. Closed space (cave).**
**E. Outside space (any amount).**
**Measurements of time and space are not required.**
**When performed with another activity which has a**
**given time-length (or on a program where a given**
**amount of time is available) let the performance of this**
**take a shorter amount.**
**A performer need not confine himself to a performance**
**of this piece. At any time he may do something else. And**
**others, performing something else at the same time and**
**place, may, when free to do so, enter into the**
**performance of this.**

The work gives the performer(s) an almost indescribable
amount of freedom. Normal musical questions pertaining to
length, instrumentation and content(!) are left completely open.
This score is more specific about the musical parameter of space
than any other subject. In fact the only space not to be used is
the concert stage as we know it. Cage: "It was an attempt to expel
music, just as we send children outdoors to play..." (Cage: 1981,
15).

There is no hierarchy involved among the players as they
are anonymously absent during the performance, an *art en*

*situation* (a term of André Reszler's) is created, the sum of all individual (unforeseen) activities. One thinks of the often-quoted Cage anecdote: "Complicate your garden so it's surprising like uncultivated land". This fulfills Christian Wolff's wish for spontaneity in any event. Coleridge's words on the same subject (see page 37) again come to mind. Herein lies the key to Cage's and many other contemporary composers' music.

The nihilist will take Cage literally in his view that this work is a radical experiment in motivating people to rethink what "music" is and whether music might eventually become superfluous, "if only the people learn to use their ears..." However, this "anything goes" attitude was put on paper to stimulate the musician's creativity and participation in the composition process.

Is it then such an anonymous work? Although the performance space is the only parameter discussed in the score, the opening up of space, material (on the famed recordings of the Los Angeles art gallery performance microphones were hung throughout the space including above the sidewalk and the bar, recordings were played and radios were heard throughout the space all following chance), length and form (a consequence of that which takes place) are all "Ur-Cageian".

Ironically Cage remains a composer of whom it is often said that it might be more fun to participate in his works than listen to them. Indeed participating in *Variations IV* is an unforgettable experience if one makes the effort to make something of it. But in that case it is equally stimulating to the "passive" (this depends on circumstances) listener. The success of the Los Angeles recordings is a case in point.

To make the circle round, that which Cage and many others have opened is that which too few have looked into and taken advantage of. This subject is the concern of part 5.

## 5. THE MUSICIAN AS EXTENDED INSTRUMENTALIST

In every phase of music history the addition of new vocal and instrumental techniques has known a slow evolution. The exponential growth of new vocal and instrumental sounds of the last thirty-five years is no exception. How much trouble did Wagner have finding singers who could handle the register and techniques he wrote for? How many singers can handle Luciano Berio's *Sequenza III* or pianists who can perform Pierre Boulez's *Second Piano Sonata* or flutists who have learned the techniques for Robert Dick's "other flute", etc.?

Certainly there are enough musicians around; there should be no problems posed by the above questions, but relatively few have been open to these new challenges. Undoubtedly some scores are unplayable, but in general it was then the composer's goal to have decisions made during performance (see Cage's *Concert* yet again). But most composers looking to expand an instrument's horizon work out the technique and its potential notation in the laboratory before writing a score. The *Sequenze* were based on this principle (see also part 6 chapter XVIb). Dick is a flautist himself and can play everything described in his textbooks.

Many feel that new techniques are the sole possession of their inventors. In fact the number of composer-performers today (today's Franz Liszt's) is extremely high. But it is assumed and to be hoped that these musicians do not feel they are playing as if they were at the Olympic Games, looking for positions (sounds) and speeds no one else can attain. They are introducing techniques which are to be musically fused with those of the established order. That should be their personal experiment. As long as others hesitate to learn these techniques, these new techniques will retire with their composer-performers. As many of today's pieces call for one or more new instrumental techniques, the lack of musicians who take the trouble to learn them cuts down potential performances drastically. Talent or the lack thereof cannot be the reason, for the number of excellent musicians for the classics has not dropped. There must be another place where these techniques are put away into vaults; vaults only a few are allowed to open. Might that be the nursery of all creation, the place of learning?

## 6. OUR CONCERN: AVANT-GARDE EXPERIMENTAL MUSIC VERSUS MUSIC EDUCATION

"My music is often just material. But not raw material exactly. It's set up in such a way as to require anyone who wants to seriously deal with it to exert themselves in a particular way" (Christian Wolff calling for a new virtuosity in Zimmermann: 268). "What does it mean to speak of "open form"? [One must begin with form in general: it is] an organic entity which arises from a smelting of various past experiences (ideas, emotions, activities, materials, ... ). A form is a successful work, the goal of production which ... again and again is developed from various perspectives of life itself" (Eco: 9, 14).

Exerting ourselves in the discovery of virtuosity, thinking about past experiences, continually developing new ones: these are the challenges of new notation, of open form. Recently a Dutch conservatory director was heard to have said the following after hearing a proposal to have a Cage work done similar to the *Concert:* "We cannot subject these poor children [i.e., advanced music students-L.L.] to music of that difficulty."

Fortunately, slowly but surely responses of dissatisfaction are being published. In a festival catalog in Bonn, the musician Florian Tielebier-Langenscheidt (Zeller: 33-39) complains that today's music student is forcefully led away from anything resembling "do it yourself" movements, they are pushed into cages (no pun intended) in which all forms of musical surprise are neutralized. He does not understand why one has to wait until discovery (often at a relatively late age and by chance) that there is more to music than do-re-mi and thus does not understand why so little has been (is allowed to be) done in opening up the minds of the youth to the potential of contemporary music's new sounds and performance possibilities. Also in W. Germany, the composer Josef-Anton Riedl has spent time inspiring a small portion of the youth with ideas of making music with new materials. In N. America it is first and foremost the work of R. Murray Schafer that has reached yet again a select few. In his collection of didactic works, *Creative Music Education,* he proposes a partner to traditional ear training he calls "ear cleaning" which "expands traditional concepts of ear training in order to deal with both the newer forms of today's music and the acoustic environment, (our "soundscape"), at large" (Schafer: ix). Worthy of mention are a small number of composers including Barney Childs and Ben Johnston who have composed aleatoric pieces for student experimentation.

It is not the goal of this writer to take an inventory of the few methods available to us today. None is geared to all of the following concerns:

– opening new music to the very young (elementary school level) including performing simple genres of music with note *and* sound materials,

– integrating new notation into the early study of instrumental students,

– including new notation, form, and ensemble techniques as a mandatory study for all conservatory students, and above all,

– including more contemporary music on a student's recital programs. It is at this basic level that the well-guarded "secrets" of new music can be made public and that the most isolated of the modern arts can be reintegrated into our society as a dynamic, and not necessarily avant-garde art form.[4]

## 7. CONCLUSION

The techniques and the technology made possible by the composer of focus here, Cage as well as all others specialized in new notations and instrumental techniques since the early 50s have been appreciated or at least tolerated by a select public and pretty much rejected by the powers that be in music education. (During a 1988 Cage Festival at a well-known conservatory, a voice teacher was known for having recommended students not to participate in master classes of his *Songbooks* as being potentially "harmful" [!] to the voice.)

It is often heard that the cause of this rejection is the supposed (lack of) quality of much new music and its overly intellectual basis. There will always be good and bad music. There will also always be successful experiments and failures. Nevertheless new ("non-musical" instrumental or vocal as well as electroacoustic) sounds are more accepted than ever and demand new forms of notation, just like the improvisation and the aleatoric/indeterminate (and even multi-media) works as discussed above.

Finally, there will always be the mainstream artists and radicals. There is little recent music the likes of the orchestra piece R.I.P. Hayman once notated for Salvador Dali on a toothpick. The current second generation of newly notated music is one of refinement, profiting by the good and bad, the more and less successful experiments of the past. If these composers get more feedback from musicians, a future revised version of this book will perhaps be able to exclude this chapter.

1) Texts of musicologists and especially composers critical of open form, as for example György Ligeti, and those critical of new notation have not been included here as none concerns a musician's (in)ability to play a given score. These discussions instead mainly deal with the writer's taste for precision and "clarity". This may be true for these writers, but in no way influences the current presentation.

2) Recordings used: KOBY1051 – 3  *25 Year Retrospective* with David Tudor, piano and Merce Cunningham, conductor; Odeon C165-28954/7Y  *Music Before Revolution* with Ensemble Musica Negativa, Rainer Riehn, conductor.

3) Recordings used: Everest 3132, 3230 with Cage and Tudor performing.

4) The writer has plans to return to a number of these subjects of education tools at a date in the near future, especially those relevant to new notations, performance practice (workshop music-making) and electroacoustic music. It is to others to work on music appreciation for the young. (See, for example, Paynter and Aston: 1970 and Paynter: 1982.) At the moment this seems to be a "hole in the market".

It should be added here that in 1991 proposals within the British educational system have been published which could lead to introducing *all* young British students at an early age to many of the areas of discussion here, a most promising development.

# VII. Form and structure, (a)tonality and rhythm and our perception's fuse box

## 1.  GREAT PIECE! WHAT WAS I SUPPOSED TO LISTEN TO?

The following pages may seem relatively conservative to most readers in comparison to the rest of this book. The question at the basis of this chapter is: when one combines sounds as every composer does, at what point does the fuse blow out in a listener's perception? In other words, where is the borderline between the presence of any sort of model (think of the improvisation discussion in the previous chapter) and perceived chaos? Is this something dependent on melody; or form; or perhaps rhythm, tempo and meter; or even timbre, sound sources or note density?

It is hypothesized that a listener needs at least something to hold onto, to identify with in order to appreciate music. This hypothesis by no means calls for the death of anything experimental. There are adequate examples of composers who have broadened music's horizon while offering a key to the music to the listener without that fuse blowing out as alluded to above.

To illustrate this we might briefly consider György Ligeti's music of the 1960s. If the listener is not watching a conductor's arms during performance, often no perceivable beat can be followed. The likes of the A-B-A form known to any Chopin enthusiast is hardly present here. There is no melody. He has even employed microtonality through the use of quarter-tones in a few of his works. Therefore so far all of music's traditional ingredients are absent. Nevertheless, the careful allocation of density change and timbral development was his *idée fixe* at the time. Perceptible networks of expanding or contracting interval fields, slow, clear, timbral development along dynamic curves are the trademarks of these compositions. The experience of the Ligeti sonority of this period might be seen as an ear-training in beatless, colorful cluster-harmonies (i.e. simultaneities based on small (second) intervals – see further part 6, chapter XVIa).

Yet how many pieces have we all heard in which the listener gets lost after about five seconds and grits his or her teeth (hopefully silently) for the duration of the overly (un)calculated composition in which only one single parameter named in chapter I seems to be prominent, namely order-disorder? Unfortunately, disorder needs order to become clearly perceivable as a parametric limit. Continual "chaos" or "order" are in this case one-sided. (John Cage once humorously complained about the permanent collection at the Museum for Modern Art in New York: there were too many masterpieces. If there had been a few "lesser" paintings, then the masterpieces might be able to be better appreciated.) Is there something then essentially wrong with atonality? With pieces based on Hz, db and sec? And what about all those works without melody?

## 2.  A RETURN TO PARAMETER-LAND

Along with form and recognizable rhythm, tonality[1] is (re)gaining prominence in contemporary art music, for many as a *sine qua non*. The arguments used are common ones. Several aspects of tonal music seem to be as organic as sound itself. Almost all instrumental sounds are based upon the harmonic series (although whether a listener is aware of these harmonics or not is not of primary importance). The fact is that harmonic structures have been universally accepted in instrumental sounds, scales, tunings, etc. Sequences, the recognizable repetition of melodic and rhythmical patterns are familiar to us through folk music, and, for instance, bird song. But is this tonality (form, meter) necessary to make music digestible.

It never ceases to come as a surprise how many people today, when listening to a work by Anton Webern for the first time, claim that his free use of rhythm and tempo can be traced to jazz, something far from Webern's methods. The desire to appreciate anything new through past knowledge, to make it more acceptable, can lead one to false assumptions. This occurs in all fields, not only in music. Yet a listener uses this method to find the doors opening onto the complexities of contemporary music.

In the classic of the 70s, Douglas R. Hofstadter's *Gödel, Escher, Bach: an Eternal Braid* the importance is stressed of the mind's need to match things. The science dealing with this is called pattern recognition. Returning to the main question of this chapter, it has been assumed that members of many musical movements leading towards great abstraction in sound organization have sometimes ignored the limitations of the mind's capabilities. Examples can be found in a number of tonal romantic compositions of the latter half of the 19th century that are perceived as formless; later a good deal of free and serial atonal works; and more recently in a (too) large portion of electroacoustic music – all seem to have been searching in their own ways for the ultimate sound complex. Composers need to appreciate the mind's boundaries[2] when creating new works, for it is imperative that the perception reacts to a recognizable, tangible "hold" that the listener can use.

This search is a kind of combination of the technological with the local of part 2. A person's perception is "programmed" to react both to cultural input and to the subjects in which one has been trained, through repeated listening, to understand or at least appreciate. In other words, if today's non-tonal music is to take hold, it must be introduced to the listener didactically (not each composition, but groups thereof). In this way there may be something to hold onto which is analogous to a theme in a tonal work.

In 1987, Eric Clarke published his thoughts on this matter in his article, *Levels of structure in the organization of musical time*. His thesis is that the organization of durations (including meter) plays a "vital role as a cognitive framework" of musical works and that composers must take account of the consequences of the absence of such frameworks if their music is to be comprehensible for listeners (Clarke: 211). His argument is based on splitting the time dimension into three levels: low – expression, intermediate – rhythm and high – form to each and all of which his thesis may be applied. Fortunately Clarke has not made the traditional claim that the use of known meters is the only way to cognition; instead he calls for collaborations between psychologists, musicians and composers to discover the limits and potential of perception's reaction to time structures (where does the fuse blow?), concluding that composers could use the results of this type of research to organize their works profiting by these (new) frames of reference (Clarke: 236; by the way, musicologists and cyberneticians specialized in pattern recognition might be added to his list). Similar research should guide our appraising the necessity of tonality as defined here as well. With all this in mind, let's take another look at a few of our parameters.

**a. Pitch:** Obviously the clearest case of taking the listener's major guideline out of the music is to be found in compositions without melody. Schönberg saw this problem correctly when he added those two famous symbols to music notation, H̅ and N̅: *Hauptstimme* and *Nebenstimme*. In this way he took care that the listener be given the chance to follow one or more highlighted instruments playing the main voice as well as those in the middle mode, being more prominent than the other, accompanying instruments, but less prominent than the main voice. Yet did Schönberg really solve his problem? In his (non-) serial melodyless works, occasionally using his technique of *Klangfarbenmelodik,* moving the main voice from timbre to timbre, from instrument to instrument every few notes, his great expressionism abstracted that main voice to such an extent that the listener often still had (and has today) trouble grabbing onto the rope that holds such works together. Schönberg believed that the listener would get used to these new abstract *Hauptstimmen* and therefore be able to follow his works, as well as those of colleagues without difficulty. History has shown this to be a most difficult process. It is "difficult", yet not impossible. Webern, known for his greater degree of abstraction than Schönberg, applied symmetric rows more often than his teacher. In the case of three-, four- or six-tone symmetric rows (that is the sequence of intervals found in the six [or four or three]-tone segment can be found in the other segment[s] as well, which means that THE row consists solely of the single segment through symmetry – the other[s all] being a variant of the first), the amount of potential permutations and combinations is highly restricted and therefore potentially easier to follow. For example, as previously mentioned his Variations for Orchestra, Op. 30 with its clear presentation of the four-note motive from the very beginning might be used didactically in educating the listener, musician and young composer to cope with, enjoy and better understand  serial music. Webern offers that something to hold onto without writing a tonal, traditional melodic work.

The following question therefore must be raised: do we need such clearly defined structures to replace melody as the main point of reference in music today? Most likely the answer to this question might be negative, *but* it is dependent on the listener being helped in finding a way to listen to melodyless music. Every revolution in music needed to be introduced in what might be considered to be a didactic fashion. People do not tend to try to understand changes in their environment themselves, but prefer to be helped. If, indeed, the assumption is correct that our perception can handle melodyless music less clear than the Webern example (again Ligeti comes to mind), how do we do the "teaching" implied above? This is work that should be looked into by any composer interested in expanding the boundaries of melody, *Hauptstimme* and all their cousins.

Until now all of our attention has been given to single voices. What about the subjects of contrapuntal or harmonic textures? After dissonant intervals became as common as a cup of tea (think of the evolution Hugo Wolf, Arnold Schönberg, Pierre Boulez), new simultaneities of all sorts were composed as if everyone was used to every and any combination. Again, things seem to have moved too quickly in the vertical department without allowing for a new sort of harmonic music appreciation to accompany it. Those composers, as dissimilar as Igor Stravinsky, Charles Ives, Edgard Varèse, Luigi Dallapiccola and György Ligeti, who consistently used certain sorts of chords or other simultaneous textures, have proven that these advances have been of great value. Those who let the numbers do the talking, sometimes create works that may be as logical as a successful computer program, but unsuccessful in the listener department, and that is what this chapter is all about. Therefore questions similar to those presented in the technology chapter and some posed in relation to melody are equally relevant to the expanded boundaries of vertical writing today.

To continue there is the subject of new tunings and the use of any frequency in new music. When discussing this an anecdote comes to mind concerning the poor Indonesian gamelan player who "suffers" from what we call "perfect pitch". If this player can only think in terms of A = 440 Hz and in terms of our chromatic scale introduced in the time of J. S. Bach, imagine the headaches he must have playing his "untuned" gamelan which doesn't fit into "perfect pitch". Our perception can obviously readjust to any (or several) tuning(s), if it is given the chance. Being stampeded with new frequencies, often without any structured hierarchy in several new pieces, does more to confuse than help today's listener.

New notation has also played a role in freeing pitch from melody. The Morton Feldman compositions, in which he separated the register of his instruments into high, middle and low without further specification leaving choice to the performer(s), exemplify a music which is more gesture oriented, than pitch oriented. In fact, pitch hardly matters in these pieces. Regardless of that lack of specified pitch information, Feldman was able to create a sound all his own in these works. Therefore this example might be seen as an object of comparison when dealing with parameter-freeing through new notations.

By the way, the question of whether pitch is the most important, or even necessary parameter in terms of cognition has not yet been touched upon. It is believed that rhythm can be equal, if not more important (think of a good deal of African percussive music) in a given piece, but it is also believed that recently secondary parameters as well as structural developments may take equal prominence as will be shown below.

**b. Duration: rhythm, meter and tempo:** Several years ago, the current writer composed a work for percussion ensemble in which half of the short movements knew no meter, no tempo. A number of musicians complained that they were treated unfairly as the *raison d'être* of the percussionist is the capability of retaining a beat or rhythmic pattern. Their complaint was that no percussion work could be of any importance without the heartbeat of their trade.

The only way to "teach" them of their fault was to include a movement influenced by the sound of the pitter-patter of light rain. This totally unstructured rhythmical experience can be one of great beauty, if one only listens to it. Most percussionists have no trouble being inspired by rain. The slow transformation of a-rhythmic rain to a more rhythmic following section is the next step in this training – how does one go from 0 – 1 in the parameter of rhythmic order? Once this has been "learned", the world of to count or not to count is open to all. The listener needs exactly the same type of assistance in dealing with this problem as unstructured division of time is most difficult to deal with in a musical context.

Music is metric, mostly danceable. That repetitive unit known as the measure is where it all begins. Yet the free flow of some Renaissance and Medieval measureless music seems to be tolerated by many a listener. Why might this be? Obviously the answer is not only to be found in this parameter, but in its connection to text, to melody (where relevant), to harmony, in other words to convention. Parametric music like serial music often forgets these combinations working on several (mathematical) problems simultaneously. This of course can lead to the ultimate crossword puzzle or Rubik's musical cube, but must be quantifiable in one way or another to the fuse box of this chapter.

New notation is equally important here as in the case of pitch. Pieces in which time notation (without note stems, leaving the listener to think in terms of continual time [in ms]) have been composed for almost forty years, many of which have made their statement regardless of having no tempi, meter, etc. (Again, one must not forget that a number of these pieces sound no different to the listener in terms of duration than the Webern pieces with their highly developed use of metrical and tempo changes.) The Christian Wolff "playing together" works exemplify this (see part 6, chapter XVIg). Witold Lutosławski's notation for "almost sixteenth notes" (see his *String Quartet*) is another interesting example of a useful innovation.

## c. Dynamics and the secondary parameters – timbre and density:

– In the present discussion the dynamic parameter forms a problem. What is *mf* actually? It is relative to the instrument, a note within that instrument's various registers, its timbre at that moment and, last but not least, to the instrumentalist. The traditional dynamic scale is the most vague of our primary parameters.

In Olivier Messiaen's *Mode de valeurs et d'intensités* changing dynamic values per note became part of music history. In pieces the likes of the Pierre Boulez *Structures* for two pianos or Karlheinz Stockhausen's mid-50s works, dynamic diversity reached a notational extreme. How much of this complexity is perceived as notated? Suffice it to say that loudness will most likely never be the most important parameter in music in terms of the fuse box of the current discussion. It will only play a major role in connection with other parameters (and is of course of primary importance in a good deal of rock music). A study in loudness gradation may be made applying the db (and not the *mf*) scale; still, pitch and the application of the time axis can never be totally pushed into the background in this time-based art.

– Timbre, on the other hand, is one of the two most dynamic parameters in experimental music (along with musical space, see chapter IX). Timbre often walks hand in hand with the collection of sound sources used in a given work (see the following chapter for the latter). Take for example the historic leap made in the late 1940s with the birth of *musique concrete*. One might state that the jump taken with the concept of *Klangfarbenmelodik* became a small step in comparison with the quantum jump made in *musique concrète* with its *"Klangmelodik"* (where any sound may be used). Sound sources and their timbral modifications are at the base of these works.

How does one, then, compose timbral (sound) compositions when one has been restricted historically to note-oriented music? Are the other parameters: pitch, duration, loudness, form, and so on still of use given their own deep-rooted traditions? And how can one "train" the listener to appreciate this music which in general is even farther removed from a Schubert song than any early 20th century avant-garde work in terms of sound organization as well as the listening experience?

Too few composers have taken the trouble to consider cognitive problems of timbral music. This particular horizon (parameter) most likely has been further broadened than all others put together and therefore deserves an equal amount of attention from composers in terms of potential application as well as in terms of the current questions in perception.

One of those most responsible for this great development was Edgard Varèse. In his works he called sound organizations, he took great care in constructing his blocks of sound (he gave them special names like "crystal" and the like) so that timbral movement could be followed. At any given moment in any given work, one hears immediately that the work is of a Varèseian nature, and furthermore, when he realized his pieces using tape, *Poème Electronique* and *Déserts* at a late age, there were few surprised by how they sounded. If Varèse had truly had the chance to organize sounds, and not just notes, earlier in his career, we most likely would know much more today about how the mind deals with large-scale timbral developments within musical contexts due to Varèse's vision. Those analyzing electroacoustic music these days can now play a major role in this most important discussion.

– The density parameter alluded to in the Ligeti example must be mentioned here. Iannis Xenakis has been fundamental in bringing this parameter to the fore, especially through the use of what he calls sound energies which combine loudness, density, general speed of music and even timbre. (Note how duration and pitch have not been named here.) Many Xenakis-influenced musicians know nothing of his mathematics, but all swear by the application of varying energies in their music. For example, the sound development in many of Ligeti's works could be described in this way as well. In fact, the use of the density parameter as (one of) the assistant(s) to our perception exemplifies a most successful way of replacing melody and simple meter as the most prominent parameters in experimental works. Krzysztof Penderecki's compositions of the *Threnody* period illustrate this elegantly. Composers who consciously compose using the density parameter as an architectural tool are thus at an advantage. Nobody misses melody in Xenakis' *Pithoprakta* – the sonorous, multi-timbral experience of this work is musically satisfying. This exemplifies the potential of melodyless experimental music with tangible safety devices built in for the listener's perception.

**d. Formal structure and that parameter called freedom:** Until now, our primary attention has been focused on time lengths of relatively short duration. Now we must move to the work (or movement) as a whole. How does the famed fuse box react to a buildings (works) that seem to have no architecture?

Contemporary experimental music has had a bit of an odd relationship with form (on paper) and structure (our experience). Looking back to the chapter on notation, Morton Feldman has said that process is perhaps the biggest innovation of our time. Process music is not teleological music. It is, in a sense instead, "turn on the machine and we'll see where we end up" music. This is indeed a most experimental way of thinking. Very dissimilar composers have had (temporary) subscriptions to this: Steve Reich, Karlheinz Stockhausen and in his own way, Morton Feldman, himself. Thus, when talking about form and structure, about macro-time, one must never forget to consider those composers who are more process-oriented than structurally minded. Perhaps we might be able to speak of the small generating the large versus the large (e.g. a rondeau movement) being subdivided into smaller parts.

Then there are composers who are more involved with their sound sources than with what happens to them in larger frames. Unfortunately, most electroacoustic composers tend to fall under this category.

Finally, there are composers, including Xenakis who, by changing their sound materials as well as their compositional rules to such an extent, have created new forms, so different to existing ones that the listener seems to need to hear a work several times before even discovering what sorts of structural boundaries are to be reckoned with.

In fact in this last sentence we hit upon something of great importance. How many pieces are heard more than once? How many pieces *need* to be heard more than once to be discovered at all? (But how many pieces *do* get listened to twice?) This is an aside, but something no one can ignore nor underestimate.

It is a rarity that experimental composers recycle old forms while searching for new roads in other parameters. Lejaren Hiller's hour long *Electronic Sonata* is one of the very few examples of note here.

Reiterating: there seems to be one of three routes followed in most experimental works: the process composition, the composition in which form is not of great importance, and the work in which a new form has been of fundamental importance. Let's look at a few examples.

– *Process:* Although it was Steve Reich who once wrote a manifesto-like text entitled *Music as Process*, the idea of a process as a form generator predates minimalism and the work of pop musicians like Brian Eno. Schönberg serialism is no more process-oriented than Bach fugues are in the sense that something starts and unravels until it has been completed. Schönberg's row method calls for choice every twelve notes. Bach may have had less choice given the rigid fugue model, but also, for example, had to fill in the voices containing neither subject nor answer. Although at any given moment there are restrictions of choice in all cases, there is no given point at which a concrete prediction may be made concerning a moment "x" measures away in a serial or fugal work.

It is in the theory of Stockhausen that process music is laid out in all of its potential. His theories of groups, moments and points as well as that super-parameter *Formel* all refer to serial processes used to create music in large dimensions. In the case of his "moment works" it has been said that these works have no beginning nor end and that the listener can "drop in" and therefore also leave a work at any time. In practice there are very few composers who take on this attitude (Stockhausen least of all!), but the implication of the experience of the moment (tune in/tune out) is something which may seem evident in a process situation, but which also demands a new sort of musical listening. Composers of moment-music should be warned that their listeners need help in reducing their musical experiences to a sum of "x" number of moments. In his "Formel works", Stockhausen allows a given – his *Formel* – to be reduced to micro-sounds or stretched to week-long lasting compositions. It is not to be questioned here whether this is a technique of universal appeal; instead, the problem mentioned in every section of this chapter must be repeated – what does the listener do with this Formel generator? Must one hear and recognize a two second version/compression of a two minute melody? Or the two hour form generated by the same melody?

Granted new experiences of time are often very rewarding. A two hour raga can sometimes be mesmerizing for the Western victim of the fast-food culture. But works in which the sophistication of content reaches levels that almost no listener can grab onto after one hearing need to be accompanied by some sort of "how to" text in terms of its appreciation. At some point that text may no longer seem necessary – we are by no means near that point at present.

The minimalists (see section 4, below), and especially Steve Reich have worked with process in a way that almost every listener can follow the simplicity of their procedures and experience new sound complexes by shutting out overly recognizable themes due to the repetition schemes involved. The experimental phase works exemplify this (see also part 6, chapter XVIe). One literally climbs into the sounds of the instruments in question when the main theme is simply taken for granted and no longer listened to. Here active and passive listening as a parameter of perception plays a role. The basic material is so clear to the listener (something missing in the case of the "moments") that it can almost be ignored at any given point. In conclusion process music has been of great use in adding to our scale of formal approaches in the latter half of the century. (By the way compliments may be given to folk musicians from many other cultures who unconsciously greatly influenced this development through their centuries' old folk traditions based on process.)

 – *No clear form:* With apologies to the readers, no composers will be named here as it is believed that these composers have often done more harm than good for experimental music by being too lax about structural problems. Think of the many heavy dissonant works which avoid identifiable rows or subsets thereof, which employ chords which fit only on the Webernian scale of mildly dissonant to extremely dissonant, which avoid any form of repetition, especially in the duration domain, which do not possess a clear curve of tension and relaxation. One could say, "Sit back and experience this new dissonant music", but the mind works on trying to hold onto that little something it can identify with *or* the piece must be repeated often enough so that that little something may be discovered. Otherwise, a composition becomes a train ride through so many landscapes that no single one remains in the memory of the traveler who has experienced an overdose on information.

This problem becomes even more difficult in the case of electroacoustic music in which most of the sound sources and therefore timbres are new. This adds a degree of discovery, but also of complexity to the listener, one which might just add aggravation to aggravation of the lack of identifiable form, rhythm and pitch. Again, this concerns composers who do not create (new) structures consciously (or by chance) in their works. Even programmatic electroacoustic works can make life easier to the listener.

– *New forms:* As mentioned above Edgard Varese once wrote about his music as being influenced by crystals. The centers of the crystals have a similar, identifiable character; their outsides are all different. In this way, Varèse was able to utilize a not too large number of basic ideas in such a way that his œuvre might be seen to be an excellent example of theme and variations. In fact isn't this a goal all composers should have? It is in this way that the listener can become acquainted with and enjoy experiencing new forms and structures in music composition.

But let's return to the serialists of the 50s and 60s. In some cases, books were filled with numbers which were translated at the last minute into notated sound. Many a Darmstadt composer or American East-coast (serial) composition student worked in this manner. By definition we were constantly confronted with new forms at every performance of new music, often several times per evening. But how well could we appreciate what we were hearing? How sophisticated were these new forms? Answer: often, extremely sophisticated and almost always impossible to follow. The form on paper was the substantiation of a work's quality. The fact that no one could ever hear it didn't seem to interest anyone.

This same story can be told of many a work in open form or even more radical notation. Here the parameter freedom again enters the discussion. These works can change so substantially each time they are played that they may leave one of two effects. The "piece" is what was played (like a recording of an improvisation), or the piece has been heard so often, that the experience of the work is the comparison of one performance to another. (How often do we have the luxury of belonging to this second group?) In chapter VI, many thoughts were presented concerning the potential advantages of process and open form. Yet all composers involved seemed to stress the importance of the key opening up the secret of a work to its listeners. Without this key, open form adds little to our perception of macro-time.

One composer who understood Varèse's thought of crystals and was able to often find a key for the listener in spite of sophisticated calculations involved with form is Xenakis. He achieved this without any bind to tonality or atonality, as was the case with Varèse, without any bind to meter and several other conventions. His parameter of order combined with his "energies" plus his own sound of highly divergent dynamics, loads of glissandi, quickly changing densities, each in clearly definable modules, is his addition to our building blocks of form, one which, after a few hearings, can be followed by any listener (see also part 6, chapter XVId).

– *In conclusion:* We have limited the macro-time discussion to three categories. These categories could be further refined; many composers could be called upon to exemplify renovation in musical structure. Those musicians and musicologists who apply techniques derived from linguistics while looking for grammars and for morphologies of musical corpora will contribute a great deal in terms of this detective novel of finding the missing clues in many a work of contemporary music.

One last remark is of great importance here, namely, the warning that this writer, like many composers he has called upon to illustrate tendencies, has been too easygoing about these parameters, separating them here at will as if they are rarely combined in contemporary works. Other than a small number of composers of the *Nouvelles Structures* school of thought (no, it doesn't exist; it just seems like a good nickname here referring to Pierre Boulez's highly abstract serial work *Structures*), few are dedicated to the formal separation of time, frequency, loudness, structure, etc. Luciano Berio is a typical counter-example of someone who thinks in unities, and less so in the separate parts. With this in mind, problems and solutions of the combination of the small with the small and the small (e.g. pitch and time) with the large (e.g. melody and form) are of equal relevance to this chapter.

## 3. A COMPOSER'S VISION = A COMPOSER'S "SOUND"?

Perhaps the moral to the stories here is not to be found directly in the detective novel referred to above, but instead in the example of the crystal. Many pieces of Feldman's sound somewhat enigmatic on first hearing, certainly for those who are unacquainted with his music, especially the pieces of the 60s and early 70s. The more you listen to Feldman, the more you realize that one of his goals in life was to find the same sort of model to use and remodel as did his friend, the painter Mark Rothko so often. The works of the last decade of his life reflect his discovery. His earlier works all lean toward that discovery, but his model became most clear in the mid-70s. His theme and variations generated an œuvre of experimental pieces all based on the enigmatic, but highly identifiable, meditative Feldman sound. His crystal was not a scientific one and certainly not one of formalization. This is of course of no relevance. What is important here is that he found that model and assumed its further use in each work which made life easier for him as well as for his listeners. He did not have to compromise anything experimental in his works.

Composers with equally enigmatic styles, who change style often may be highly talented, but are avoiding that crystal. This can have a negative influence in terms of their music's reception.

Elliott Carter exemplifies an exception here. The composer of the *Double Concerto* creates highly dense, seemingly unpenetrable music which somehow fascinates without allowing for clear cognitive understanding. This author can not categorize this exceptional composer's music and has remained frustrated by and attracted to his music for more than twenty years. Carter must be named for his music succeeds despite its complexity (see also part 6, chapter XVIc) and use of an intuitive approach to a music which tends to demand a structural one. He knows extremely few equals.

One name has been conspicuously absent in this story, Cage. For it is here where his well-articulated total avoidance of any key leads to the liberation of the perception or to a closed door of misunderstanding. Cage the *provocateur* has helped the modern listener in getting used to anything being music. His longer works based on pure randomness do tend to sound aimless as they are so. The liberated perception accepts this and lets the sounds come without any form of further treatment as it were. Following his way, one might someday reach the world of no masterpieces as random works can hardly shock time and again (except the fully indeterminate ones). His addition here is in fact the addition of indeterminacy as an alternative, an extreme end point belonging to the parameter, determinism. Otherwise, Cage will remain the *provocateur* of chapter VII.

In contrast, Ligeti, our first example of the chapter is one who consistently has offered the listener with the key to his often experimental works, what is know as the Ligeti-sound. In general he has used his own version of the Varèseian crystal to great results. In other words, one goal of this chapter has been to present the crystal concept. Implied, but not stated and impossible to formulate, is that this crystal must be treated in a *musical* fashion.[3] In other words: the crystal + musicality = that something to hold onto applied in such a way that it very well might be at the base of a rewarding musical experience.

## 4. THE MINIMALISTS' 20TH BIRTHDAY, A SPECIAL CASE

If any movement in contemporary movement may be termed successful in terms of popular appeal, it is minimalism. It has been written that these composers continued an evolution against dialectic, teleological thinking of the classics as was first consciously formalized by Schönberg and strengthened by Webern. They profited further by the moment idea of Stockhausen and the anti-work, music as process ideas of Cage (see Wim Mertens' book on the minimalist school and their background for the complete argumentation for the above claim). Most listeners agree that these composers, with few exceptions, moved their music from the seemingly untouchable "in" radical dissonant to the highly tangible (no problems for the fuse box here) currently "in" radical consonant. In fact, the music became so consonant that early Terry Riley records were brought out simultaneously on the pop and classical markets. The Steve Reich and Philip Glass ensembles not only play extremely tonal (or modal) music, but also highly rhythmic, often loud music – all of which may be said of today's popular genres.

It is true that the early phase works of Reich and many a fluxus work of LaMonte Young were in their own way highly experimental calling for the construction of musical entities out of repeated (phased) modules. Michael Nyman dedicates an entire chapter to the minimalist school in his book entitled *Experimental Music*. But how experimental is their more recent music after all?

The good news is that our musical art which suffers from so much less popularity than all other contemporary arts (with the possible exception of video art or perhaps contemporary poetry) has finally found a group with wide appeal. In a sense it may be stated that it is remarkable that a pop music-like group of musicians has been able to keep it going with relatively few musical ideas for so many years. Yet the fact that their formulae resemble those of musics of a lighter quality is not the point; the fact that this music is hardly experimental is.

Perhaps experimental music should be separated from its current most popular school. Why? Because minimalism's easy-to-digestness has been used to help many of experimental music's greatest critics in their calling non-minimal experimental music too complex, too abstract and intangible, further polarizing an already difficult situation.

The appreciation of these composers is due to the simplicity and the nature of their works. The keys to their music are offered on a silver platter. Opera and other larger podiums of music had been looking for marketable modern composers for years. The minimalism of Philip Glass and John Adams was the obvious solution. The musical genres their works resemble, often non-Western ones (which has fortunately opened many an ear to what is known today as "World Music"), are clearly audible. In a sense these composers are the opposites of the *Nouvelles Structures*. They may be found at the other end of the parameter "predictability" in music. Credit should be given to the successful (remember the media discussion). Still, this writer would prefer the minimal to coexist with the experimental instead of claiming to participate from within.

If there is one sort of music that isn't avant-garde, then it is minimal music. With Cage also being a member of an extreme of the predictability scale, one might consider assimilating the repetitive with the anti-repetitive. Herein lies the potential experimental use of minimal thought along with the process and fuse box discussions above.

## 5. A CLOSING WORD

This chapter is of importance to the lot of experimental music in calling for the coexistence of pushing borders in all directions with the careful treatment of the question of our perception's fuse box. We can conclude that it *is* possible to write db, Hz, ms music in which the listener is offered the key to its story. Our parameters can be treated in an infinite variety of ways as long as there is something to hold onto (with the exception of indeterminism). These somethings to hold onto lead us to perhaps the most intriguing challenge in today's music, without question one of the most important and too often set aside subjects. The solutions are open to all; our avoiding solutions will be fatal to experimental music's future.

1) This term tonality will be applied here in a rather broad sense. The Dutch composer Peter Schat has used the term *tonicality*, which embraces all music, be it modal, strict tonal, pentatonic, or whatever, as long as it is based on tone centers. It is in fact tonicality that is the subject here. – Several ideas in these four paragraphs are derived from (Landy: 1984, chapter 5).
2) "Boundaries" has been written here for obvious reasons in the plural. Each individual perceives apparent (dis)order differently; this is often due to experience and training. What is being asked of the composer here is not "complexity for complexity's sake", but instead some notion of what a listener *can* follow and wants/needs to be able to better appreciate or understand a work.
3) With all respect, no attempt will be made to define musicality. The point here is that neither musicality, nor the crystal alone insures that a composition be successful.

# VIII. Sound sources, color

In this chapter issues surrounding the art of (experimental) music based on sounds – and not just notes – will be the focus. In the introduction the subject area will be delineated and a small number of remarks made concerning the slow tempo of development of compositional techniques as well as concerning the relative lack of musicological scholarship in terms of sound music analysis and aesthetics. The second part of the chapter specifically confronts two subjects the author considers particularly problematic at this point: 1) the propagation and appreciation of sound-compositions as well as 2) the creation of a solid terminology for the description thereof. (In fact this might be seen to complement the musical content issues raised in the last chapter.) The brief conclusion links the second section to the introduction by providing a few subjects of study to musicologists interested in this area as well as suggestions for frustrated fellow composers.

## 1. INTRODUCTION

"Be not afeard –
this isle is full of *noises*."
**William Shakespeare** (*Tempest*)

"... of *organized sound*."
**Edgard Varèse**

Of all the advances in (late) 20th century music, the one shared by most is within the realm of timbre.[1] As instrumental music offers a limited, though fast growing, amount of potential sound colors, experimentation with potential new sound sources inevitably became integrated with timbral research. Chronologically, the most important developments of growth in sound (color) sources used in musical contexts can be summarized in the work of four artists: Luigi Russolo with his noise orchestra "Intonarumori", Edgard Varèse with his extended use of percussion as a means of organizing sounds, Pierre Schaeffer with the introduction of *musique concrète,* and John Cage with his attempt to liberate all sounds. Through the musical results of the international movements of electro-acoustic music born around 1950, the liberation of the sound was fact. Through applying computer techniques originating from the early 1960s, the concept of music comprising all possible timbres has become reality.

Despite the often heard comment, "Don't worry, I can still write instrumental music as notes are sounds, too" – notes are a subset of all sounds after all – there are more than a few musicians who indeed have trouble combining their "sound" with "note" music.[2]

To illustrate this curious state of affairs, since 1982 the direction of the Paris Biennale has felt the need to include separate departments for music and sonic art. (Vocal music is included in the  latter! – see their catalogs for further information.) Furthermore, composers have been known to call their tape works "audio art" saving themselves the problem of having to defend their pieces as musical compositions. And to make this tale even more confusing, some composers, including Helmut Lachenmann, differentiate their sound works (*Klangkomposition*) from their timbre compositions (*Klangfarbenkomposition*).

The late 1980s is a good moment for (re-)appraisal, to look at and look back. As Simon Emmerson mentions in the introduction of his compilation, *The Language of Electro-acoustic Music,* the 60s was a decade of more or less mandatory experimentation; in the 80s one can finally talk about successes as well as failures (Emmerson: 2). It is a decade in which specific experiments are assimilated and applied to more general musical situations. It is in fact this concept of reappraisal and assimilation that stimulated the current writing.

There is some concern that content in and appreciation of sound-works have not developed as quickly as the technical potential of its realization. Furthermore, one of the biggest "holes in the market" in the musicological area is that of macro-analysis (focusing on the music itself and not just on how sounds are constructed) and aesthetics research of this musical corpus (see chapter VII – now we are referring to our reception of sound works as a whole; this is the problem of the fuse box as seen through a looking glass). These are the topics of the following section.

## 2. TWO PROBLEMS: PROPAGATION AND TERMINOLOGY

### a. The "stages" of sound works

> "... failure of teaching institutions."
> **Simon Emmerson**

#### – Lower education
What does the young child learn about the music of sounds? What does he learn about contemporary music at all? Classical music? Music? The 20th century has been good for the creation of a handful of pedagogical methods for introducing the young to all sorts of music. In the case of the Kodály method, young children may become acquainted with music, be it local, foreign, international – folk, popular, jazz, classical: old or new and be given the choice to participate in music making (and dance) at a young age. In this way, new music does not necessarily have to be "confronted" for the first time during a later phase of life and seen as the music of acquired taste.

There are only too few methods which specifically tackle the problems of the music of sound for the young, the best known being that of R. Murray Schafer. It is the opinion of this writer that when the young are given a chance to hear and make music with sounds, the appreciation (short-term effect) and quality (long-term effect of those dealing with sound music since childhood) would grow enormously.

#### – Higher education
Are mature students of music that much better off? Relatively speaking, music education has become more liberal and especially "tolerant" of contemporary music in the last twenty-five years, but are there specific techniques for preparing musicologists to study works the likes of *Gesang der Jünglinge*

and our case in point in chapter VI, *Variations IV*? Do young performers learn enough about improvisation to handle the graphic scores of Anestis Logothetis as well as other forms of scored improvisation? These types of scores have been around for a couple of decades, but there has been relatively little response as to how they may be dealt with. Virtuosity is only 50% of what is required for the performance of a good deal of new music. Where experimental techniques of interpretation (musically as well as analytically) are not developed, the appreciation thereof must eventually suffer. Finally, where and when does the young composer learn criteria to choose materials and sort them into musical categories in his early pieces? Obviously with all the available sonic resources and the lack of contemporary "schools" these choices are critical. Where is today's Arnold Schönberg to write "The Art of *Sound Composition*"?

## – The communications media

How much time is allocated to new music's dispersion on radio and especially on the super-media, television? How is this music presented: a few names and dates or a "seminar" on the various influences leading to...? As too few people are acquainted with new music through their education, these two media have a seemingly almighty power to make or break contemporary music's propagation. Without a clear aesthetics and terminology for sound works, a good deal of faith is given to the programmers who are often primarily interested in success through more listeners (and that most contemporary music cannot yet guarantee – a vicious circle).

Modern technology allows for a good deal of research to be done concerning new music's presentation via the air waves. Modern radiophonic and video art works using new music compositions as sound material and dance with contemporary scores for the television are alas the only successful examples of note (see also chapter X for more on this subject).

## – The written word

Many newspapers and a few weeklies allocate some space to new music.[3] But as new music is seen as the music of a few, many writings are left unread by the majority of its readers while others consult reviews just to "keep up". Lengthy discussions of the music itself are exceptional, isolating the reviews to the province of new music.

There are too few popular books introducing this repertoire to those who are willing to give new music a try. The radio producer, John Schaefer, has broken ground with his exemplary discographic survey, *New Sounds*, a book of interest to beginners and connoisseurs of sound pieces. Schaefer has categorized this music and showed how popular, experimental, jazz and even folk music all seem to cross boundaries.

### – On stage

In most countries new music, be it performed on concert stage or in alternative spaces, has the smallest public of all the contemporary arts, with the possible exception of video art and poetry. Too many complain that it is a question of a lack of quality and exaggerated complexity. The author is of the opinion that the fault originates from those involved in the first four categories listed above.

In a simple economical sense, the making of a new music work is hardly a lucrative enterprise. Many work for months on a small commission with one or two performances for ca. one hundred spectators as the temporary final goal. The gift of a third performance is a jewel known to a small minority. The French critic, Maurice Fleuret once called our period, the "Kleenex epic" – use music once and throw it away. As will be discussed in chapter X there is another way (through various audio-visual media) which is followed by an ever increasing group of composers and musicians; still, the continual evolution of Kleenex works is the disastrous reflexion of the so-called over-production of art of our time.

In sum it is no wonder that the appreciation of new music is in poor shape. It is also not surprising that, despite great technical breakthroughs, composers have a good deal of trouble finding their ways through the mazes of new music. Now that the guilty have been named, the search should be to collectively improve the status quo. Let's now return to the musician and those closest to the musician, the musicologist.

## b.  Absence of analytical models and aesthetic norms

> "Writing has covered ... analysis of the technical means. Little has been written ... on the musical aims, the ethic and aesthetic of [electroacoustic] music."
>
> **Simon Emmerson**

Emmerson's words above immediately reach the heart of this entire chapter. Those employing and interested in the music of sound have every opportunity to read about each and every technical advance, tested or not. What is achieved employing the technique or applying new sound sources is apparently seen to be less important. Nothing could be further from the truth. If musicians and music scholars had had a better working terminology for our still very young musical area as well as analytical tools for scores, improvisational works, recordings (through the use of post-scriptive notation) as well as reception, a good number of problems summed up above might have known a different recent history.

### – A few recent publications of note

The Emmerson remark appeared in the introduction to the above-mentioned compilation. His goal is to participate and inspire others to join in creating a new basis or bases for analysis of and aesthetic research in the music of sounds. His own contribution to that book consists of a description of a three by three matrix allowing for the categorization of sound – and thus non-instrumental – works through their form and sound sources. (The axes range from the use of clearly perceivable sound objects to unidentifiable ones and from overt form concepts to the total absence thereof. The middle mode on both axes is the combination mode.) Denis Smalley's contribution assembles a number of terms and symbols which might help in creating a morphology of sound music. These are useful in post-scriptive notation of sound works as well as to the composer realizing such works. Finally, Tod Machover's contribution praises new possibilities in digital sound generation as new continuities (parameters) of sound and its content may be realized, formalized and experimented with.

One of the often treated composers in Emmerson's work, Bernard Parmegiani, is the subject of an analysis and semiotic discussion in the exposé on his composition, *De Natura Sonorum* (see Philippe Mion *et al.*). The book may have its flaws (especially when the analyses attempt to penetrate the surface structure of the work), but it is one of the first lengthy discussions of a single piece which extends beyond lists of sources and machines used for the realization of the work. A new term, *objets composites,* whose attacks are concrete and whose resonance is electronic and therefore ambiguous, is added to the *objets sonores* and *objets musicaux* known from Pierre Schaeffer. Jean-Jacques Nattiez's semiotic discussion of Parmegiani's composition is the first step along a long path leading to a greater understanding of the signifiers and signified of *musique concrète* and all related sound-oriented musics.

The book *On Sonic Art* written by the British composer, Trevor Wishart (who also contributed to the Emmerson book) is one of the most informative how-to books in the entire field of experimental music. He delineates his field of sonic arts, discussing sound source and structure categories and problems composers (and all others involved in this area) will confront in the music of sounds. The inclusion of two cassettes means that many ideas are illustrated using contemporary works including several of his own. He also gives special emphasis to what is known today as extended vocal techniques (one thinks of the Paris Biennale example of combining new vocal and sound music), recording a huge number of vocal utterances for musical application.

Finally the recent book written by Michel Chion, systematizing Pierre Schaeffer's *Traité des objets musicaux,* is a long awaited treatise formalizing (for as much as any method for new music can be formalized without becoming too limiting) the theory and solfeggio of the founder of the *Groupe de recherches musicales* at the Paris radio studios which led to his "Solfège de la musique concrète".

As the first dissertations are appearing or are in preparation in the areas of analysis, systematic formulation of composition techniques, reception and aesthetics, there is a good deal of hope for the future. Obviously we can learn from the successes and failures of almost forty years of sonological composition and research; these studies potentially can influence the destiny of sound works at and on all its stages.

## 3. QUO VADIMUS?

> "The utopian moment can be found in the form."
>
> **Heiner Müller**

The first and last quotations included in the present text are from dramatists. Perhaps the partners within "Other Media, Inc." are more aware of musical problems than we often claim. Although Heiner Müller was referring to a dramaturgical problem with this remark, he concurrently reaches the crux of this eighth chapter. Without concentrated work on form in sound works and the forms of their presentation, many will continue to suffer the effects of the Kleenex era.

This chapter has been written to incite composers and musicians to consider not only the technical aspects of their music, but also its form, its aesthetics and its potential dissemination. Indeed many modern musicians today must spend as much time playing the role of impresario as that of musician, but this may change as: 1) education from the early stages is improved and 2) the sound musician collaborates with musicologists so that the media partners have less difficulty presenting and discussing their work. More opportunities should arise as more place is given to the underdog of the modern arts leading to a better balance between promotion and creativity.

The musicologist's role here is by no means unimportant. Musicology has been fundamental in providing specialists and general listeners with basic information as well as advanced analytic and aesthetic tools so that music can be written and talked about and better understood. The understanding of a given musical corpus has never been as poor as that with the music of sounds. The note and sound schizophrenia alluded to in the introduction is in desperate need of treatment.

Ignoring this problem may lead to the materializing of a view once heard from the ethnomusicologist, John Blacking, who claimed that modern music was simply "a hiccup in music history" – something unpleasant which you temporarily have to live with, but it will go away, sooner or later. We must do our best to avoid having Blacking's joke turn to reality.

1) This subject was mentioned but not elaborated upon in the parameters chapter. We have discussed continuities of pitch in Hz, dynamics in db and time in ms. Color, on the other hand, may be determined by a sum of sine tones, but what might its scale be? As so many composers have been timbre-oriented, this question could be quite useful. Fortunately, some excellent work has been done within the musicological world, leading to – among others – two recent publications of merit concerning systematizing sound colors and sound structures (see the books by Wayne Slawson and Peter Wilson).

2) In current digitally generated music, the difference between additive synthesis (i.e., the larger, more sophisticated systems based on sounds built as a sum of sine tones) and MIDI-synthesis (the less costly, more commercial systems most often using a piano-like keyboard as its focus – see chapter XIII) is comparable leading to two distinctive types of computer music. The first theoretically can generate all sounds; the second is note-oriented, based on a huge assortment of sound colors.

3) The lot of music journals and books for those involved in the sounds of music is the subject of section b (page 100), below.

# IX. The "parameter" space

Throughout music history there have been principally two "stages" for music, the podium and spaces for participatory music be it the street, a concert area or wherever. Western art music has rarely been known to be interested in the latter category, being an art in which (almost) all participants are in front of their audiences, in a concert hall or in a church. (Exceptions are organists and responsorial choirs – the most spatial music-makers until the mid-20th century.) Spatial breakthroughs through serial, indeterminate, multi-media thinking as well as through the performance, fluxus and happenings movements not to mention electroacoustic performance (and installation) environments have changed that picture radically. How radically? We are no longer shocked by concerts or performances being given on a beach, around a lake, or just anywhere. But how influential has the expansion of potential performance spaces been?

This chapter hopes to show that: when a space or use thereof is essential to a work, this can be most effective. In contrast, alternative spaces chosen just to leave the concert hall have been less successful.

Let's go back to that very important statement from Antonin Artaud that was called on in the local music chapter, "The idea is to feed, furnish and let the space speak for itself," and superficially compare two extremely different examples: any Bach cantata with Alvin Lucier's composition *I am Sitting in a Room* in which both composers were clearly dealing with musical space.

Bach probably could not calculate exact reverberation times in each church he worked in, nor was he likely to be aware of reverberation differences with churches in other cities. Still these works somehow sound wrong when presented in acoustically drier concert halls. One might say that Bach's religious works were written with a harmonization of genre and space in mind.

Lucier's work must be briefly described for those who are not yet acquainted with it. In this work, the composer reads a text aloud and records it in the room in which he is sitting. He says he does this to try to free himself from a speech impediment. The careful listener is aware that several sorts of speech sounds are produced that may be of great use in this unusual theme and variations work. Once the text has been recorded, the recording is played in the same room and rerecorded. The combination of quality loss through the sound system with the more important gain of the physical reaction of the room to the sounds is multiplied with each rerecording. In the last variation, one only hears the resonance frequencies of the room, itself. Lucier's voice is lost; only the amplitude curve still exists as the room, the space in question plays the solo final variation.

For the cantata, the space is fundamental to the character of the piece, but as in most cases in music is itself not used. With Lucier, the space is integrated into the work to the point that it is one of the two final parameters at the end (the other being loudness). Lucier exemplifies therefore an elegant musical translation of Artaud's modern theater space.

## 1. THE CONCERT HALL = ONE SPACE

What has the traditional concert hall experienced in experimental music in terms of a listener's spatial awareness?

– *Musician placement:*   Any book on Charles Ives includes the anecdote of his father's experiment in which two marching bands moved in opposite directions while playing two different tunes. One can imagine the experience of these two ensembles approaching one another in Ives' backyard and the cacophony when the two tunes "met" and crossed. Many consider this experiment to have inspired Charles Ives to his poly-anything ideas in his compositions, including have different instruments in different areas playing various layers of a single score.

Also the father of sound organization, Edgard Varèse was most interested in music and space. His scores written in the 20s and 30s often included a seating chart for the musicians to reach a maximal spatial sound quality. Varèse never took the step taken by Stockhausen and Xenakis of placing musicians throughout and/or surrounding the audience (or Cage's step in *Variations IV* placing the musician[s] outside of the space) although with Xenakis' help Varèse did achieve similar spatiality in the 1958 Philips Pavilion at the Brussels World's Fair with his *Poème Electronique* performed on hundreds of loudspeakers in a spatial multi-media show. It was of course Stockhausen who first formally handles space as a parameter at the time of his large-scale orchestral work *Gruppen*.

These composers and many others have helped the public reorient their listening through the addition of the dimension of sound depth by spreading out their musicians. This is the obvious first step on the road to spatial awareness.

Do take note that the space is still always seen to be the "podium", as opposed to the group participatory context known primarily from folk musics. In fact, most of the important examples of participatory music can be found at happenings or fluxus events (see below) or in (electronic) hands-on sound installations, which are placed in a space, rarely profiting by the special qualities of the space it is placed in. With this in mind one can conclude that in almost all cases, the addition of space to our musical parameters has been done as an extension to frontal podium practice and not as part of a potential search for a more vague boundary between podium and participation art.

These additions to frontal attention most likely led the way to quadraphonics, one of the subjects below. Quadraphonic sound tries to approach the spatiality of a hall by way of a tape recorder system, technologically an inevitable development. Still, we should note that there is somehow a limit to our perception"s growing awareness of space in the box or semi-circle known as the concert hall as opposed to the spatial potential of alternative spaces, for example the several mountain tops envisioned in Ives' never completed *Universe Symphony*.

– *Loudspeaker placement:* With the arrival of electro-acoustic music, the loudspeaker was added to the *tableau de la troupe* of almost all concert spaces. In the 1950s the first musicianless electronic and *musique concrète* concerts were heard. Some composers have no problems in writing solely audio, and therefore non-visual music. However, many a listener has complained about the sterile atmosphere of watching two, often specially lit loudspeakers "play" a piece. In reaction to this a number of composers decided to make a performance of mixing his or her piece on the spot; others wrote new works for for live musician(s) and tape, that sometimes difficult mix of sound and note music.

Whatever the case may be, stereo frontal concert music added little to our spatial awareness. It was simply the translation of all those musicians sitting in front of the audience. Some groups, among them composers from several French studios, started adding speakers all over the space. Although still employing a stereo image, the spatiality could be mixed in during a performance through a choreographed sound diffusion. Even more important is the use of quadraphonics in electroacoustic music.

Quadraphonic sound as a consumer article is a funny beast. When we go to a concert, most sounds do come from up front; only a fraction of the sound bounces back from the sides or the rear of a space. Therefore a correct quadraphonic recording is "top (front) heavy". Still, for the few who have quadraphonic recordings at home, the spatial recording is indeed more realistic.

Nevertheless, quadraphonics really becomes interesting when musical sounds are made to be heard as coming from any point within a space. One of the best known examples of spatial research can be found in John Chowning's composition *Turenas*. This computer music work employs a quadraphonic environment giving a listener, located not too far from the center of the space, the feeling that certain sounds travel around along circular paths. Other sounds come from distinct points within the space. This is all achieved using a good deal of mathematics, knowing about the acoustics of a space and profiting by having four loudspeakers distributed throughout the space in the form of a square. The concept parallels the placement of musicians sitting throughout a space, but can do something non-Olympic musicians cannot do, namely have its sounds move around at lightning speeds during a performance.

Again Alvin Lucier will be called upon for an example. In the case of his *Birdcage* (a homage to guess who), Lucier wears binaural microphones which look like headphones placed on both sides of his head and walks around the audience picking up the sounds of an electronic bird in a birdcage. This somewhat disturbing sound is repeated continually during the length of the performance. Somehow Lucier is aware of how (in what doses) the sound is sent to his loudspeakers given his ever-changing position. All of a sudden, at one point of the performance, the electronic bird knocks at the back of your head, moves around to one ear and seems to fly from one ear to another *inside*. In this case one is not particularly involved in the space as a whole, but is treated to a private moment, given the listener's own space.

The use of loudspeakers in the concert hall has meant a very large step in spatial awareness in music.

– *IRCAM's concert space – everything placement*: IRCAM, the music department of the Centre Georges Pompidou in Paris, sometimes known as the house of Boulez (its director), celebrated its 10th birthday in 1987. IRCAM is without question the most prestigious music research center in the world today, especially as far as modern performance and electroacoustic technical advances and composition are concerned. One of the most fascinating, yet curious parts of the underground IRCAM complex is its concert hall, built in the building's sub-subbasement, near one the medieval underground canals of Paris. This relatively small space is the most high-tech concert hall in the world. Its walls move, its floor can be moved as well as the ceiling. It is the modular architect's dream. The IRCAM staff members that give tours in this space often say with pride that the acoustics of the hall may be changed from the sound within a thimble to that of the Notre Dame de Paris. Obviously when one adds the technical potential in terms of staff and equipment within IRCAM, this concert hall should be every composer's dream. But is this so?

Obviously the advantages of this hall to anyone with imagination should be clear. One might be able to change the reverberation characteristic *during* performance making what might be called spatial transformation music in the literal and figurative senses. But this hall has known two disadvantages. The first is an economical one and is less interesting. The space is expensive and relatively small. Here, many concerts do have to be repeated more than once to give those interested the chance to hear a particular concert. If none of the works of a given program was especially written for this space, a church or museum in Paris is often chosen to get the entire public inside in one evening. This version of the "Kleenex epic" is an odd one indeed. The second problem applies the kleenex thought in yet another way. The composer who writes a piece for this space can only have the piece performed there and nowhere else.

This problem should be less negative than one thinks. The hypothesis in this chapter is that spatial music made with specific spaces in mind are the best examples of experimental spatial music. Therefore, music written for this space should potentially lead to interesting results. But how many composers are willing to write or realize a work for only one locale having those one to three performances. And then? One possible reaction to this question is that if a piece is good enough to be repeated, it most likely will be. If it was written for the IRCAM space or equivalent, it will be repeated there. Contemporary music calls for a good deal of patience, to put it mildly. Why shouldn't one have patience in waiting for the second round of concerts in this well-known unique experimental music space?

## 2. OTHER SPACES

Quite a number of composers have been infatuated with breaking away from the concert hall as their main place of employ. Some of them have made enormous contributions to the world of organized sounds. Where did they go is an obvious question. Why did they go is much more pertinent.

– *Alternative spaces:* The alternative space can be anywhere. As we already know John Cage informed all potential musicians and music enthusiasts to open up their ears. He also incites his interpreters to look for new locations for performance in many pieces. He has been known to suggest that if we indeed reach the point of "listening" ("happy new ears") then (his) music would become superfluous.

Certainly few subscribe to this last point, but what is important here is that when people are more aware of sound, in their sound environments, at home and wherever they go, the listening experience can be highly enriched.

This writer has been startled very often when visiting boat harbors in noticing how few listen to their marvelous concerts of water, wind, rope, metal, wood, rubber, voices, motors and so on. This sound experience can be more rewarding than many a composed work. But of course this is not the point. By listening to the harbor counterpoint, one is often surprised and inspired by the unexpected simultaneity of color or rhythm or even of the pitches of the surroundings.

This type of accidental simultaneity is at the basis of the more than forty year old collaboration between Cage and Merce Cunningham. The dance and the music are prepared separately after a performance length has been established. What is created is the blend of two originally independent unities. Cage and Cunningham know each other so well that the chance of such "accidental simultaneities" is statistically high. It is just like the boat harbor where such sounds can always be perceived. When exactly – no one really knows. Of course Cunningham works with many other musicians as well; the technique has caught on and evolved and is therefore applicable to more than just these two pioneers.

Cage allows the I Ching to determine location in some works. This is based on a point of view of total freedom of choice. When the main goal of a work is to get people to hear their environments, this can be a most useful way of going about things.

However, there are cases in which the composer chooses a location just to get people to see music performed in other settings. Here the concert hall is *in Frage,* but little is really done with those chosen settings, which sometimes can lead to disappointment. Let's now look at what was behind the thoughts of a few schools involved in the exodus from our concert halls.

– *Alternative movements:* Members of a small number of movements took music to the streets in the 1960s. Some did this in reaction to "élitist" concert practice; others because the music would lose effect elsewhere.

A handful of politically oriented composers made music for factories and for schools. In general this music has a socio-political justification. Most often these works are hardly experimental and will be ignored here.

The *Happenings* movement, a group of musicians, artists of all sorts and a few members of literary background, created just what their name says, happenings (an excellent reference is Hans Sohm's *Happening & Fluxus*). These were (dis)organized events often taking place in galleries and lofts in which the unexpected was the call of the day, events often performed before a public hardly knowing what was going on and why. Here art is brought closer to "the people" just like with the political composers. To what extent the guests could really appreciate more than be amused/alienated by these often highly unusual events is hard to say. (It should be mentioned though that many happenings were of a participatory nature, a rare example of participation art.)

The happenings were clearly influenced by the Cageian thought of extending boundaries to the no boundary zone. In fact it was Alan Kaprow, a major figure in the movement who initiated these happenings after having attended Cage's classes at the New School in New York. Musicians made art works, artists made merry music and a good (at least odd) time was had by all. The most radical element of the happenings, apart from some of the almost surrealists actions that took part, was their voluntary ephemeral nature – these were "works played" once and left. One might think of the ancient Taoist call for unity of life and nature. Unfortunately the comparison ends there for the most pure quality of happenings was their estrangement. Happenings might be seen to be the art of the counter-culture in the years just preceding flower power. What sort of happening would be a reflection of the vastly changed cultures of the late 80s?

*Fluxus*, the partner to the happenings, was a movement which was famed for its shock factor among other reasons. Fluxus events are also often participatory (take for example a group of "listeners" throwing beans into an open harpsichord in a work by Alison Knowles), in general of unusual lengths (in one work of LaMonte Young a piece lasts as long/as short as a bit of hay is fed to a piano, in another an open fifth is held as long as possible – think of the organ version!). In any event, at these unique events anyone from one to one hundred years old gets plenty of opportunities to laugh in this special combination of theater and music. Many have been known to think of the fluxus artists as a group of people playing a game called art.

In the case of the happenings, being there, wherever it was, was a major part of the event. The locale was of great importance, although its own specific location was usually not the focus, nor did the choice have much to do with Cage's vision in terms of new ways of listening. These events concerned taking art away from its holy shrines and succeeded in making many an artist free to expose his or her wares outside of the normal circuits.

The fluxus group was not as free in its choice of performance space. First of all performances (plural) did take place (today's "performance art" would never have existed were it not for fluxus), often at concert halls, simultaneously parodying the pretentiousness of various concert formalities. The highly fluxus oriented New York Avant-Garde Festivals organized by Charlotte Moorman did take place in the most ridiculous surroundings – in a train, at an empty airport or baseball stadium – but the activities rarely seemed to have much to do with these unusual temporary halls of culture.

In other words, the many artists, who, inspired by multimedia works such as Cage's *Theater Piece* and Stockhausen's *Originale*, took art away from the concert hall, were reacting to convention more than profiting by their new performance surroundings. It is in this sense that their breakthroughs were of greater importance to a contemporary artist's attitude than to his or her awareness of space. The difference between throwing beans into a harpsichord in the Wiener Oper or at Grand Central Railroad Station was probably not accounted for when Alison Knowles conceived that work. Being able to invent such a work was the strength of fluxus.

– *Soundscape artists:*[1] The boat harbor tale told above was not written because the author tends to dream of the sea. It is the link to one of the most interesting developments in experimental music's history. A small number of sometimes highly resourceful composers has spent a good deal of time creating, and often more time organizing concert performances for specific (types of) spaces far away from the concert hall. Mr. Soundscape, R. Murray Schafer and Alvin Curran are two of the major figures here. Both have made pieces to be played at boat harbors, on rivers, lakes and the like.

Such performances are of course happenings in their own right, for the environmental sounds they do not compose are often unforeseen. In this way, these composers try to make the listener more aware of their soundscapes through music as a stimulus. In such cases the composers first try to become acquainted with their performance space at least as well as Bach knew his churches; once in awhile the music takes special advantages of the characteristics of a given location.

In this way we have been led to one of the most radical developments in spatial awareness in modern music, which sometimes turns out to be most effective. Here a question will be asked as food for thought: is it not so that the steps taken in spatial awareness within the limits of the concert hall can be extended in equal proportion to the size of the space called for in a space-dependent work?

Soundscape compositions are most important to the hypothesis of this chapter, for here spatial experimentation walks hand in hand with the search for the musicality of the space itself in the sense of Artaud. Perhaps Cage's plea for better listening has been aided more by these composers than in many of his own works, for where can one better try to apply the Cageian "art as imitation of nature in its mode of operation" than on a mountainside, around a lake, in an empty apartment building, or even ... in a concert hall?

With all this in mind, what is left of these developments in terms of alternative spaces today? Are they still relevant?

Essentially one can conclude that the most successful experimentation with and development of spatial music took place in works which were specially made with a space in mind or, as in the case of John Chowning, with the particular treatment of a space in mind. Chowning does this within the concert hall. Schafer does it best elsewhere.

The search for alternative spaces has not really failed, although its relevance seems to be slight at the moment. This might be due to the fact that the flight towards alternative spaces was more due to the 60s reaction to the establishment than to the benefits of those particular spaces. Today, there are fewer performance possibilities. Many Schafer-like events do tend to be a bit costly. Therefore, almost all music or performances take place at the established addresses.

Still, one cannot speak of failure for two reasons. As stated, the attitude of almost all artists was changed by the happenings/fluxus participants who through their events not only added a drop of humorous provocation, but also a greater feeling for reflecting our daily reality as part of our artistic materials. More important, the composers of the soundscape school have indeed given many a listener the opportunity and the pleasure of encountering organized sound in new ways by experiencing that counterpoint derived from the sounds of the composer and those of the surroundings of the performance (two for the price of one!).

Alternative for alternative's sake is a losing proposition. But what about the following suggestion? In the chapter focusing on local music the following question was posed: Could a player "X" from society "Y1" interpret a piece of music of the composer "Z" from society "Y2" in a way that communicates it to an audience in society "Y3"? If experimental composers would give more thought to this question in works written for specific (types of) spaces, wouldn't we have a lot of interesting musical soundscapes to look forward to? Those who have ever experienced such works as a listener, performer or composer most likely would answer in the affirmative.

## 3. ADDENDUM-1: HOME = YET ANOTHER SPACE

Everyone is aware of the fact that our media world has provided us with an extra concert hall, namely the home. Almost everybody does most of his or her listening at home or at work with its omnipresent radios. The "performer" we know best is most often a loudspeaker; in some cases it is even a pair of headphones. This fact is in itself not particularly relevant to this chapter. But where listening in the Cage sense calls for an increase of awareness, might we conclude that through these television or radio/CD loudspeakers some listeners' awareness of sound and space is possibly decreased? The following addendum is even more pessimistic as far as spatial perception is concerned.

## 4. ADDENDUM-2: SPACE VERSUS NO SPACE – THE WALKMAN

Surely there must have been a scientific study questioning the percentage of loss of reception to the sounds around us when we use walkmen outside on our bicycles, in our cars, walking around. The danger involved is clear, yet so many seem not to be disturbed. The asocial quality is beyond question (happy no ears?).[2] The media win yet again; our masses "tune out" in broad daylight. The beat goes on and on and even our books are read for us as we commute. The walkman is handy in several senses and hazardous to everything this chapter has stood for in several others.

Fortunately there are a few good words left for the media. This is the subject of chapter X.

1)  Soundscape here is used in the sense of performances taking place on location or of untreated recordings of sound from a certain locale. Trevor Wishart's "soundscape" works use highly sophisticated studio techniques and are thus not part of this discussion. In the case of Luc Ferrari's *Presque rien* works, one speaks of "audio environments".
2)  The Dutch fluxus artist Willem de Ridder's participatory walkman pieces using cassettes or broadcast live on the radio, form a unique artistic exception in the middle of this picture of walkman antisocial behavior.

# X. The media/2:
# How often have you <u>seen</u> your compositions performed?

## 1. INTRODUCTION: A PLEA FOR MORE AUDIO-VISUAL COLLABORATIONS IN EXPERIMENTAL MUSIC [1]

The following text represents an attempt to stimulate a growth of interest within musical circles in the application of experimental music's potential in connection with the audio-visual arts. Today, contemporary music is primarily an autonomous genre, like literature and the plastic arts. But, unlike many of the sister arts, experimental modern music has not succeeded in reaching the public it deserves. The basic hypothesis of this chapter is to demonstrate that through active participation in audio-visual works, a much wider audience can be reached which in turn could lead to more attention being given to new music. Music's position in various audio-visual arts has been a sorrowful, undervalued one. The technology exists, yet there is still much to be developed in terms of its application, its potential being ignored by too many in general. The following is a call to musicians to explore and utilize these possibilities while redefining music's importance in various audio-visual contexts.

It should be noted that this chapter is more genre than content-oriented in comparison to all others in part 3. Nevertheless it binds a number of questions together relating to the media and to technology posed in part 2 as well as propagation questions repeated so often in chapters VI to IX. In fact this chapter treats a number of questions left open in

117

chapter II profiting by discoveries derived from the last five chapters.

## 2.  THE BACKGROUND: OUR "IMAGE CULTURE"

Today's consumers, especially those born after the birth of television, tend to be more visually than audio-oriented. New technology is obviously partly responsible for developments which led to what is often called today's image culture. Analogously electroacoustic and live contemporary music are also experiencing a period in which technological advances are becoming more and more prominent. The question to be raised here is: can music, especially experimental, sound-based music, profit by a greater presence within our image culture by applying contemporary techniques to audio-visual contexts? The following section of this chapter, while presenting a number of pro's and con's, argues that it might be worth a try.

## 3.  A CHOICE OF RELEVANT AUDIO-VISUAL ART FORMS

> "In this marriage of music and time-variant image lies one of the greatest artistic adventures, and promises, of our age."
>
> **Tod Machover**

In the following pages, a number of audio-visual disciplines will be discussed one by one to see what might be of interest to today's composer and where things have been difficult in the past, leading to points for future development.

It is clear that the composer, who in all cases has been trained to work independently – leaving a score and/or tape to his conductor, musicians or technician and thereby having an enormous freedom of movement – will have to "share the wealth" in a given work. The loss of sole creative leadership can be compensated by two factors: satisfaction in terms of artistic result and participation in the crushing of deeply-rooted traditions which have treated music in an at best amateurish fashion. (How many audio-visual artists are truly up to date where new music's repertoire and potential are concerned?)

These two factors translate in music's playing a greater role in each individual art form.

It is also true that in order to be able to participate in such collaborations, many composers might have to undergo supplementary training to become professional in the new visual field. This does not mean that the composer must become a double specialist. The author is of the opinion that very, very few have the capacity to specialize in both areas at once. Exceptions the likes of Mauricio Kagel, who composes music as well as "composing" video, film and theater (see for example Werner Klüppelholz and Lothar Prox's anthology which includes examples of Kagel's important audio-visual notation), are quite rare and should not be seen as exemplary as far as this discussion is concerned. What is important here is the general knowledge of an audio-visual discipline, including its history as well as its specific current technical vocabulary.

## a. Theater

There's an anecdote which circulates among West German musicians: the composer, Gottfried von Einem (of One), could never make music for the theater.[2] If he were to do so, he would have to change his name to von Allem (of All, be it kept in the singular for poetic reasons: "von Allem und Jenem"). This joke is painful in two senses: first of all it shows how the theater composer is expected to write like a chameleon, changing color constantly; he is to be a "jack of all trades"; furthermore, it shows how the theater composer often must adjust his (or her) standards to the wishes of his almighty director. Many film composers' destinies are no different.

Certainly the role of the composer in spoken theater does not necessarily have to be a major one; ironically when this is the case, most pieces are written for the opera. There are very few composers who have no interest in being either primarily an opera composer, or a "theater composer", the von Allem – but instead to be a "musical dramaturge", someone who attempts to introduce music as one of the main characters in a given dramatic performance. An ideal situation is where the composer collaborates directly with a playwright (think of Kurt Weill/Bertolt Brecht and Philip Glass/Robert Wilson) in creating a new work in which the music is permanently integrated. The question is when, if desired, can one also find a similar amount of space within new productions of existent theater works for which there is no pre-composed music?

Returning to Artaud's quotation concerning "furnishing" a space for the third time, one might say that this thought is of particular interest to the composer of new music for the theater. How might one sonorously furnish the theatrical space? To begin with, we have already discussed recent advances in experimental music, especially the important radical increase of musical materials, which used to consist earlier only of notes and now include all sounds as well as the liberation of the spatial dimension in music (in terms of new performance spaces, multichannel recordings, spatial placement of musicians and loudspeakers). These two musical advances, combined with Artaud's plea, lead to an interesting potential starting-point for today's composer working in the theater. In fact, the von Allem joke isn't all that irrelevant after all when one considers the potential sources of sound one can employ within a (theater) composition: all instruments found throughout the world, new vocal techniques – this is of special interest when the composer can work with the actors' speech and singing techniques – and all sounds recordable via the microphone or produced electronically. The challenge is to bring together (i.e., assimilate) diverse sound sources and styles that are compatible to the composer and to the given dramatic situations.

A comparison is apropos: if one were to call Robert Wilson's theater, the "theater of images", does the audio-visual "theater of sound" exist and is it in turn a potential partner of this image-theater as well as of the more traditional spoken theater?[3] This question may be answered in the affirmative when the composer liberally approaches music as the organization of sounds (specifically made in relationship to images and dramatic texts) while constantly working in collaboration with the direction team and with the actors as far as the non-visual portion of theater is concerned.

Theater is perhaps the oldest of all the art forms to be discussed here. It might be called the toughest nut to crack for today's composer as any musician with theatrical experience, especially in larger theaters, will know. It is most fascinating to see how little music has found its way into contemporary theater with the exception of well-known musicals and the 20th century equivalents of the operette (Brecht's theater is therefore not particularly modern in this sense). Music has not at all kept pace with the enormous breakthroughs in scene designing and lighting of the past thirty-five years. Most theater managers, dramaturges and directors – not to mention actors – have never taken part in the preparation of a play during which time the composer participates in general interpretation, specific execution (vocal techniques) and, of course, musical (sound) elements. This leaves the composer with the above-mentioned problem of trying to find a common language with which to communicate with his colleagues while attempting to free music from its role of *musique d'ameublement* (a scene change, atmosphere music for accompaniment) or just a number of songs. Once this common language is found, a slow, tedious but often rewarding process begins (theater work is not for today's Bachs and Mozarts who enjoy completing orchestral works weekly).

Personal experience has demonstrated that smaller theaters with relatively low budgets are more interested in "taking risks" experimenting with music and drama. Alas, many of these theaters are not equipped to take on the challenges of producing and mixing multichannel works complex enough to "furnish" and "feed" a particular dramatic work. When it does prove feasible, a great deal of possibilities arise which are not always present in a large hall (for purely acoustical reasons: relative proximity of speakers, the creation of a more "intimate" atmosphere, and so on). Larger theaters generally offer a better technical potential, but often have all sorts of taboos, for example where loudspeakers may (not) be placed.

Then there is the question of the public. Personal experience has again demonstrated, ironically, a much larger "tolerance" as well as appreciation for new sounds and music from a general theater audience than from the equivalent music public. (The small circles already close to modern music are not being referred to here.) This openness is surely due to the marriage between sound, image and dramatic action, the goal of any composer working in the theater. While perceiving visual elements, the viewer discovers different meanings for (abstract) sounds, something often found to be (too) difficult in non-visualized music.

An important choice for composers potentially interested in music for the theater is that between artistic globe-trotting and a monogamous bind to a single  ensemble theater. This choice is important, especially early on in this period of "tradition-smashing", because doing work in several cities in several theaters entails introducing the audience to new music in theatrical contexts with almost every new piece. (A theater which already possesses an experimental musical tradition is indeed hard to find.) Those who participate in several productions in one house often acquire respect for having added something to that theater's artistic content; expectations are raised and music can thus become a fundamental part of many of that theater's productions. Until now this has remained the exception as most theaters do not have a sufficient number of directors who are open-minded enough to maintain a music-drama continuity. Most musicians are therefore left leading a gypsy life. Teams such as Glass and Wilson, who have collaborated several times, are most important. The more such pairs work together, the more understanding will be developed within the theater world, and the greater will be the available audience.

Another interesting question, which is by no means unique to the theater, is the recycling of music composed for one specific production. If music is highly integrated within a given production, can it have any use elsewhere after the theater group has terminated its run? Suffice to say that each composer has his own answer to this question; fortunately, the answer is not a uniform "yes" or "no".

Theater is one of the oldest audio-visual disciplines and one of the hardest to enter. Contemporary music is the underdeveloped child of the theater, but will inevitably gain in importance as its technology and aesthetics are fused to those of the other disciplines present in this richer (in terms of subsidy), better visited (than contemporary music) branch of the audio-visual arts.

## b. Film

The state of modern film may be said to be similar to that of contemporary music as far as the deep divide between the more popular and the more experimental is concerned. There exists a special circuit of experimental film houses, museums and festivals. Even those often considered to be "art films", which are indeed sometimes shown at commercial film theaters, are mainly of a literary nature; new visual and sound techniques are almost always of lesser importance to these so-called art films.

There is another important parallel with music. We have seen an enormous increase in terms of technical potential in recent years (think of recent Hollywood science fiction spectacles). Yet how many non-commercial composers have had the opportunity to apply this potential? Happily there are some important sound hunters in recent film history, not the least of whom was the late Andrei Tarkovsky.

This division between very large and very small audiences dates from early film history. Composers like Erik Satie and George Antheil made music for the silent films of René Clair/Francis Picabia and Fernand Léger. Antheil, along with composers the likes of Aaron Copland and William Walton, later landed up working in Hollywood as well. With the Antheil/Otto Preminger partnership, a much larger public was reached than with his infinitely more interesting early work *Ballet Méchanique*. There is, of course, a rich history of film music, which has led to the tradition of elegant, safe music produced for today's popular films. However, the number of *sound* specialists for (experimental) films is fairly small and consists to a large extent of film makers, who have themselves (like the Canadian pioneer Norman McLaren), made a hobby of working with sound.

A number of questions raised in the theater and music discussion above are of course equally relevant to film and will therefore not be repeated. In short it may be concluded that making movies, especially those for a large public, is an exceedingly expensive venture in which few (commercial) risks are taken.[4] The (financially poorer) experimental film is in contrast quite different as it is based on the aesthetic, and therefore commercial unknown. As long as the gap between the two remains so large, the audio-visual composer will most likely have to restrict himself to the above-mentioned relatively marginal circuits.

## c. Video

Video, like film, is an art of modern times, an art made feasible through the availability of electricity. In the early years of cinema, an experimental mood prevailed; everything was new. Television, being younger than the movie, has seemed to skip the early experimental phase and has become in general an even more commercial medium. Video art is younger still. It was born of the necessity to apply the potential of video technology without being dependent upon commercial (or state) television demands. The experimental freedom evident in the works of (among others) Nam June Paik is perhaps a sophisticated variation of that present in early films of Man Ray or Luis Buñuel.

Video is a potential best friend of music as there are several points of intersection in recent image and sound technology. The word synthesizer, for example, is not solely applicable to music. Earlier, video artists either simply recorded existent music on the sound tracks of their tapes (like today's video clip) or tried to add home-made sounds themselves. In other words, a tape of images was made and music was then injected later or, conversely, the music recording presented the basic rhythm for the later mounted images.

The exceptional video works were first made by the multi-artists, such as Kagel, Steina and Woody Vasulka and Paik. Recently, new credits have been popping up in video art. Not only are composers named but, alternatively, new specialists known as "sound organizers", "sound designers" and "sound dramaturges" are listed as having co-realized a video work, and thus partnerships comparable to those between composers and playwrights are slowly but surely gaining ground.

Due to video's youth and enormous technological dynamic, this may very well be the most powerful discipline for the audio-visual minded composer. Works *a due* are being made more and more. The sound studios in video studios (like film) are in general of excellent quality and manned by technicians who, by the nature of their work, are at home in merging sounds and images. The only aspect which may be difficult concerns the problem that arises when video tapes are shown on television or on small monitors (at video centers). When the high-quality soundtrack(s) are not heard through high quality speakers, one may see beautiful images and hear low-fidelity sound. The technology exists, but one is never sure whether a good sound system will be available. For the fortunate few whose video pieces are shown on television one is, of course, certain of inferior sound quality in most private homes. (A good sound technician of course does attempt to account for both possibilities while preparing final copies of a new video work.)

Due to the growing success of video art (audio-visual studies are being offered in a growing number of countries), video artists are finding new collaborators from other disciplines as well. Video is being used more and more in dance and in staged music works. Very important, too, is the young genre of *video theater* in which music almost invariably plays a major role, thereby adding depth to Artaud's theater space through loudspeaker placement.

A final word concerning television: video art has not had an easy time sharing the television medium with Dallas and weekend sports programs. This will of course change to an extent as society's discontent with television seems to be growing (at long last). Nevertheless, while television is the medium with the most viewers, it is not necessarily always the best method of disseminating video. The problem of the reception quality has been mentioned. Many video installations and high resolution video tapes being created these days simply cannot be presented like the eight o'clock news. Videothèques, the equivalent of the movie theater, are beginning to appear here and there. They will at least be able to present works as the makers desire. The composer able to work at twenty-five images/second (MM 1500) is invited to join in developing this younger art form.

### d. Traditional disciplines
This title refers specifically to the modernization of two genres, opera and ballet. The first coexists today with what is called "music theater", "performance art", and others. The latter coexists with modern dance and the newer dance theater.

So far most attempts to find an experimental equivalent to opera (the stage genre of music) have originated from that small minority of musicians who have talents in the visual arts: examples include Mauricio Kagel's famous *Staatstheater* and Laurie Anderson's one woman performances. In both cases a good deal of the non-sound ideas were thought up by the composers, themselves.

More and more composers are considering making staged works in which music plays the central role. Few have had success. Why might this be so? Most likely, the primary reason is the high cost of organizing such works. Composers are in general low-budget artists. Opera is ultra-high budget art. Reputation and perseverance are the most likely roads leading to the realization of such works. Perhaps there will be more of such undertakings when composers have proven themselves within the organization of theatrical and video works, both of which belong to much more expensive art forms than the world of the string quartet or even the symphony orchestra.

In any event, newcomers should be warned if they have illusions of making large-scale staged works without a stage reputation. Kagel has yet to restage his highly controversial, if not successful, *Staatstheater* (at the time of writing this book there are rumors of this work being restaged). The ability to create such works must be seen as the climax of many years' labor within the world of staged music. (Operas for traditional ensembles form the exception as they of course are commissioned with some regularity. Yet how many of these new operas might one truly call experimental?)

The story of modern dance is a totally different one and is in fact one of the most gratifying audio-visual genres for today's experimental composer. The story may begin with Sergei Diaghilev, with Martha Graham, with George Balanchine, and accelerates with Merce Cunningham. How many contemporary composers have had the opportunity to collaborate and thereby participate in the many successes of the latter choreographer? (A positive sign is the growing number of such collaborative efforts currently in France, for example in the recent works of Carolyn Carlson.)

Throughout the world more and more choreographers decide to use a broad selection of (electroacoustic) music and audio environments for their new pieces. Many of these choreographers have a considerable renown, several of their pieces are performed for months on end in large performing spaces. Other than a few dance (theater, film, video) critics, there are not many spectators who seem to ignore the music they are hearing. In fact, in the author's experience, some electroacoustic works not originally intended for the dance seem to acquire an added dimension of depth when performed as part of a choreographed work. Better yet are the pieces written for the special desires and needs of the modern dancer.

Dance and music have been partners in all periods of history, in all world cultures. It is therefore no wonder that modern composers who have worked with choreographers have been able to profit by ages of experience. What is of particular interest here is when the composer and choreographer (scene, lighting and costume designers as well) work together so that all forces of contemporary dance can merge.

A special development within modern dance is noteworthy, that of the birth of the *dance theater* (e.g. that of Pina Bausch). It is in this branch of modern dance that all audio-visual possibilities meet (film or video is often used in performance). The composer with some dance and theater experience has an important voice in dance theater because of the dramatic as well as dance-accompanying role that the music usually plays in these works. Dance theater is a young art. There is room for a great number of pioneers here.

### e. And also Hörspiel/radiophonic works
This last category theoretically does not belong in this chapter at all. Nevertheless, it is included for two reasons: its historic relevancy and its advanced state of development and appreciation.

Before television existed, radio plays were so rich in sound that one could "see" the piece. One can speak of audio-visual art without images. In the early phases of this history, few experimental radio plays were made which stressed contemporary experimental music techniques. *But*, the enormous amount of knowledge needed in order to allow small pieces of wood to sound like the entire Soviet army led to the art of the "bruiteur". Given the tradition of the important role given to these sounds within radio plays, the request was made at the French radio in the late 1940s that led to the birth of *musique concrète*. Today radio plays obviously occupy a much smaller role in media world, but radiophonic art has (perhaps unexpectedly) not diminished.

Radio stations such as the WDR3 in Cologne have successful weekly programs for experimental *Hörspiele*. In this way contemporary artists from various branches have been able to learn and develop this genre. Musicians have played a very important role in radiophonic history and have thus helped in widening new music's boundaries. Also, combined forms such as radiophonic text sound works (sound poetry – see Henri Chopin's anthology in which many composers are mentioned) have been developed at such radio stations over the years.

The makers of the radio play improvised with concrete sounds in a much more sophisticated fashion than Edgard Varèse did in his earliest scores. Had he had the knowledge of the bruiteur, the technical resources of the radio of the 30s and the interest, his *Déserts* and *Poème électronique* might not have been his first and only works in which he truly organized sounds. Radiophonic art is audio art with an often implied visual level. It is a fascinating discipline which, after its rebirth in the late 1940s, has been dynamic enough to continue to grow in quantity and quality with new ideas and technical resources. It is the closest art form to "pure" music presented here and is therefore a great training ground for musicians who hesitate to jump immediately into the lion's den known as theater or cinema.

## 4. ... AND THEREFORE

This entire text might have taken on a more manifesto-like character in which the author analyzed experiences and specifically described various technical breakthroughs in these audio-visual disciplines while fighting for the "cause". But participation by experimental musicians in audio-visual art is not at all a cause. It is instead an important broadening of the spectrum of new music in terms of content and dissemination. One could be criticized of a certain cowardliness, of not sticking to the holy domain of an audio-only new music, working in collective teams, perhaps even taking on an "if you can't beat 'em, join 'em" mentality.

Those who prefer to continue working outside of the image culture should certainly continue to do so. Those willing to take the risk of participating in an evolution from within are invited. A continuing coexistence of "pure" and audio-visual music? Obviously. Collaboration between experimental musicians and visual specialists? Why not?

1) This chapter is a mildly revised version of the article *How often have you seen your compositions performed?* (Landy: 1988).

2) The following four paragraphs are the most general sections of a text which discussed the author's musical work leading to a February 1987 première of Heiner Müller's *Philoctetes*. The entire text appeared (in German) in the March/April 1987 Basle, Switzerland theater magazine. This text is not only relevant to theater; it has been included here to introduce several general points of interest.

3) For the sake of clarity, it should be mentioned that works the likes of Ligeti's *Aventures* are not what is meant here by the term "theater of sound". This work is a theatrical musical composition and has been written for the concert hall. What is being discussed here is a *Gesamtkunstwerk* utilizing the theater as venue; had Ligeti chosen an approach including special lighting, scene design, directing the actors (singers in this case), etc., then this work would have been an ideal example. For performance art, see below.

4) To be honest, there have been more risks taken in music than in many other aspects in Hollywood films. Sonic experimentation has led to various sorts of mood creation. This is risky compared to Hollywood text treatment and the like, but not when compared to musical experimentation in general.

# Part 4 –
# Contemporary music today

We have often repeated the opinion of many that the decrease in experimental activities, beginning in the 1970s and continuing today, is due to a failure of the music. Failure in the sense of lack of quality. Failure in the sense of lack of large-scale appreciation.

As has been suggested several times in the first three parts of this book, it seems that criteria for judging quality do not really exist. Furthermore, the give and take involved in popularity in today's consumer culture has been found to be a most troublesome topic.

The author is not of the opinion that "failure" is the correct word, otherwise this book need not have been written. In part 5 suggestions will be made for a potential future for experimentalism. This part 4 takes an inventory, be it far from complete, of what is around at the moment and how it fits into musical and socio-economical developments which we are now familiar with.

# XI. Survey: One step forwards, two steps backwards?

## 1. THE WHOLE = THE SUM OF ALL ITS PARTS?

This perhaps silly title does typify what most consider the state of music today. Schools of composers are out of fashion in the "no-nonsense 80s". Individualism reigns supreme. Therefore, most successful artists must show and promote their individualism as part of their talent.

But is this in fact so? It is believed that there are a number of very clear directions, be they progressive or more conservative, being followed by a majority of today's composers (there are, of course, still exceptions). Most categories begin with the prefix "neo" and tend to be somewhat conservative. There are the neo-romanticists who tend to conserve elements of the past as well as the creators of neo-simplicity (*Neue Einfachkeit*). Perhaps the only exception to this can be found in the minimalists who have been placed in the neo-tonal group. These composers have cleared a path towards fusion with non-art musics, the subject of chapter XIV.

Also, the return of orchestral and operatic works as two genres of (more conservative) contemporary music as well as the frequent use of classical chamber ensembles will also be looked into separately here.

Besides the neo-groups and fusion music, musicians involved in the best known sorts of the music of sounds, electroacoustic music and new extended vocal techniques, although not always independent of subjects mentioned above, will be given special attention in chapter XIII.

## 2. NEO = MORE OLD THAN NEW

When one considers a list of a few of the "neos" around today – neo-romanticism, neo-tonality, neo-simplicity, neo-melodic writing, neo-atonality and neo-virtuosity, many of which have never been clearly defined – it is certain that the thought will arise that experimental music is not at the forefront of today's music. This is indeed correct. But to isolate what is left of experimentation today and what might be expected of it in the future, we must briefly inspect the daily diet of most of today's composers.[1]

– *Neo-romanticism, neo-tonality and neo-simplicity:* Of all the "neos" listed here, *neo-romanticism* is the most vague. Literally, a typical piece of neo-romanticism might be the Dutch composer Simeon ten Holt's *Canto Ostinato* for four pianos which sounds like a synthesis of Robert Schumann with Philip Glass. But in fact this work forms an exception to compositional approaches which are often bunched together within the broad field of neo-romanticism.

The majority of today's contemporary music concerts contains at least one work with a traditional title the likes of Sonata, Variations on ..., String Quartet or a programatic title which comes closer to Claude Debussy's *La Mer* than to Steve Reich's *Pendulum Music,* a piece in which the programatic title also concerns its cast of characters. Of course it's what one does with the program that counts; most program works today do tend to be highly romantic and expressive. Perhaps we should consider this neo-romanticism in fact to be neo-neo-classicism (not to mention a-atonality and post-post-modernism), as the points of departure of the neo-classic movement of the 1920s have not been changed. As will now be shown neo-classicism was based on renewing established forms, genres or even existent musics (think of the difference between Igor Stravinsky's *Pulcinella*, a Pergolesi orchestration, be it highly revised, and his *Symphony of Psalms* with its updated use of fugal techniques). The "classic" part of the "neo" by no means is fixed to the time of the first Viennese school (again, one may use Stravinsky as an example in considering his jazzy *Ebony Concerto* on the one hand and his highly romantic *Jeu de Cartes* on the other hand. In fact, one might even say that his *Movements for Orchestra* belong to neo-classic thinking as a variation on atonal techniques of Anton Webern's – this latter piece is better placed as belonging to neo-atonality, see below). Analogously, the "romantic" in this overly used term does not necessarily have to relate to the likes of a Hector Berlioz.

We might attempt to define neo-romanticism today as music in which tonality (or at least the tonic) in some form is present *and* the craftsmanship of the composer is more in the forefront than any progressive or experimental element. In fact, neo-romantic music might therefore be seen to be the antithesis of experimental music.

*Neo-tonality*[2] and *neo-simplicity:* These two terms will never win a prize for their clarity as well. They all even seem to be interchangeable at times. Of course experimentalism knew its share of tonal works: think of Karlheinz Stockhausen's *Stimmung,* a vocal work based on the overtones of a single pitch, Luciano Berio's *Sinfonia,* the work containing the famous super-quotation section using a Mahler symphonic movement as a frame in which to glue together an indescribable number of pieces (quotations) from several other composers, and a large number of works written by Henri Pousseur and Bernd Alois Zimmermann in which tonality came in direct confrontation with experimental thought, to name just a few. These composers' works are not the subject of the current chapter if we apply the definition of experimental music provided in chapter I. For, with the exception of a number of the minimalists, none of the "neo" musicians is particularly interested in experimentalism.

Neo-tonality arose as a term (describing a movement) to include those composers who reacted, or at least opposed the large-scale group of second generation composers of atonal works born in the Darmstadt 50s. Neo-tonality knows its parallel in the plastic arts where abstraction has diminished in importance since the 50s (although there has been in resurgence in the plastic arts) and where realism in one form or another is again taking prominence. This neo-tonality was not founded to search for new systems. It is also not a set of techniques or methods; many composers prefer to call neo-tonality an attitude. It is often called harmonic music (in the sense of overtones), allowing prominence to the lesser overtones, the consonant intervals[3] (although a good deal of this music does tend to be mildly or even highly dissonant). Neo-tonal works are rarely written in a specific key. They often disregard those harmonic relations which were at the base of traditional European tonality. They often profit by our growing knowledge of non-European musics. Also they seem to include most minimal music.

But shouldn't minimalism be the foundation of what is known as *neo-simplicity*? Minimal art was based of course on the reduction of material to a minimum. LaMonte Young's early music was analogous to minimal art with its use of minimal sound material. Nevertheless, minimal music officially belongs to neo-tonality and to an extent to neo-romanticism (e.g. the ten Holt example), but hardly to neo-simplicity which is, as stated, a translation of the German *Neue Einfachkeit;* it is something this writer would prefer to call neo-expressionism. Composers, the likes of the very often performed Wolfgang Rihm as well as Detlev Müller-Siemens and many others in West Germany as well as a number of Italians and to a lesser extent composers in other countries, are those behind neo-simplicity. They seem to have taken over where the *Blaue Reiter* composer, Arnold Schönberg left off in the early 1910s with compositions the likes of the *Piano Pieces,* Op. 19, *Herzgewächse,* Op. 20 and *Pierrot Lunaire,* Op. 21. Their works tend to be highly dissonant although they avoid serialism, reminiscent of the great struggle in tonal thinking around the turn of the century with a dose of mild *Verfremdung* (alienation) typical of an Oskar Kokoschka painting and the expressionist self-portrait painter Schönberg.

The final remark concerning neo-romanticism in terms of the presence of a tonic and in terms of its leaning towards craftsmanship above experimentation is most often equally true to almost all of the neo-tonalists with the exception of the fusion composers (see chapter XIV) who do indeed form exceptions. This final remark is also pertinent to those composers belonging to the neo-simplicity category regardless of their strong atonal leanings.

There are literally hundreds of composers all worthy of attention when it comes to the various approaches to neo-tonality: George Crumb the American eclectic; Ton de Leeuw who established his own variant of Olivier Messiaen's *Modes à transpositions limitées*; Arvo Pärt the Estonian who composes many a work which sounds more like Medieval or Renaissance music than music of the 1980s; Per Nørgård the Dane who, having left serialism and repetitive music, has found new tonal applications of the Fibonacci series and the Golden Mean; Alfred Schnittke the Soviet composer who seems to have made an about-face from experimentalism Russian style to march forward into the past. He calls his manner of composition poly-stylism, an attempt to find unity among a variety of historical musical traditions. Doesn't this sound similar to the original Stravinsky notion of neo-classicism? These are examples of important contemporary composers who may have invested in experimentation in their earlier years, but who currently have little to do with experimental thought.

And then there are the *neo-nationalists*, many of whom are located in the traditionally nationalist countries of Eastern Europe, in Great Britain and so on, as well as the "neo-...s" (i.e. any other "neo" school), the composers who consciously choose proven successful formulae to be safe, who by definition are always to be found worldwide in huge quantities. These "neo" composers form a majority of today's *Tonkünstler* offering a large selection of hardly progressive music today.

– *Neo-melodic writing:* What happened to the melody early on in the century? Schönberg used his *Hauptstimme* as a melody replacement; Webern thrived without melody; highly diverse figures the likes of Cage, Xenakis, Reich and Boulez have written important melodyless works. Yet around 1970, there must have been a convention held somewhere where almost by acclamation the melody was taken out of hibernation and reintroduced to the musical society known as contemporary music. This is particularly of note in the works of the maestros of experimental music of the 1950s and 1960s – see the following chapter; this subject will be further discussed there. The "rediscovery" of melody obviously has something to do with that little something we need to hold onto when listening to music (referring of course to the lengthy discussion in chapter VII), but in general has gone hand in hand with the "neos" presented here.

- *Neo-atonality and neo-virtuosity:* Too many departments of musicology throughout the world tend to stop teaching music of around 1920 onwards as it is found to be too young to be placed into an acceptable historic perspective. This author doubts this to be so. In any event many composers have been able to place serial thinking of the 20s into a historic perspective as they are neo-ing it in ways similar to our neo-tonalists. An interesting phenomenon in neo-atonal thought is that there are still two clear subgroups: one more dissonant (Webern) oriented and one less dissonant (Berg) oriented. Brian Ferneyhough belongs to the first group as well as many of Elliott Carter's followers; George Perle and Peter Schat clearly belong to the latter group. Eastern Germany has created a good deal of atonal composers who seem to span the range of both groups. In fact one might state that the reaction is no longer to the 1920s, but instead against the highly (too?) complex developments of the Darmstadt years in Europe and the fruitful Milton Babbitt/Carter years in the United States. Still, what is most surprising is that most atonalists today are indeed "neo" in the senses described above. Ferneyhough is in fact one of the few who has provided a significant addition to atonal thinking in the last two decades.

This significant addition can be found in the level of difficulty for the musician(s) and the extremely high density of notes in many of his works. Surely *Pierrot Lunaire* broke records in terms of rehearsal time before its première, but this Schönberg score looks like an easy *étude* compared to some of Ferneyhough's compositions. Perhaps one might think of the over-complexity of the Carter works discussed in chapter VII (see also part 6, chapter XVIc); yet Ferneyhough's sound is quite different and earns a place in atonal writing without the qualifier "neo", as craftsmanship and development seem to be at equilibrium in many of his pieces.

Brian Ferneyhough is also an example of a *neo-virtuoso* composer.[4] This term is a ridiculous one as the "neo" here is useless. Every period has known its (performer-) composers who showed off their talents in many ways, one of which being the high level of interpretative difficulty. These members of the Olympic team of music history generally tend to add something to the musical alphabet as it were – new sounds through sophisticated (physical) performance techniques breaking previous instrumental "records" – originating in the difficulty itself instead of through making knowns more difficult. Think of Wagnerian singing: ranges were expanded and techniques developed hand in hand with new tonal thinking; of Xenakis who writes seemingly impossible sounds to play while creating new timbres. And then there are the performer-composers: Liszt, Bartók and the hundreds of performer-composers today writing in general almost exclusively for their own instruments. Their music is almost always part "show" in the sense of performance gymnastics, but hopefully a large part is taken up by our key word, musicality. As neo-virtuosity is quite prominent, it has been included here, but it is the only subject of the current chapter which is still pertinent to experimental music today as it does not, in general, satisfy the definition of the other "neos" where more accent is given to proven forms of craftsmanship than to development.

– The return of the orchestra and the opera, etc.: getting back to our real "neos" and briefly referring to the postponed subject of socio-economics, many composers' return to the musical ensembles and genres of yesteryear, not to mention yestercentury, was unavoidable. Does the orchestra have the sound needed for today's music? The string quartet? Obviously the answer to both questions are "Yes *and* no".

"No *and* yes" is actually more correct. These ensembles were created with certain types of music and acoustical givens in mind. They are dynamic only to a small extent as the basis of the sound of such ensembles is the first music written for them. Some composers seem to be able to penetrate this and write highly innovative music for our historic ensembles: Xenakis' orchestral works, the string quartets of Ligeti, Carter and Penderecki, Henze oratorios, Kagel's opera.

But these exceptions are not the point here. "No *and* yes" is the better answer, for these ensembles clearly are more available for "neo" works than non-"neo" works. Many of these ensembles are funded; some request new works, others are pleased when new works are written for them. It is probably easier to get a commission from and a performance organized by a chamber orchestra than for that work you always wanted to compose for triple brass quartet and boat harbor.

In other words, limited funding and established ensembles (as well as concert halls with their varied series) combine to insure a continuity for new music made for tradition ensembles in traditional spaces. An experimentalist might say: musical theater, not opera; large ensemble, not orchestra; string quartet for kora, koto, sitar and fender bass and not that other one. That experimentalist will have to find another source of income and demonstrate a good deal of patience.

It is the belief of this writer that this seemingly vicious circle benefitting established ensembles and genres is unhealthy for music's progress, for even when these ensembles would be free to try their hand at more experimental compositions, their music education (see chapter VI) may prove to be inadequate. This creates an unfortunate atmosphere of relative stagnation, a not too unrealistic description of the scene of a great deal of contemporary music-making today.

– And of course there are those *individuals*: All periods, be they dynamic or relatively stagnant, have always known their more individualistic composers. We have now seen that our time is actually not determined by a sum of its individuals; in fact there are only too few. For it is from these people that a good deal of invention is still to be found.

Certainly there have also been some groups conforming to a single sort of experimentation. There is no reason why each development must be totally invented, decomposed and (re-) composed by just one composer. But the individual must, almost by definition, seek out a world for himself or herself. Giacinto Scelsi and and the player piano specialist, Conlon Nancarrow represent two individuals who preserved their individualism in their late years (something which is not true to all experimentalists – see the following chapter). Luigi Nono seems to represent one of the exceptions of the following middle generation. Jean-Claude Risset may be named here as well as he is currently in the vanguard of today's composers specialized in computer music synthesis. The younger Finnish composer, Kaija Saariaho, who uses the computer to aid her in, among other things, her vertical compositional techniques, has already created a special place for herself in the generation of composers in their thirties and forties. She has only too few colleagues who have also suceeded in creating such places for themselves, their techniques and their "sounds". (The electroacoustic composers Denis Smalley and Trevor Wishart in England deserve mention here as well.) These individuals may be thought to belong to one of the neo-groups in one way or other, but this is generally not the case. For example Scelsi's "one tone" works could be seen to belong to neo-tonal thinking. That there is *the* tone at the basis of these pieces is true; still those acquainted with his highly unusual music realize that the claim that he participated in what we call neo-tonal thinking is most unlikely.

That something at the basis of their individuality is what has made them known; their experiment plays a large role therein.

## 3. CONCLUSION

In general it might be said that since ca. 1970 the amount of timbral works has dropped and the number of spatial works has also decreased significantly, these being the two most dynamic parameters of experimental music at the time. Again, the economics behind these developments is clear. Or has it just been a taking-stock time? Even a number of heroes of experimentalism have slowed down if not stopped altogether with their progressive thinking and sound organizing, as will be discussed in the following pages.

Our time has often been called a time of synthesis, as the available information is so great. The Canadian musician who writes a theme and variations for wind quintet based on an Ibo melody from Nigeria is quite likely to be a member of one the neo-synthesis schools of music. The musicians who will be called upon in the conclusion of this book will be their partner of the other gender, namely members of the experimental synthesis musicians guild.

"Neo" is survival. It is the vitamin of the majority of musicians. Those who live from their art, eat "neo" at breakfast, lunch and dinner daily.

This book has been written to look into what is the matter with experimental music today. The fact that far more than 90% of today's contemporary music belongs to the "neos" is perhaps the clearest statement of what is wrong with our subject of focus. If we accept that experimentalism lies at the foundation of cultural development, of progress, this statistic is shocking and must be brought back into balance at some point. But of course several have bid a final *adieu* to experimental thought many years ago.

It is true that too few profited by experimentalism's offerings (in terms of composers, musicians, and listeners). Still, we have now shown that this is not *only* due to the said lack of quality of experimental works.

In a highly dynamic world, one in which consumerism is so overly present and abundant, contemporary music should offer a cozy shelter. Instead it, too, conforms and marches to the beat of the symphony orchestra playing its second "successful" season of neo-romantic "classics". This is also what's the matter with experimental music.

1) Two remarks must be made concerning this chapter. First of all, the systematic approach of the first ten chapters has been loosened here as the current goal is to emphasize one single point, namely that the *"neo"* presence in contemporary music is relatively overwhelming. Secondly, a number of better-known composers will remain unnamed here as they are treated separately in the following chapter.

2) The subject of neo-tonality was treated in *MusikTexte nr. 14* (1986) by four writers: Reinhard Febel, Wolfgang Rihm, Herman Sabbe and Peter Sloterdijk. Those interested in this subject will find useful information there.

3) Ironically, Arnold Schönberg made many statements in which he proved the natural quality of his twelve-tone row based on their presence in the harmonic series. The most atonal Stockhausen works are based on (sub-)harmonic relations in pitch and rhythm. In other words, it seems natural to use all twelve tones, and even more natural to give prominence to the consonant intervals. But which nature is being referred to: mother nature or human nature?

4) The British composer, Michael Finnissey deserves mention here as well.

# XII. The maestros of the 50s and 60s in 1989

## 1. BEFORE AND AFTER PHOTOS

You have all seen those advertisements in various periodicals: advertisements for diet pills or hair growing remedies with their over-satisfied clients who looked "wrong" in the before picture and "right" in the after picture. In this chapter we will briefly look into how many "cures" have been followed by the pioneers of early experimentalism.

Many an article has been written and many an evening discussion has focused on the attention given to composers who reached maturity in the late 1930s who had to deal with that very difficult decision: "Who will be my guiding light? Will it be Stravinsky (neo-classicism) or Schönberg (atonality)? Or will it be Bartók (nationalism is the traditional name: multi-regionalism is perhaps a better description of his work) or perhaps even Hindemith (*Gebrauchsmusik et al.*)?" The first pair was of special importance as it was they who set up that important division between consonance and dissonance that was in every composer's mind in the second quarter of this century.

Few articles have been written, but still there has been many a discussion about composers reaching maturity in the late 60s or later. Their question was: "Will it be Cage (indeterminacy), Stockhausen (or Boulez or Babbitt – serialism) or Xenakis (mathematics and physics)? Or perhaps Berio (experimentalism with a human face) or those who hardly ever left the electroacoustic studios?"

This chapter wonders which questions might have been of interest to the composers themselves who came to the fore in the period of greatest experimentation – twenty years later? How much of Xenakis' timbral density is there in Penderecki's recent works? What was Boulez's *répons* (a pun intended for Boulez fans) to his *Structures*? In other words, in an era in which a number of our consumer products are gaining many partners with the suffix "light" meaning fewer calories and sometimes also meaning milder to the palate, might our elder maestros also be conforming to this new popular consumer ideal?

Our hypothesis is that instead of reaching a synthesis of earlier styles as many masters of composition tend to do at later ages, most experimentalists have become progressively less radical, perhaps by putting water in their wine, which in turn serves as a weak foundation for inspiring younger composers to profit by and continue their experimental work.

Certainly there is the example of the elder Satie who, having studied at the Schola Cantorum in Paris at a relatively late age, paid for it in his later, less radical works; but most of today's masters learned and "rejected" their training early on. Varèse's late works on the other hand were by no means *mea culpa* compositions.

In art, Salvador Dali became extremely conservative at old age, whereas Marcel Duchamp did nothing of the sort. Hopefully it is not the suicidal Jackson Pollock who provides the true example, having ended his life so tragically at the peak of his career?

All dramatic thinking set aside, it is shocking when one considers what has become of a number of major experimentalists. The following paragraphs look into just a small number of these musicians, but nevertheless attempt to illustrate a general trend. Few examples will be given, in the first place because these works are of a less experimental nature, and in the second place because there is enough published information on all of these figures concerning their recent pieces.

Two extreme examples of quitters are Krzysztof Penderecki and Toru Takemitsu. The composers, respectively of that elegantly, yet alternatively notated, highly colorful work, *Threnody for the Victims of Hiroshima* and one of the most impressive works of *musique concrète, Water Music* have heightened their successes through mildly modernizing the mass (Penderecki) and the music of Debussy and Messiaen (Takemitsu) in the 80s. There is of course nothing at all wrong with their sources of inspiration; it is the total divorce from their highly deserved earlier fame in modernizing the music of sound which is so shocking.

Penderecki's fellow Poles Witold Lutosławski, Henryk Górecki, Bogusław Schäffer, Kazimierz Serocki and Wlodziemierz Kotoński, to name just a few, all joined hands in creating the powerful Polish school of timbral music in the late 50s and 60s. Not one can be said to be continuing this tradition to a great extent in his recent works. The leader, Lutosławski was always modest in experimentation; therefore his development might be seen to be more natural. As Poland has been most tolerant of experimentalism, the lack of continuity is most painful as far as experimentalism in socialist countries is concerned.

Takemitsu is also no loner when speaking of Japanese ex-experimentalists. He, too, has joined the "neos". Toshi Ichyanagi is hardly the same composer as the earlier maestro of Japanese Fluxus music. Yuji Takahashi has gone through a similar metamorphosis. Maki Ishii's works have become more and more spectacular leaving an experimental flavor primarily to the uninformed. The highly individual composer, Makoto Shinohara is one of the few to continue his life-long search for the combination of experimental sounds with roots in his Japanese culture and in his Darmstadt training (see part 6, chapter XVIj for an analysis of one of his works). Even the well-known South Korean composer, Isang Yun, has shown that his earlier models no longer interest him; only his political message remains unchanged.

And then there is that enigmatic, highly musical György Ligeti who, beginning with his opera, *Le grand macabre,* rediscovered melody, a most significant development. He was but one of very many, including Mauricio Kagel (beginning at about the same time: e.g., his composition *1898* and continuing in almost every work since 1970 aligning him strongly to some of the "neo" schools), Karlheinz Stockhausen (beginning around the time of the work, *Mantra,* which was to lead the way to all of his future works), and very many others even including Iannis Xenakis who all chose to allow that main voice to be present in many a piece after so many had fought for its being unnecessary. (Luciano Berio was one of the few who almost continually used melody in his works.)

Was the war lost or was it a draw? Only time will tell. Ligeti's recent *Piano Concerto* shows that he was never totally separated from his earlier highly innovative works, although his *Horn Trio* (with more than a wink given to Johannes Brahms) placed his credibility *en question* as an experimental leader.

Very few composers openly admit to having been "wrong", after choosing a safer way in their compositions. This admission would at least be honest. There are those who "sell" their newest music using old progressive slogans, whereas the product is less progressive than the slogans. This is less honest. How do experimental music's major leaders fare here?

## 2. THE MAIN FIGURES OF EXPERIMENTALISM

What is fascinating about the elder statesmen of experimentalism is that they all claim to be totally consistent in terms of their earlier philosophies.[1] But how do these later versions sound?

**Karlheinz Stockhausen:** How does one compare the musical violence of the *Mikrophonie* works with the *Formel*-ized recent works, known for their clarity, most of which are related to his magnum opus, the week long lasting opera, *Licht* ? That parameter referred to in the first chapter, "compositional bearing" has known its extremes in his œuvre. Is today's Wagner truly the composer of that meditative prose score, *Aus den sieben Tagen*?

Stockhausen is still the most parameter-minded composer. He is also still, with excuses, the most arrogant, guru-like salesman of his branch of contemporary music – thus the Wagner comparison does not only concern his search for the 20th century's Bayreuth. It must be said that his recent music has lost nothing in terms of quality. It is his prominence in terms of progressive thinking that is to be questioned here.

Indeed, his *Formel* is one elegant way of going about things. An entire form may be reduced to the size of a melody and further reduced to the complex of a single sound (Xenakis does this as well, using his own tools). But his works dating from *Mantra* (1970, the year in which many things changed) onwards all tend to be milder than his heavily dissonant early works as well as many of his aggressive sound works of the late 50s and 60s. The fact that his melodies are seen to be necessary given his Formel approach is one of the finest logical bends known to history. Had he not invented this super-parameter, might he then not have returned to melodic writing and clearer, less harsh orchestration that he so clearly has chosen?

To close the composer of major expressive serial works the likes of *Kontakte* is indeed an excellent melody-maker; his *Tierkreis* offers substantial proof of this. His experimental lust of the Darmstadt years has been remarkably tempered.

**Pierre Boulez:** The word, milder, is without question also true to Stockhausen's partner in the famous struggle for Webern's prominence as a source of inspiration above Schönberg as well as above Stravinsky in the Darmstadt 50s. Boulez's recent works, many of which employ techniques utilizing computers which timbrally and spatially manipulate live instrumental sounds in real-time, are exemplary of one of the few new "sounds" of recent year of a given composer that have really caught on. Perhaps the works of the *Structures* period were too intellectually conceived and did go too far for our modest perceptions. Boulez seems to have found his *modus operandi* in which the listener is very clear about the sonorous experience being offered. He still is clearly a product of the atonal Second Viennese School; nevertheless, his experimental attitude has been taken away from his first subject of study, multi-dimensional serialism, and has been led to more timbre oriented sound manipulation of instruments by the computers of his most important address for modern music, IRCAM in Paris, a commendable evolution.

**Luciano Berio:** It is uncertain whether it would be correct to start this paragraph with "mild, milder, mildest", but Berio, the composer of those wild *Sequenze* and the milestone of *musique concrète* using only the voice as sound material, *Tema: Omaggio a Joyce,* has mellowed. He still writes exquisite music, music which clearly communicates directly with human emotions. Yet the experimental character is pretty much lost or has simply been masked in the new Berio "sound" which just might belong to the neo-romantic category discussed in the previous chapter. Why couldn't these two be combined as they used to be? Truly, the brilliant arranger of two books of *Folk Songs*, the composer of *Sinfonia*, *the* work of experimental music for a large public, always wanted to leave all doors open toward more general acceptance and popularity. Recent major works including the orchestra piece, *Formazione*, and his opera, *La vera Storia*, illustrate his enormous musicianship as well as the large distance traveled (into the past?) after the completion of *Tema* and *Visage*. The experimentation seems to be lost; the beauty remains.

**Iannis Xenakis:** Xenakis is one of the two truest composers to their original models along with John Cage. He has designed his UPIC computer system at his studio outside of Paris on which anyone can draw the most unusual sounds which are in turn converted into the real thing by the computer. A child draws freely, Xenakis draws sounds determined from mathematics.

But this is not the full story. Even he has rediscovered melody in his own way. Furthermore, his recent works tend to be somewhat less rich in contrast (loud/quiet, staccato/legato, glissandi/points/lines) than many of his earlier works. He has even been known for his modal thinking in recent years.[2]

Xenakis, too, has become milder, at least in his vocal and instrumental works. One might say that he has been true to his own cause of music's being based on numbers; the translation of those numbers was always influenced by his own strategies. Earlier translations led to that peculiar and fascinating early Xenakis sound. It is not totally lost, he has just given his probability tables higher weights for round (consonant?) numbers.

**John Cage:** Cage's sources of inspiration have not changed one iota since the composition of his *Music of Changes* in 1951. He is the only composer on this list who did not become noticeably milder in the 1970s. It is true, that many recent works do demonstrate a rediscovery of precise notation. Perhaps, he, too, was disenchanted by the too high number of poor performances of his works utilizing new notations.

The only other noticeable change of the John Cage of recent years has to do with his enjoyment of performing. Many works call for (or even features his own) vocalizing, his *Empty Words* being a typical example. His love for mesostics (an alternatively notated graphic poem in which the name of the person in homage can be read from top to bottom) which are nice to read, but also to hear, exemplifies this as well. His works are almost all based on the *I Ching*. Some works are based on star maps, but this does not influence our tale of aleatory and indeterminacy. His sources of inspiration, Satie, Thoreau, Duchamp, Buckminster Fuller, Suzuki, just to name a few quite dissimilar figures, have not been replaced.

The only noticeable, and somewhat unexpected development may have something to do with his somewhat atechnical background. Most of Cage's recent works are vocal or instrumental. This means that there are fewer "any sound will do" pieces than earlier. Cage claims that these instrumental works are sound works as well; however, many a listener thinks that an organ sounds like ... an organ and a violin sounds like ... a violin. In this one case, Cage seems to be doing little good to his liberation of sounds, that liberation R. Murray Schafer calls "ear cleaning".

Again, spatial and timbral thinking have been reduced in the work of most composers above. The tempo of development in these areas of experimental music has been slowed down. This author considers this to be disappointing to put it mildly and unhealthy in terms of keeping contemporary music dynamic.

Furthermore, the maestros – with few exceptions – do not serve the purpose of leading younger, potential experimentalists in any particular directions. If Xenakis can compose mathematical modal music for a wider audience, if the battle is no longer between the sound and the note, but instead perhaps yet again between the dissonant and the consonant, it is clear why no new experimental schools have been formed. It must be hard to become experimental and conform to well-known composers who have become more careful in their thinking after what now looks to have been extended youths. Young people need and deserve examples from which they can develop new visions. The foundation of experimental thinking has now become very weak, as current inspirational examples are, in general, noticeably absent. This in turn contributes to the miserable statistic mentioned at the end of the previous chapter.

The only good news that can be stated at the end of this discussion is:

– 1) for those interested in further experimentation regardless of the findings of chapter XII, the information is there in the form of recordings, scores, documents and musicological literature for all interested. Experimental synthesis is open to all.

– 2) the road is quite free for individual choice, as there are so few examples of note anno 1989. Again, those who do not want to be programmed in that second season of neo-romantic classics will have relatively more difficulty finding performance possibilities. This author believes that the pleasure of putting an experimental piece together under these circumstances is about the most satisfying artistic experience possible.
　　Or should we just all become musically milder as we get older?

1) Getting back to our definition of experimentalism, one might conclude that this concept is limited to a composer's attitude/intention. Perhaps practice is another means to the end: how does one compose? How does the composer work with musicians? What is the composer's lifestyle? In a single case (Cage), the latter question is relevant. But still our interest is in experimental composition and music-making; it is here that in general these composers have cut back on the seasonings.
2) In 1987 Ivanka Stoianova wrote the following concerning a performance of the work *Akea* (1986) for piano quintet. "It was already known that (Xenakis') musical language had changed in recent years. ....Where one might expect sound masses and cluster movements, one instead experiences a flow of melodic polyphony; instead of the known formal gestures of sound masses, there were relatively transparent musical fragments which often included textures of repetition or quasi-modal figures. ... The work begins with virtuoso arabesques, with arpeggio chords on the piano which remind one of Brahms to an extent  ...  vague memories of Messiaen; these illustrate Xenakis' recent tendency towards looking for simplicity of texture ..." (Stoianova: 54).

# XIII. Today's music of sounds: Electroacoustic music and extended vocal techniques

## 1. A VAST MAJORITY OF OUR MUSIC IS PRODUCED ELECTRONICALLY

Our relationship with music may have become passive in this century in the senses proposed in the media chapter. Still, music has by no means become less present than in earlier times. Radios blast at you when you enter clothing stores; Muzak paces you at the supermarket; in the Balkan countries some radios are kept on outside on terraces playing music day and night regardless of whether anyone is at home. The omnipresent television uses music for all sorts of things, not the least of which being advertising.

Although we have already established that some 90% of today's art music belongs to the "neos", only a fraction hereof is electroacoustic. As art music is but a tiny fraction of all music consumed daily, this statistic does not in any way contradict the following one: a vast majority of our music consumed daily is produced electronically.

Electronic music was born, partially due to its inevitable technological use in music – think of the electric organ as the modernization of older models – partially due to the growing need to broaden the horizon of musical resources. Pierre Schaeffer's dream was to systematize all sounds as *objets sonores* and *objets musicaux* leading to the coexistence of *musique abstraite* – instrumental sounds are abstract – and *musique concrète* – recorded sounds are not. The work of

Karlheinz Stockhausen and others in the Cologne electronic music studio of the 50s which was based on the building up of sine waves, or conversely the filtering of white noise, clearly was created to expand timbral sources.

What has been the lot of these highly pioneering thoughts? Is the work of the musician of electroacoustic music indeed so totally different than the work of the poor old instrumental composer? Is the only difference between an acoustic guitar and an electric one to be found in the loudness parameter?

## 2.  DIDN'T YOU KNOW THAT COMPUTER MUSIC IS NUMBER 1?

Let's begin with what might be considered the most recent major technology for musical application, the technology of computer music. It is in fact computer music[1] which covers most electroacoustic music today – practically every synthesizer in use currently is a digital instrument belonging to the category of computer music synthesis. Computer music instruments are truly – and this is said with a tear in the eye – a form of consumerism *pur sang*, perhaps unavoidably. Computer technology is renewed (prices tend to be cut in half, potential is doubled) per computer generation which lasts approximately four years. Often when one has mastered a new technique or digital instrument, it is already out of fashion.

If we scan through the history of sound synthesis with the computer we see that the first forms of computer sound generation (ca. 1960) were highly similar to the Cologne analog electronic music experiments begun a decade earlier. These included *additive synthesis* which is based on the creation of sound built up from sine waves and *subtractive synthesis*, the filtering down of noise (the presence of all frequencies simultaneously) to the desired timbres. The first attempts at speech synthesis and instrument imitation through computer synthesis utilized one or both of these varieties.

Later on two very important developments took place. In reversed chronological order *sampling* will be discussed first. Sampling provides the musician with the possibility of entering an existent sound into the computer where it can be "played back" in a variety of ways or modified and then resynthesized. For users who are interested in using such (instrumental, vocal or recorded) sounds as a *point du départ*, sampling provides the possibility of modifying any acoustic sound, a great advance for those who could not create similar timbres through other methods. This has been added to the larger additive and subtractive synthesis languages, such as CSound and CMusic, but is also best known through certain more expensive digital synthesizers or less expensive sampling units which can be connected to synthesizers and other digital equipment.

Secondly, John Chowning pioneered the research leading to what is known today as *FM* (frequency modulation) *synthesis*. Additive and subtractive synthesis are highly, perhaps ultimately precise, but are very inefficient, time consuming and use huge amounts of space in the computer for computation and storage. Take for example a stereo synthesized work the length of an ordinary Bruckner Symphony sampled at the compact disk sampling rate of 44.1 kilobytes/second (88.2 kilobytes [2 channels] x 60 seconds/minute x the length of the work in minutes). FM synthesis, which is hard to program but highly efficient – today it works on most systems in real-time, i.e. play the MIDI synthesizer key or strike the MIDI drumhead and hear its computed result – sped up the work and cut down drastically the amount of information to be computed. We know the FM-sound today as primarily coming from those synthesizers which have a very natural sounding bell and wood drum sound, where all other "realistic" timbres are at best approximations.

Obviously anyone working with computing prefers to save money on huge hard disks needed for that synthesized Bruckner symphony and time waiting for it to be computed and stored. FM synthesis is actually extremely flexible; its variety known to us through synthesizers, the best known being the Yamaha DX-7, is unfortunately less so. The reason for this is called MIDI (the abbreviation for Musical Instrument Digital Interface).

MIDI was created in the 1980s. It has the advantage of having brought computer music to an enormous number of users as it is used in synthesizers of all sorts from the relatively cheap to many of the highly expensive models. But it brings along a disadvantage which brings us immediately to one of the main subjects of this book, namely that it is more note- than sound-oriented.

MIDI is essentially the encoding of note information most often originating from a keyboard synthesizer. Among other things, time, frequency, loudness, timbre and vibrato/tremolo codes can be sent and received. This is a minute amount of information compared to what is recorded on a CD. MIDI allows for a great spectrum of potential timbres, especially when sampling is available. The restriction of MIDI is that with very few exceptions, one has been brought back to the chromatic world, leaving all those continuous scales of frequencies, lengths, dynamics, etc. far behind. Iannis Xenakis once told this author that the maker of electronic music should always be conscious of making something new as the technology invites this. He most likely was shocked when MIDI took on so quickly, not with the musicians of pop music and jazz which was to be expected as they are more note- than sound-oriented, but by composers of contemporary music who seem to willingly accept the restriction of the note as basis in place of the sound. Through its restriction, MIDI has led to some fusion between contemporary music thought on the one hand and rock and jazz on the other. It is experimentation that has been reduced in the process in general; therefore, we are essentially back to our "neos" (computer music "neos" in this case).

Essentially the state of the art is the following: "Traditional" computer sound synthesis is almost thirty years old. It has grown relatively slowly; its basic principles have hardly changed (which is logical as sounds have not changed either!). As the apparatus has gotten smaller, cheaper, faster, more people have been able to appreciate and utilize these methods of sound generation. There have unfortunately been relatively few works of true importance,[2] but this is not as awful as it sounds. Learning to cope with this new technology is hardly simple. Changing the rules of hundreds of years of note music is a revolution which cannot take place in a day. (This is of course true for analog music as well.) It is expected that the use of languages the likes of CSound and of digital signal processors, those user unfriendly units of incredible application potential and speed, will continue to grow slowly as they become more and more user friendly and also easier to use while musicians gain more experience with them, therefore playing an important role in the future music of sound. The fact that sampled sounds can be read in as input to these traditionally additive languages means that a great deal of the brainstorming as to how to create (new) timbres can be reduced. A whole world is now open to the user of the small system. The only cost problem still is that of the hard disk needed for the huge number of generated samples – these hard disks can cost as much as four times the price of the computer or synthesizer in question.

One special subject of interest must be added here. Chowning and others have spent some twenty years doing research and composing with the computer focusing on quadraphonic *sound placement* (see chapter IX). Those composers profiting by timbral and spatial sound research with these systems are, by definition, at the heart of today's experimentalism – these are the two most dynamic parameters of the post-war era.

Still, such kinds of computer music synthesis are marginal; the "number 1" hinted at above has nothing to do with this subfield of musical computing.

The "didn't you know that computer music is number 1" composers are those using MIDI. Simple MIDI instruments are used for jingles on the radio as well as in most pop music. But first a noteworthy, more complex example will be presented. Michel Waisvisz's composition *Archaic Symphony,* in which he wears two "hands" that look like metallic gloves while performing a simple choreography, is an example of a sort of live computer music. Pierre Boulez uses the computer to modify sounds performed by instruments in real-time. Waisvisz conducts a couple of computers which in turn are sending MIDI parameters, manipulated by his hand movements (lateral hand movements, finger movements, changes of proximity of the two "hands" are just a few ways of his controlling several MIDI parameters at once). He uses FM generated and sampled sounds coming from several synthesizers simultaneously and played back on a barrage of loudspeakers for a visual and sound-spatial effect. Here MIDI note music comes pleasantly close to the music of sound.

Waisvisz is nevertheless an exception in the world of MIDI users. Most are content with the keyboard (or MIDI drum set) as performance medium, which more or less by definition rejects the idea of the music of sounds and as already stated brings us back to the music of notes.

MIDI music is quite often not only note music, but also fairly consonant music as well (again, here the old battles of the early 20th century are fought! The overlapping with the previous two chapters should by now be clear). But MIDI music is affordable music and is also "being up to date" music as well. Here, users tend to follow the yearly music instrument shows to see what has just come out and discover all the "fasters" and "betters" they can do. Computer "freaks" making music generally belong to the MIDI team and not to the additive synthesis et al team. These people swear by new sequencers with up to twenty thousand notes, new samplers of up to twelve seconds/sound, new violin and drum synthesizers etc. They mix their (digital) music digitally on multi-track recorders saving themselves union scale pay to musicians by playing all their parts themselves or even having the computer play for them. Some are even beginning to laugh at those poor *démodés de la musique* who still play an instrument at all.

In short, it is wonderful that MIDI has brought many musicians to digital music and its potential; it is a shame that the limitations have taken reign above questions of content. In fact, we can conclude that most pioneering from the 50s to the late-70s was done in the experimental sector in collaboration with technicians of varying backgrounds. Now, the moves are made in the commercial music world as there as simply more buyers there. Modern composers who use these machines are therefore allowing themselves to accept the restrictions we have spent so much time trying to overcome. One might consider this a form of fusion as the technology has grown similar to a majority of users. Whether this has done more harm than good is another story.

## 3.  IS ANALOG ELECTRONIC MUSIC ALREADY "OLD-FASHIONED"?

Have you ever heard of an obsolete violin? Probably not, at least as far as those manufactured in the last centuries are concerned. An obsolete synthesizer? Perhaps not, but many instruments used in what is today called analog electronic music are no longer being built, having been replaced by their more contemporary, but not always similar or compatible digital partners. Analog electronic music is just ten years older than computer-generated sound synthesis. It was a music that called for a good deal of hand work. This means changing patches, turning knobs and splicing tapes in the most usual sense. It called for building, even soldering, electronic instruments for the live electronics composers. Has this music become old-fashioned? The answer is "yes" in terms of its hardware and "no" in terms of its aesthetic goals.

One clear example of continuity can be found in new sampling techniques with MIDI or those present on more sophisticated installations. Sampling is usually used to play an instrument sound using the notes of a digital keyboard, but not in all cases. Many composers have found the potential of sampling useful for they can now continue making *musique concrète* works with all the advantages of digital technology. In this case, the developments are most compatible with the more traditional analog techniques. As a matter of fact, in some sampling programs, there are commands like "Splice" or "Reverse the Sounds" – these obviously have been derived from the old reel tape days. With digital recorders, the PCMs and DATs, most people have left their old stereo tape recorders to rust. Machines with four or more tracks are still used for pre-mastering, but then again these are not found everywhere.

Continuity may also be found in the fact that at the base of additive and subtractive synthesis, old hand-controlled or voltage-controlled electronic music techniques became programable. Still, as all users of analog apparatus have experienced at one time or another, the potential of commanding the dials with your hands sometimes lends itself better to the creation of more naturally vibrating "acoustic" sounds than through programing the same sounds, where that wee bit of untuned trilling is hard to simulate. The studios at the University of Amsterdam where this writer teaches still include an "old-fashioned" tape and analog synthesizer studio so that all newcomers, and interested veterans, get a chance to create sounds by hand, record them and then manipulate their recordings themselves.

There have been so many excellent pieces of analog music created over the last forty years, it seems a shame that such works are now virtually impossible to compose as most of the electronic machines they were made on can only be found in store rooms, museums or on junk piles. Most electroacoustic composers over thirty will have had some experience in the analog studio. Many have trouble automatically switching over to computer music, but look for more hybrid means of making the music of sound. This is especially clear, for example, in Britain where the main analog/digital generation, slightly more than ten years removed from their studies, has shown a great deal of dynamic in musical as well as hardware developments in recent years. The old Moog synthesizers may be lost to us; the musical movements begun in the late 40s are fortunately still very much alive.

## 4.  NEW VOCAL MUSIC DOES TEND TO BELONG TO THE ART OF SOUNDS

Why has the voice seemed to evolve more in the direction of the music of sounds than any other instrument? Some say that this has to do with the fact that the voice is the most natural of all instruments, in the sense of bird song belonging to nature (i.e. concrete sounds). Otherwise there is little difference in terms of new music between the sound of those harsh oboe multiphonics and vocal multiphonics. The point is that the voice has been undoubtedly the most dynamic and flexible in terms of development in comparison with all other instruments.

Three groups involved with extended vocal techniques will be mentioned and illustrated here: composers specialized in new vocal techniques, text sound poets and performer-composer vocalists. The reason for the following paragraphs' inclusion is to underline the importance of these techniques within the world of experimentalism in the art of sounds. There are members of all three groups who use electronics to record and/or modify the voice, but in fact the inclusion of these voice-specialized artists here is due to this music's inclusion in many a survey of the art of sound.

*– The composers:* among others Georges Aperghis, Charles Dodge, Kenneth Gaburo, Sten Hanson, Daniel Lentz and Trevor Wishart.

As mentioned in the chapter on the music of sounds, Wishart has written a book entitled *On Sonic Art* which includes two cassette recordings, one of which deals exclusively with (practically) every sound a human can vocalize. Certainly there have been similar surveys written for the flute, oboe, contrabass and so on; what is of importance here is the incredible range of potential vocal sounds which may be used in a musical context. In this sense, one sees that the voice is the instrument with the widest register of sound potential. Wishart has proven this elegantly in the cycle of *Vox* works he has been working on for several years. In this sense he has been important to experimental music through his creative work, including works for solo voice, vocal ensemble with or without electronics and/or tape, as well as through his exemplary writings which describe and analyze phenomena, but which also can be used didactically. His early tape work *Red Bird* illustrates his application of his experiences in *musique concrète* with the use of analog electronic techniques while combining these with his own personal extended vocal approach.

The Greek/French composer Aperghis has excelled in creating experimental vocal works in theatrical contexts which are simultaneously highly innovative as well as humorous. The Americans Lentz and Gaburo have, like Wishart, written many multi-voiced works employing new vocal techniques.

Important to the composers Hanson and Dodge is the combination of normal vocal sounds with techniques derived from analog music or in the case of Dodge, computer speech synthesis. This latter area is one of the major areas of focus in computer music currently with major projects being executed in the U.S., France, and The Netherlands.

*– The text-sound poets:* among others Charles Amirkhanian, Henri Chopin, Bernard Heidsieck, Gerhard Rühm and Carles Santos.

Actually all of the composers in the first category have also been named as text-sound poets at one point or another. Text-sound poetry was born at the time of Luigi Russolo and

Filippo Tommaso Marinetti futurism and reached its first climax with Kurt Schwitters' tour de force, the *Ursonate*. Since the period of dadaism, this variety of poetry, which is to be heard more than read, has been most dynamic. Theoretically its members were all poets, creating a new poetry of sound, phonetic poetry and the like. But since the 1960s, artists of all sorts have joined this movement, (obviously) including musicians as well as people from the worlds of theater and literature.

What is then the borderline between this poetry of sound and the art of organized sound? Answer – there isn't one really. It is surprising how musical some of the poets are (and how unmusical others are despite their highly musical works). In the case of Chopin (who according to his own anecdote decided at a young age not to become a musician because of his name, and still got close through his chosen art), a huge number of phonemes have been transcribed and recorded which are of potential use in text-sound/phonetic works. The comparison with Wishart is then obvious given their creativity working hand in hand with their documentation.

Amirkhanian, who is also one of the most important figures in the U.S. as far as getting new music onto the radio waves is concerned, and Santos are in fact musicians who have made their fame within this movement. Both profit by their performance experience using vocalized texts as substitute (and sometimes imitate) instruments often in a highly emotional and virtuosic manner.

Heidsieck has made many works which have clearly furthered Marcel Duchamp's idea of the "ready-made". He has used existent texts or simply recorded the radio using this information as a basis of his sound poetry works. Rühm is known for a number of his radiophonic works. Here again the comparison with *musique concrète* as well as with audio-visual works (of which he has made a few) is important.

Although we have discussed two categories so far, they really do form a unity, as the poets here have added as much to their own art as to music and therefore have created new possibilities equally important to those of their partner composers.

– *The performer-composers:* among others Diamanda Galas, Joan LaBarbara and the late Demetrio Stratos.

The composer often needs an interpreter. The text-sound poets most often interpret their own works. The performer-composer is therefore more comparable with the latter. Virtuosity plays an enormous role with both. The comments made in chapter XI concerning neo-virtuosity are relevant here as well.

Virtuosity may come across to the listener like gymnastics; it may also be placed in a highly musical context. Galas, LaBarbara and the late Stratos are just three of several extended vocalists of highly deserved fame, creating new sounds and new directions in vocal performance, each in a very different manner. Surely there is the inspiration (to the Westerner) of less-known vocal techniques from Indonesia, Korea, Africa, So. America, from the Inuit and so on. There is an equally large inspiration derived from the the work of the Wishart's and Chopin's who have made inventories of vocal sounds for use in extended vocal contexts.

In the case of Diamanda Galas, some of her (sometimes amplified, though not modified) vocal sounds are comparable with those generated by electronic instruments. Perhaps it is through her highly volatile form of performance that the connection finally can be made between our main subject of this chapter, electroacoustic music and these new vocal techniques.

It is curious that the voice has often been separated from other instruments. Still, it is aurally clear that a good deal of contemporary vocal techniques do indeed belong to the music of sound.

## 5. THE ART OF SOUNDS ≠ THE ART OF NOTES?

That electroacoustic music with all its new possibilities is a microcosm of all of today's music might be seen as ironic. Nevertheless, the battles of note versus sound, consonant versus dissonant, popular versus, well, less popular are all to be found here. Still, these problems only begin to touch on the main fascinating question of this chapter, how does one compose with sounds? Clearly, some of our traditional musical experience is relevant; a good deal of potential and techniques have (yet) to be discovered.

Is there a difference between the acoustic and electric guitar? Of course. The latter lacks the finesse of the former; it can also be played ultimately louder. Loudness is after all one of the most prominent "parameters" of popular music.

But the difference between these two instruments has been proven to be infinitely smaller than the difference between composing music of additive synthesis and music for traditional instruments. Electroacoustic music will continue to move relatively slowly in its development due to its ultimately different background. The sonata form is truly not very interesting to the composer in this branch of music. New structures are needed and are continually being realized. MIDI instruments and electric organs are more easily taken into the mainstream of music today due to their similarity to instrumental givens we have known for centuries.

Still, one can say that the greatest deal of experimental activity is taking place within the worlds of electroacoustic music at the moment. The quantity of "neo" activities here is relatively less than in contemporary instrumental music. And given the trends that have been sketched in the last three chapters, it is expected that most experimental activities will remain in this field.

Fortunately, vocal music serves as an area of experimentation in which one need not be dependent on electronic media, for otherwise many great vocal-instrumental advances of this century would be lost to the past. In both sorts of music, expansion of potential sonorities, be it through new timbres or new sound sources, is still taking place. As said, in electroacoustic music, the parameter space has not yet been forgotten. In fact, all parameters seem to be alive and well in this branch of new music.

Why has instrumental music divorced itself from its vocal and electroacoustic partners? How can the contemporary instrumental composer seemingly ignore so many great advances of our century? It has already been recounted that the Paris Biennale has separated their "music" and "sound/vocal" departments. At the time it was mentioned, this divorce seemed silly and superfluous. It may be found in time that the organizers of this important festival may have been correct.

This would be a shame, but it is an honest reflection of the current state of our experimental musical art.

1) The computer is used by a number of composers to "assist" in the composition process. This concerns composers of formalized, often mathematical music. Those that also use the computer for sound generation are of relevance here. Those who use the computer to generate instrumental scores may be of equal interest, but are not the subject of this chapter.

2) Recently Jean-Claude Risset has done his share of broadening respect for computer composition. His works are recommended as a good starting point for those unacquainted with this repertoire (see also part 6, chapter XVIi).

# XIV. Fusion music

## 1. AFTER ALL THE SCREAMING, THOSE BORDERLINES *ARE* BECOMING MORE VAGUE

Experimentalism expands horizons. Fusion brings things together. Both can use and are perhaps in need of new forms of synthesis; this is the essence of this chapter.

It doesn't happen every day, but the following tale is true. It was in the early 80s that a small group of "punks", having heard that something special was going on, attended an electronic music concert in which a couple of Gottfried Michael Koenig's electronic pieces from the 60s were performed. These works are highly original. They are also pretty loud. The "punks" were in ecstasy and most attending (i.e. the "traditional" electronic music listeners), after their initial surprise, finally understood why. (Koenig obviously belongs to the category of composers able to compose interesting music that is also pretty loud and thus interesting to another segment of music lovers.)

As the above example was unexpected, the fact that there are many music lovers of Brian Eno or Sting who also enjoy, for example, Philip Glass's highly tonal minimal works is very much to be expected.

Where does a composer "belong"? Must he or she belong somewhere? Or may one transcend categories? What about Laurie Anderson who used to be so experimental, and who, since her hit single *Superman*, knows what top of the pops means? Are the experimentalists going pop selling out in the way those who went "neo" did? And what about those like Eno or Frank Zappa, or even Ornette Coleman and Duke Ellington who came from those other musical backgrounds and approached contemporary music through the back door?

Jazz is still jazz and pop is pop; both know their subcategories as well. Modern music is another type of music with its own demographics. No one wants them to become one single super-music most likely, but many are at least filing down the boundaries; and this may be of benefit to all.

## 2.  FUSION/1: POP MUSIC

Frank Zappa was probably the first pop musician with true fusion tendencies when he winked an eye (through quotation, pastiche) at the likes of Igor Stravinsky in his early recordings. It was Brian Eno and many of his English associates including Richard Toop who take the thought further by creating works which certainly could be considered as contemporary music works aimed primarily at the (marginal) pop music public, which are also potentially of interest to the experimental music enthusiast.

Eno comes from the art world and has been known to make video installations. His fairly experimental "ambient sounds" seem to be most effective there. He belongs on any list of contemporary electroacoustic composers. Rhys Chatham on the other hand, composer-performer and also earlier one of the directors of the concert space called The Kitchen in New York, has dropped his flute and toured playing electric guitar in recent years primarily to the (pop lovers of the) experimental music public.

David Byrne of the group Talking Heads has made scores for the film *The Last Emperor* as well as audio-visual spectacles with Robert Wilson including one of the parts of *CIVIL warS* as well as a work entitled *The Forest*. And then there is the phenomenon known as Glenn Branca who writes *Symphonies* so loud that the old Grand Funk Railroad – may it truly rest in peace, having rewritten their loudness record in the Guiness Book of Records several times – must seem left out. Branca's music has been performed at a number of modern music festivals scaring the daylights out of some listeners and pleasing many others. As loudness has rarely been characteristic of experimental music although often characteristic of pop music, the border has been made to overlap.

Of all potential fusion partners for today's composer, pop music is obvious on the one hand (experimental music's public is too small and deserves to be increased – the pop music market is the largest there is) and almost unthinkable on the other (pop music is based on extremely few formulae and is in general fairly unsophisticated in comparison to some forms of folk music and most jazz – experimental music may sometimes be based on one or a few ideas, but does tend to be fairly complex, if not downright enigmatic).

In any case it is understandable that the Eno's do exist. They have applied developments from the experimental sector while creating their own experimental pop sector. Its reverse is often hard to digest, at least as far as this author is concerned, as many examples of pop-like music coming from within contemporary music circles just might belong to neo-pop music. (One assumes that there was no other way to get famous or at least to survive.)

Brian Eno has proved that there is at least one intersection between these two music worlds. This writer believes that there are probably very few others.

## 3. FUSION/2: MINIMAL MUSIC

In chapter VII attention was given to the place minimal music has earned after twenty years. Whether we accept this music as highly experimental or not does not take away the fact that minimal composers have by far the largest public in contemporary music today. Their overt, often saccharine tonality is one of the reasons. The music often swings and has ingredients of orchestration that do tend to remind the listener of non-experimental musicians from the pop world, or from India, South America, Africa, or in the case of some of the minimal composers who emphasize brass instruments, even jazz. Terry Riley with his synthesizers and newly (oldly well-) tuned pianos seems to have kept Indian and some rock music in his pen throughout the years. Philip Glass is not shy of loudness. Steve Reich has often been known to orchestrate in a popular manner.

And then there are those who have added their own little somethings to minimal music. Here are a few: Louis Andriessen brought minimal music closer to the experimental music world with his piece *De Staat* ("The State") based on Plato. His now defunct Hoketus Ensemble with its pairs of panpipe players, electric basses, keyboards, etc. sounded like a rock band profiting by a new translation of tape loop techniques derived from the old *musique concrète* studios of the 50s. Michael Nyman and John Adams are writing many works for stage like Philip Glass. Both create their own blends of "neo", mostly romantic ones. And there seem to be more young composers in Hungary today writing minimal music than anything else.

Minimal music is an obvious genre of music for the stage, especially for the dance (it is the most cyclical and rhythmic of modern music) and therefore does seem to have staying power within art music circuits. It has brought people who avoided new music like to plague to try their music and those of others; in this sense it has had a stimulating function.

Minimal music is highly popular startling many a supporter of experimental music who believed this music to be doomed to live a brief life. As already stated our consumer society prefers lighter, more digestible music for the palate today. Minimal music seems dynamic and diverse enough to suit the needs of those who prefer this particular diet.

## 4. FUSION/3: PERFORMANCE ART

When fluxus died (its supporters will highly disagree with these three words),[1] performance art was born. Performance art has also diminished in recent years, at least as far as those one-time events are concerned. Today's performances are more streamlined, more virtuoso, even more attractive (that is to say less interested in conscious alienation). Excluding recent plastic artists' performances which are becoming more and more rare anyway, although they do come closer to the older performance tradition, we can briefly mention a couple of examples of performance artists today.

The Pole Zygmunt Krauze graduated from minimalism and started giving performances on his own instrument, the piano, in the early 70s. He has been touring for years with a performance of Lisztian dimensions of playing power which is in a sense a medley of the "hits and heavies" of contemporary music from Webern to himself. In the case of this convincing "performance", perhaps the term "recital" might be more appropriate.

Laurie Anderson is probably today's most successful performance artist. Beginning in the early 70s she had been working in mixed media performances with film, video, and sound aspects, often with a feminist undertone. She has created some radical instruments including a violin played with a bow consisting of a magnetic tape played above a contact microphone. She bows recordings of her voice forwards and backwards creating two understandable phrases on her instrument. (In a non-performance situation she is known to have designed a table which creates sounds only to be heard when the visitors place their elbows at certain points on the table while placing their hands on their ears.) Since cutting her hair and recording that single alluded to above, the glitter has been extended, the message tampered mildly, and the success amplified exponentially. She has brought performance art to the masses (they call it a show, a one woman theater work or simply an evening out) through fusion.

Robert Ashley, who once was responsible for some of the most controversial live electronic works ever made, might be considered today to be a pre-rap experimentalist. His music is certainly easy listening, laid back pop-like tones with the most fascinating blasé voice recital (even more so than Cage's) in modern music. He carries on the Harry Partch American tradition reflecting his deep affection for his country's culture of the post-60s as opposed to that of the 40s Partch was so much a part of. Ashley's video opera, *Private Parts* is fusion of genres, musical styles with his own special way of articulation. This author is surprised that he has not become even more successful in the commercial sense as his show is equally streamlined and digestible as Laurie Anderson's.

## 5. FUSION/4: JAZZ

Fusion with jazz is hardly new. Just think of Ravel, Gershwin, Stravinsky, Hindemith, even Bartók. We know that it took very little time in jazz history for it to penetrate non-improvised music. American composers the likes of Copland and Bernstein have been extremely important in fusing these two genres. Even composer musicians from the jazz world took the trouble to fully notate works for soloists and ensembles without jazz training. Duke Ellington's *A Single Petal of a Rose* for solo harpsichord is a clear example here.

But today this fusion has taken on a new dimension. At its base is the common area of jazz and experimental music, that is the freeing of parameters also known as improvisation. John Zorn is at the forefront of this development enticing many a musician from the jazz world as well as from the world of contemporary music to play together.

Due to this music's sophistication, this sort of fusion should be the most obvious one. But since improvising has become the common denominator and not just the sound of jazz, it is interesting to see how few musicians and composers can in fact display their talents within this special branch of fusion. Referring back to the brief discussion in chapter IV, jazz reflects the fusion most of interest to an experimental music of technology and local values. But can we handle the new notations, the new models? Can we handle our new freedoms? If answered in the affirmative, there will be a good deal of growth to be expected here.

## 6. FUSION/5: ETC. OR "ALL TOGETHER NOW "

In our age of synthesis, fusion is obvious and desirable. The Dutch radio broadcasts a weekly four-hour-long program which treats fusion musics in all their aspects. John Schaefer's book, *New Sounds*, does just what the title suggests; it gives an inventory of the music around us in terms of new sounds. The likes of a Ravi Shankar, new age types, the West German pop group Kraftwerk with its 70s computer-mechanical, political fusion sound, a Luc Ferrari with his *Presque rien no. 1* recorded and left pretty much unedited as an experimental work of the sounds found at a Yugoslavian beach, African musicians as well as jazz, (neo-tonal or even neo-romantic) minimal and performance artists are all fused in the contents of this book.

Symmetry for symmetry's sake: experimentalism expands horizons. Fusion brings things together. Both can use and are perhaps in need of new forms of synthesis; this is the essence of this chapter. Experimentalism can expand in this way. Other genres can be enriched as a consequence.

1) To save face, I will quote Peter Frank (personal letter): "Fluxus did die ... fluxism, the fluxus spirit and praxis, lives".

# Part 5 – Conclusion

The cast of characters in experimental music has been introduced, has been shown off or perhaps frowned upon. The musical themes have been played and analyzed in terms of their content. The non-musical themes have been juxtaposed, made dialectic and sometimes torn apart. The music, the politics of the music, the success of the music or lack thereof and the musicians have interpreted and been interpreted.

The only thing left is to summarize and more importantly to look into the future. For at the basis of this book is the title, and in the title is the thought that something is wrong. Where there's a wrong, there might perhaps be a right. **What** it is specifically will most likely not be found in this final chapter. **Where** it might be sought is its subject.

# XV. A possible future
# for experimental music

Experimental music has become yet more marginal in the 70s and the 80s than it already was, but it is not yet forgotten. Experimentalism has known its phases throughout history. The 70s brought on a phase of no-phase as it were. The economy hurt most developments and the ensuing conservatism covered up most of the rest. For diehards like the current writer, the words perseverance and patience must play a role.

This final chapter has been written in the form of a cookbook recipe (pointing to ingredients, not naming them – we might call it Zen cooking) summarizing the main points of this book while making a few extra suggestions at the same time. It is hoped that the readers who have made it this far might think of trying this recipe out for themselves.

## Reprise in the form of a cookbook

### Ingredients/1: Extra-musical

#### Music and our schools

##### – Music and our lower schools (VI, VIII)[1]
What is wrong with experimental music begins at the basis, with our youths. What is unknown is foreign and can only be gained as an "acquired taste".

*Kodaly's method* calls for young children to be presented with all sorts of music so that they know they exist and that they can be most varied. Choices made are then not only due to

175

hit parades, but also due to tastes developed early on. *Schafer's method* calls for young children to get a chance to experience music as sound organization. Both methods stimulate the activity of making music as opposed to the growing *passivity* (II) or *music-taking* very much alive today. Through such methods, more people can come in contact with and be better informed about and even become proud of musicians creating new forms of *note* and *sound works* today. This in turn makes new music more understandable to more people and therefore more accessible to more listeners as well as to more future musicians. Without this basis, the lot of contemporary music will remain most problematic.

### – Music and our music schools/higher education

Is contemporary music really bad for your health as orchestra musicians have occassionally been known to say? Why is higher education in experimental music, if given at all, so poor in general? *Avant-gardism* is alive and well as far as interpretation of challenging new notations and instrumental techniques are concerned. What is unfortunately still avant-garde is that too few musicians can handle these works. Is it all the fault of "poor" quality or "impossible to understand" composition techniques? This writer believes that the fault can also be found elsewhere.

Criteria for criticism, aesthetics and analysis are necessary and should go hand in hand with new didactic techniques for offering future musicians, musicologists and music journalists a solid base on which to build new and future musics. People from these fields should work together to widen the discussion instead of sending off all interested individually into the wild uncertain yonder. Without this basis derived from higher education experiments will mostly be destined to be seen as curiosities of music-making and will never be integrated into music as a whole. Obviously no experimentalist is happy with this form of isolation.

## Music and the media (II, X)

### – Music and the mass media

As 99% of today's listeners have not had the music education described in the last paragraph, the powers that be within the *communications media* are almost all-encompassing. What is not put on radio, television or record/cassette/CD virtually doesn't exist. If no better criteria for selection are found and, more importantly, more media attention be given to today's modern musics, the epitaphs of many a work in the *Kleenex Era* (VIII) may have already been written.

And what about the lot of *live music*? Why can't live music play a major role any more in a music society thriving on passivity? Furthermore, hasn't enough harm been done by our overwhelming drives toward an almost mechanical *perfection* of performance and recording? Why can't the sickness known as *media envy* be transformed into a better form of collaboration between the powers that be within the media and musicians? Is a recording on DGG the ultimate goal, the proof of *success,* or can we profit by using smaller labels that get around to those who are most interested in a particular music, our *musical community*?

Marcuse has called for all to use our media in a constructive way. Experimental music should be an ideal case in point. This has hardly been the case so far. For example radio recordings should be an ideal way of developing *radiophonics* as a genre of experimental music. Even experimentation with the "idiot box", the television, e.g. through video art, has hardly been exploited by experimental musicians who have not adequately reacted to our *image culture.* These problems have grown due to the naivety from the point of view of the musicians and from the negative support coming from media professionals. But of course, at the heart of these developments there is the much greater political problem of the suppression of a famed non-commercial art.

### – Music and the audio-visual media

One must take into account that we are living in our era of the *image culture.* This author does truly believe in an "if you can't beat 'em, join 'em" mentality, not due to cowardliness, but because there is so much to be developed musically which can be of use to the audio-visual arts including theater, film, video, modern dance and musical theater/opera as well as to experimental music itself. Collaborations must be sought out and given the chance to grow. It is a shame that the successful examples of this have recently remained so few. Our music will reach a larger public and will finally reach artists from other arts as well, who might never have come into contact with experimental music. This in turn could expand the size and breadth of the musical community. New audio-visual techniques will have to be invented. There is still a good deal to be done here.

### Music and technology (III)

First of all, all potential musicians should become better informed about what *technology* is and how it might be applied. To reiterate, the most important questions of chapter III were: what can be the justification for using technology as a compositional tool? Where can one define the boundary between using technology, and being bound (even enslaved) by it? Which aspects of technology are applicable to modern music, and in what ways? Are we therefore able to keep technology in the right perspective vis-à-vis music?

We can only succeed in answering these questions if we consciously ask ourselves the following questions each time we apply technology in an artistic context: why use a certain technique? Do we understand the technique? And what do we expect of it? This is indeed the heart of experimentation, itself.

Furthermore, musicians must continue to take a stance in the discussion which is currently taking place looking for the ideal choice between the more universal *Global Village* and the more local *musical community*, the latter being based on our reactions to the *nature* seen from any window today. Can we combine our technologies with *local values*?

### Music and local values (IV)

Why have local values become so taboo in current times at least in our Western societies? Is there something wrong with being Italian, Swedish or Dutch? Do we have an answer to the

"Americanization" of the consumer culture? Do we want to find that answer?

What has been the fate of many folk musics? What have been the advantages and disadvantages of finding all forms of *exotic musics* at our music stores along with more local varieties? Has small-scale *acculturation* died? Are all cultural boundaries doomed to be lost? Is the universal music of today's Wagners (e.g., Madonna and Co.) what it's truly all about?

Using *jazz* as an example it was found that there is a possibility to take on a model originating from one society and develop it into local variants leaving a breathing space for *local* and *individual* development.

The *musical community* appreciating any given sort of music may be a local one or may be one based on a common denominator, e.g. experimentalism. Therefore the following question should be given due attention: Can a player "X" from society "Y1" interpret a piece of music from the composer "Z" from society "Y2" in a way that it communicates to an audience in society "Y3"?

When the local or regional thinking can be consciously focused upon as well as the above-mentioned technological aspects of music, what might be optimal combinations? One of the goals of this book is to stimulate this very research.

## Music and politics (V)

### – Politics in terms of society and its music

Shouldn't we spend more time using our democratic right of having a greater say in the activities of *"Music, Inc."* ? It is after all a society's politics which dictates most of what transpires in its musical milieus. Participation is the best way for evolutionary change to take place in each and every extra-musical area.

### – Politics in music-making

Participation in political decision making can concern *hierarchical* questions among musicians as well. These questions are most often influenced by political circumstances dependent on the first category. This subject was found to be less important than the first one, though as far as this book's subject matter is concerned.

### – Politics of the composer

Again here a set of questions should be referred to more and more often: why does one compose? For whom? What factors might be pertinent of one's style? Are social factors of relevance? What do we want to communicate with our works (if anything at all)? Most important, can we verbalize the "dramaturgy" of our new musics?

Assuming that the sound of music, with the exception of vocal texts, does not contain a unique political message, the *idealists,* be they of democratic socialist, communist or anarchist persuasion, should perhaps invest more political energy into the first category, politics in terms of society and its music, than in the sole creation of political musical situations that clash with their outside worlds. Again, the idealists in Western society have contributed greatly by adding to musicians' and listeners' thinking, but have not really influenced the politics of music as a whole to any great extent.

These three music-political subjects are in fact 50% of the challenge to today's experimental musician. If these issues are ignored, any solution found for problems of content will remain relatively anonymous. The experimental musicians and their partners in the fields of musicology, music journalism, concert programing, subsidies, publishing, recording, radio-television and rights organizations should team up to find new roads towards positive action for today's experimental music instead of falling into the traditional Darwinian trap of large scale competition, jealousy and professional hatred. Herein lies the heart of this ultimately important subject.

### The experiment: the object of all these subjects

If we can except our definition of *experimental music* (I), then there are very many areas in which experimentation has and can still take place. Most experiments primarily concern musical issues, some extra-musical. This book has attempted to show that successful experimentation involves both, for without the knowledge necessary for acceptance and the appreciation gained through performances, experimental results easily fade into obscurity.

### *Ingredients/2: Musical*

#### **Our parameters** (I)

##### **– Primary parameters** (VII)

We now think of music in terms of *continua* (Hz, db, ms, etc.) as well as in discrete scales (diatonic/chromatic, pp/mf/ff, quarter notes/half notes, etc.). We think of music in terms of *sounds* and we also think in terms of one of its subsets, *notes*.

Beginning with the domain of our primary parameters, there is so much research still to be done, one could literally continue forever while restricting experimentation to these elements of sound. Still, it has been shown that many, if not a majority of significant discoveries have been made in areas such as *timbre, density,* and even *form/structure*, not to mention *sound sources* and *space*.

Whatever the subject or subjects of experimental focus may be, the most important moral of this story in terms of musical questions can be found in the chapter focusing on the *fuse box* of our perception which reacts best to some sort of tenable ordering. It was shown that the presence of melody and other constants of music history is not necessary to reach this goal. Edgard Varèse did this by liberating the percussion instruments in his early works. Hundreds of others have proven this possible through the use of other sound sources, new approaches, new techniques.

Those who prefer writing purely subjectively find dealing with the fuse box perhaps more difficult than those who prefer total formalization. The former group often works against the fuse box; the latter group should attempt to apply criteria which in principle should offer clues to the listeners. There are too few of the Carter and Ferneyhough school of ultimate complexity that are able to overdose the fuse box and still create their own recognizable styles. In any event, perceivable foci should be present to the listener; these foci gain a status of importance when the musicality of a composer is well combined with the experiment. As they say in the computer world, "garbage in, garbage out": the formalization is not in itself the goal, nor is the melody or whatever handrail is offered. It is the musical vision, that dramaturgy combined with the above which lies at the heart of important experimental works.

### – Sound sources (VIII)

The hottest item in the music of sounds is the fact that we have too few *criteria* and a lack of a usable *terminology* with which we can communicate about new sound works. Again, the understanding of sonological explorations is mostly restricted to the true connoisseurs, which might be positive for internal growth, most negative for propagation.

New works should be analyzed, new terminologies created and of course new works composed. In this way a common language will evolve for every musician, for teachers and students at our schools, for members of the media, of the press, for the organizers at our concert halls, and for the musicians in our ensembles. They in turn will be able to get the message out and share (understandable) information outside of the tiny province of experimental music studios.

Along similar lines, questions the likes of – is composing the music of sound truly different than composing note music? – must be further researched to avoid the continuation of that divorce illustrated by the Paris Biennale. Currently there is a clear split between the electroacoustic and instrumental provinces. They are not the same, but are they two different art forms?

Furthermore, there are two ways of showing off experimental works: first, by what is different about them, and second, by showing what they have in common with other music. The listener needs to know about both and is generally only informed about the former. This leads not only to insufficient information, but also to the experiment's isolation so often referred to.

### – Space (IX)

The concert hall, the mountainside, the living room, even the walkman. These are our musical spaces. Antonin Artaud suggests we furnish them and have them speak for themselves.

It is not the space that counts in the first place, it is what is done with it. There is an enormous amount of fascinating work waiting to be developed in this area, an area in which the media will play a very minor role, for spatial music is live music, and that does not necessarily have to be such a bad thing.

## – Notation, improvisation, new instrument techniques (VI)

Along with the huge amount of developments in the golden age of experimental music in the domains of sound sources, colors and spaces, notation and performance techniques grew almost exponentially. Just like in the case of new electroacoustic instruments, the rate of the speed of change has often been proven to be too great, leaving too little time to absorb – absorb in the sense of learning how to use these notations or techniques, absorb in the sense of appreciating and further developing them. The aim was to be new, to be different, to be up to date. Instead of going into more depth in one of these areas, something always had to be unique. This has led us to the absurd situation of having many experiments doomed to failure due to underexposure and lack of appreciation. Quality does not necessarily play an important role here.

If works the likes of the two Cage pieces discussed in chapter VI can rarely be played intelligently, it may be due to his call for musicians to participate in the creation of – and not only interpretation of – new music, to add their "Y2" to his "Y1" as it were. Many of these musicians are trying to improvise in various new ensembles. If they cannot handle Cage, they probably will not be able to handle improvisation because not enough time and creative effort is given to learn to perform these very challenging techniques well.

Too little attention is given to learning new models. Jazz knows but a few, experimental music perhaps too many. Quality is obviously important to both but there is often more quality found in a jazz improvisation than those performed in an experimental context. Composers like Cage have invited musicians to live and learn; too few have applied themselves. Adding insult to injury the schools of music have done their best to hold works of this sort outside of the curriculum, making solutions even more difficult.

Composers and performers creating new notated techniques for all known instruments have often encountered similar problems. Too often the techniques are developed and popularized by one single performer who enjoys playing the role of Olympic musician more than musical musician. Those who have combined technique and musicality best have found that they do create a *Nachwuchs*. It is assumed that those who develop new techniques want them to be playable by more than one person. Or does the uniqueness problem play a role here as well?

New notations, new improvisation techniques, new instrument techniques should be defined, described, rehearsed, spoken about, performed, revised, further developed. There is too much information available now. Choices must be made or a great deal of significant innovations in these areas will disappear within a few years.

## The "sound" of a composer, experimental or not

We have discussed musicality, formalization, experimental actions, the perception, notations, spaces, "new" sounds and many other subjects. Schönberg said that the "idea" of the composer is what makes him or her new. It may be added that the idea is indeed the nucleus, but only when it is translatable into an identifiable "sound". Most composers, fortunately, are conscious of this.

Morton Feldman once said that a composer who does not find that one idea sinks into a sea of over-information. That one idea found by a composer may not be substantial, but it is at least the axis around which all other musical activities revolve (the Varèseian crystal). There are very few successful composers today who do not have their own sound. This is what distinguishes the composer, but also what integrates an experiment with all other music at large. For we can talk about the sound of a composer, it's done every day.

## The movements

### – "Neo": a necessary evil (XI, XII)

Every thesis has its antithesis, and "neo" is the antithesis of experimentalism. Much attention was given to this subject to highlight its contrast with experimental activities and to reflect the general conservative direction our (musical) societies have taken on in the last two decades. The "neos" have always been present; it is their numbers that are so astonishing today as well as the fact that some experimental leaders seem to have joined them as well.

### – Overpopulation of composers = no new leaders?

It has been said that there are as many scientists alive today as there have been throughout the sum of the history of the world. Might this be true of composers as well? If there are so many composers and so few "slots" in which to be performed, is there still room for leaders? Obviously there is.

There is a need for exemplary figures in every field from which others may be compared. There are of course several names of major composers today, but their number is substantially lower than the number that should reflect the larger number of active composers. This is most curious indeed, but does reflect the extra-musical subject of too few opportunities mentioned above as well as the heavy accent on "neo" activities for which few (living) leaders are necessary.

Where are those stimulating ideas behind potential new leaders? Where are the propagators of those ideas? This is a very unhappy situation.

### – Fusion: move inwards (XIV)

One may speak of fusion as an antithesis of experimental activities taking place in the world of the music of sounds. The latter theoretically concerns music moving outwards.

Our time should be characterized as one of synthesis. The "neos" synthesize in some ways, the fusion artists in many others. It all belongs to our time and in the case of fusion can lead to new forms of music and redefinition of musical boundaries. It is not expected that much experimentation will take place in fusion musics, not because it is not possible – the fusion should call for experimentation – but because fusion is often called for to gain access to a larger public. In any event it consists of a number of movements well worth following. Perhaps the 90s will provide interesting and unexpected developments in new fusions. That would reflect our spirit of synthesis.

### – Electroacoustic and vocal musics: move outwards (XIII)

It has been shown that electroacoustic music is surprisingly a microcosm of the wider field of music in general, fighting the same battles fought in instrumental music as well. It has also been shown that up-to-dateness is not always a useful *modus operandi* as many recent technological "gains" have sent electroacoustic music from a forward march to a jump backwards in terms of potential applications.

It is expected that a majority of the developments in the experimental music of the future will take place in the music of sounds as well as in vocal music as timbral research is more obvious here. This is especially true in the case of the forty year old (or, better said, young) electroacoustic music where there is so much still to be learned, developed, discovered, created.

Experimental music is not only based on these two branches of music-making, but moving outward does play a major role. If the musical and extra-musical problems of the art of sound are carefully treated, a new wave of experimentation may be expected within the foreseeable future. Economic pointers do tend to stimulate this forecast.

### *The recipe: experimental synthesis*

#### Synthesis: move both ways

"Neo" is synthesis (it was also antithesis), fusion is synthesis (it too was antithesis), experimental synthesis *is* the final synthesis of this book. Most extremes have at one point or another been reached musically in terms of sound materials, sound organizations, sound spaces, technological *curiosa* like simulcast works for five countries with a chorus in each one singing to the tune of the coordinating satellite. Certainly there are some unexpected discoveries still to be found, but synthesis based on experimentation (these are *not* antonyms) is the way of the near future.

Digest, appreciate, learn and relearn some of the experimental results of the latter half of our century, utilize the information at large to be found in our super-archives, learn the old instruments, the exotic ones, the new ones, record sounds, modify them or make new ones. Do all this and more remembering that fuse box, treating technological and eventually local aspects carefully as well while building up that dramaturgy which is behind the final sound of this experimental synthesis. This is the recipe of this book.

There's much work to be done, certainly in the political area, more importantly in the didactic and musicological areas and not the least of all in the creative area. Idealism should not be thrown overboard, but a touch of realism is necessary to go on.

What's the matter with experimental music? Plenty. Is it a terminal case? Not at all.

1) In this chapter roman numerals in parentheses refer to the chapter in which the main discussion took place. Words in italics refer to subjects treated in these chapters.

# Part 6 – Work descriptions and cues for the listener

This final part is one of illustration. Though not intended to add any incites to current musicological literature as far as experimental music analysis is concerned, the following pages may be seen as the appendix to the first five parts of this book. It is hoped that concepts introduced in the text may become clearer while a few of the problems mentioned most often are exemplified.

Not all major composers will be treated, nor all issues. As questions of new notation (with the exception of notations for multi-media and electroacoustic works) have been adequately treated in chapter VI and the parameter space has been given sufficient attention in chapter IX, they have not been included. Composers the likes of Pierre Boulez and Karlheinz Stockhausen who have received substantial attention in publications of all sorts will also not be treated here. Furthermore, non-experimental "neo" composers the likes of Arvo Pärt who have known great success in recent years through the creation of a personal, often light modal or tonal "sound" are skipped and only experimental works have been chosen.

Chapter XVI consists of the following areas: sound color and density as alternative to melody (Ligeti), new vocal (and instrumental) techniques and new virtuosity (Berio), ultra-complexity (Carter), new perceivable formal structures (Xenakis), process music (Reich), open form (Brown), music-making influenced by political vision (Wolff), the combination of note and sound music (de Leeuw), electroacoustic music

189

*(Risset), and assimilation including the use of non-Western music (Shinohara).*

*As the last example coincides the most with the main theses of the book, it is only this final composition which will be analyzed in depth. All other illustrative discussions are specifically geared to aspects already presented in parts 1 to 5.*

# XVIa. Melodylessness and beatlessness – Ligeti's *Ten Pieces for Wind Quintet*

## 1. INTRODUCTION

In the main part of this book, György Ligeti has been called upon a great number of times as a representative of experimental thought with a clearly personal "sound" based on a good deal of musicality. The following pages may serve as a primer for those who have never looked into his works, for the choice of the ninth piece of the *Ten Pieces for Wind Quintet* (completed in 1969) is what one may call a didactic example of Ligeti's style. We will try to show how Ligeti has replaced melody with what might be called a timbral weaving. To do this Ligeti's personal combination of contemporary counterpoint and harmony (simultaneities) will be described. His conscious avoidance of the beat will also be demonstrated. When this is done, the major Ligeti terms "micro-polyphony" and "movement types" will be presented before a few hints to the listener are provided in the final section.

## 2. THE NINTH OF THE *TEN PIECES* [1]

The *Ten Pieces* include five ensemble pieces and five pieces in which each instrumentalist individually can be said to have the *Hauptstimme*. Number 9 (see score published by Schott on the following page) belongs to the ensemble group, but uses only three instruments: piccolo, oboe and b-flat clarinet.

191

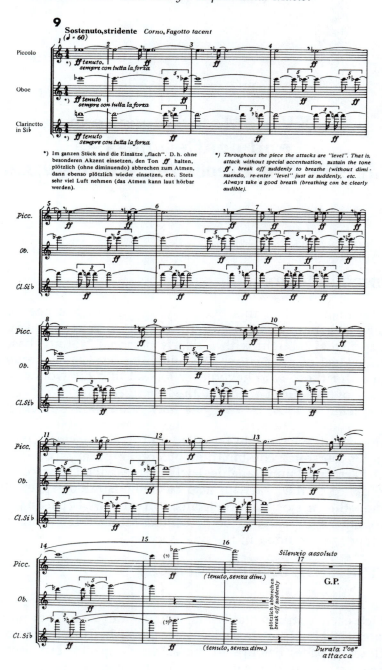

Dynamically there is nothing to be said about this miniature of slightly more than one minute. There are no accents, all attacks are to be "level", all dynamics are *ff*.

    – *No melody:* Looking quickly through these seventeen measures, one discovers that none of the instruments is at any moment in the foreground. Perhaps it would be more correct to say that each instrument is in the foreground each time a pitch is changed. Only the final note of the piccolo being so high may be called prominent, but this has been cleverly masked by the composer as the clarinet arrives at the same pitch, be it an octave lower, at the same time. In fact this is the first simultaneity after the very first beat! Since melody is clearly absent, we will have to find that something to hold onto elsewhere. It is not to be found in the dynamics as has already been shown. Although the time axis must play a role in a composer's sound, there is no beat that the listener can follow as will now be explained.

    – *No beat:* The piccolo's attacks take place based on sixteenth movement. In other words, any attack can begin on the beat or any sixteenth within a given beat. The oboe's attacks take place within quintuplets, though none falls on the beat itself which "belongs" to the piccolo (one might speak of twentieth movement – quintuplet times quarter). Likewise the clarinet's attacks are based on triplet sixteenth movement (twenty-fourth notes). Here no attack begins on the beat or the half beat (the fourth sixteenth within the triplet) as these points both "belong" to the piccolo according to Ligeti's scheme.

    These attacks appear irregularly; it seems as if no symmetry between attacks can be discovered. (This can be a bit misleading: e.g., the attacks of the piccolo at the end of measure 7 until measure 10 are equidistant – 15/16th durations.) With the slow tempo (one quarter note = one second), and the various subdivisions described above with their "scattered" attack-points, as there is no conductor's arm to watch, the listener hears non-metrical time, perceives beatlessness although the three musicians are counting constantly. This is but one way in which Ligeti consciously avoids the listener's perception of a beat. Please note that nothing has been said about pitch here, for this has nothing to do with the question of Ligeti's treatment of the beat.

– *The voices, one at a time:* Each voice begins with the pitch E-flat. This pitch is also repeated in all three voices for several measures. Beginning at the end of measure 7, when the piccolo moves up a minor second to the E, no more new attacks of the E-flat take place.

At this point each voices follows a path of interval expansion at their own pace: E-flat – E (up a minor second) – D (down a major second from the E) – F (up a minor third from the D) – D-flat (down a major third) – G-flat (up a fourth). Here one would now expect the C, a tritone below the G-flat, but the diabolus in musica will not appear. The oboe's pitch development ends here. The clarinet, after the G-flat, will play both G and A-flat (twice a rising minor second), the last being played synchronously with the piccolo. The piccolo also has the G-flat – G movement, but then plays the missing C, not a fifth below as would be expected in this interval expansion, but instead a fourth higher as a preparation for another rising interval in the sequence, the minor sixth towards that final very high A-flat, concluding the piece (before the "Silenzio assoluto"/ G.P. in bar 17).

The twelve-tone specialists among the readers will cleverly note that had this interval expansion continued on for three more notes, all twelve tones would have been used. But this is clearly not of primary interest to this composer of timbral weaving. Before looking at Ligeti's use of counterpoint, the attacks must be presented schematically.

Disregarding the first seven measures (unison E-flat's) which introduce the common timbral texture and create the atmosphere of no-beat (the attacks here should hardly be noticeable), the pitch movement is the following one (the numbers represent how long the preceding pitch continues in that measure – e.g. 3–3/4 = three-quarters and three-sixteenths):

| measure | 7 | 8 | 9 | |
|---|---|---|---|---|
| piccolo | -> E-flat —> 3-3/4 E | | —> 3-1/2 D —> 3-1/4 -> | |
| oboe | -> E-flat | | —> 1-2/5 E ——> | |
| clarinet | -> E-flat ——> 1-5/16 E | | —> 2-1/2 D ——> | |

| measure | 10 | 11 | 12 | |
|---|---|---|---|---|
| piccolo | ——> 3 D-flat —> 1-3/4 G-flat | —> 1-1/2 G ——> | | |
| oboe | ——> 1/5 D —> 3-4/5 F ——> | | | |
| clarinet | —> 1-2/3-F ——> 2-1/3 D-flat —> 3-5/6 G-flat | | | |

| measure | 13 | 14 | 15 | 16 17 |
|---|---|---|---|---|
| piccolo | ——> 3-1/4 C —> 1 A-flat —>3 *rest* -> | | | |
| oboe | —> 2-2/5 D-flat —> 1-1/5 G-flat —> 1 *rest* -> | | | |
| clarinet | ——> 2/3 G —> 1 A-flat—> 3 *rest* -> | | | |

— *The horizontal movement:* As mentioned, the first seven measures are played at unison. Between measures 7 and the end of 10, the general motion calls for two voices to be at (ever-changing) unisons; this occurs through one voice's moving away from a unison immediately creating another one or shortly thereafter having a new one created by yet another voice's arrival at a new unison pitch. After this point there is a three-voice non-unison "counterpoint" lasting until the final octave A-flat is reached.

In this way a texture is created which becomes more and more complex until the sudden climax (the octave) is reached. In other Ligeti works, after a maximum density is reached, a period of thinning-out begins, similar to the pattern of breathing (-> maximum density = inhale; -> thinning-out = exhale).

This breathing effect can be found in the collections of pitches notated above along the time axis. For example look at measures 11–13. As we cross the bar line to measure 12 there is a trichord based on D-flat-F-G-flat (in ascending order); within measure 12 this becomes a tight cluster, F-G-flat-G; in measure 13 the spread becomes wide, particularly due to the C coming in the "wrong" octave, with the trichord D-flat-G-flat-C. This is thus another sort of fluctuation of texture. The widening could be expected due to the expanding intervals. It is Ligeti's clever use of attack points which makes this ever-changing color (be it slight) seem somewhat unpredictable. Perhaps one could call this "non-mechanical process music". How does Ligeti and those who write about him describe this type of writing? This is our next subject.

 – *Micropolyphony and movement types:* What here has been called timbral weaving – the most important characteristic the listener holds onto – has officially been given the name micropolyphony.[2] This might be defined as a polyphonic sound fabric comprising several voices all of which join in the formation of a single total sound. Each part has its own subtle, differentiated rhythmic movement (see above). Where earlier elements such as motivic development were essential to form, here these elements are not to be differentiated as they all form that total sound entity. Therefore the general movement of sound masses takes over the function of the various single recognizable elements of older music.

The time dimension is determined by various movements of sound groups, movements which in turn determine the totality of a work. These sound masses have their own characteristic properties which are based on density, timbre, instrumentation, etc. The general movement of these sound masses with their own specific characteristics is sometimes known as "movement types". Ligeti has been known to call them "form types" as well. These form types are not the likes of a rondeau, but instead the external characteristics of a movement type.

In principle there are four main movement types in Ligeti's works of the 1960s: the *static* form – this is the case in the ninth piece of the *Ten Pieces* (other examples are *Atmosphères* and *Lontano*). Here a balanced musical situation seems to make the listener feel that the form is being postponed as if time were being extended. The music moves through small internal changes, but gives a stable impression. The second is the *dynamic* (or restless) form (see both *Aventures* works as well as the third movement of the *Requiem*). A number of contrasting musical givens are treated simultaneously or sequentially. Here again there is no feeling of development (therefore in the dynamism, there is stasis - this is a not too distant cousin of the first type); the notes are most often short in duration and abruptly cut off (see also measure 16 of our current example). Micropolyphony is often present here as well. The third type is called the *mechanico* type (see the

*Continuum*, third movement of the *Second String Quartet* and the *Chamber Concerto*, not to mention his work for one hundred metronomes, the *Poème symphonique*). The movement is quasi-mechanic. Ligeti refers to several superimposed lattices working simultaneously. The fourth type is the *kaleidoscopic* type (see other movements of the *Second String Quartet* and the *Chamber Concerto*; Ligeti says that the *Ten Pieces* as an entirety represent this type as well!). Here a collection of contrasting givens form a unity through continual change in their combinations, which is just the same thing as looking at one image while turning a kaleidoscope.

Obviously our current example clearly belongs to the first type. Nevertheless, for those who would like the tools to investigate further this very important composer, an understanding of all four movement types is of fundamental importance.

## 3. WHAT TO LISTEN FOR

Ligeti is a composer with an excellent ear for color, for density, for cluster harmonies, for that breathing dynamic movement described above. Static timbre leads to a sound mass's slow development which is perceived as one sound whose focus dial is ever being tampered with. As the "crystal" in this case is the basic color(s) + the movement type(s), Ligeti listeners have more than enough to hold onto despite the lack of perceivable pulse and melody. Ligeti is without doubt one of the most successful composers of experimental music. Success is being used here in the sense of making this music accessible to the listener.[3]

1) Recording used: Wergo WER60059 performed by the Wind Quintet of the Südwestfunk – Baden Baden.
2) The main source used for these three paragraphs is ten Hoopen (pp. 14-15, 49). For those interested in a more detailed analysis of another (the first) movement of this work, see Sabbe.
3) Few complaints were heard about that most unusual film music in Kubrick's *2001: a Space Odyssey*.

# XVIb. Extended vocal techniques, new instrumental techniques and new virtuosity – Berio's *Sequenza III*

## 1. INTRODUCTION

It would perhaps have been obvious to choose a more recent work to illustrate the most relevant points here, but Luciano Berio's piece written in 1966 is not only historically very important in terms of new virtuosic techniques, it is also important in terms of a number of other subjects brought up in the first five parts. Its title makes one think of Darmstadt parametric thinking. Whether this is true or not will become clear in the next few pages.

## 2. A WORK CONSISTING OF ORGANIZED VOCAL SOUNDS

By the mid-60s Berio had become what might be called a "liberated" composer. He was not "limited" to either instrumental and vocal music one the one hand or "just" electroacoustic techniques on the other. In fact, in this period it seems that his techniques in the more note-oriented pieces had effect on his more sound-oriented tape works and vice versa.

In the case of *Sequenza III*[1] a technique derived from his experiences in electroacoustic studios is quite evident. This calls for a composer's creation of a data bank of source materials (Pierre Schaeffer calls them *objets sonores*). Once this collection has been made, potential musical combinations of these materials (*objets musicaux*) are sought. At the same time a global structure begins to take form; this structure may be said to be generated, at least in part, by the character of the source materials.

The technique is quite different from that which is necessary to write in sonata form for example, which in itself is not particularly dependent on the sound sources used. In the more contemporary world, this technique differs from aleatoric composing which can be used to create piano sonatas or music for any sounds.

What we are describing here calls for the interrelation between form and material, an interrelation which has been proven useful in a good deal of electroacoustic music. In the case of the *Sequenza* for voice, Berio's primary research consisted of three elements: the sound sources (a sum of a large number of vocal techniques), the text (its content? its program? – see below) and the presentation of the work (its live performance aspects). Synthesizing the three was the main experiment here.

Some writers (musical iconographers?) have tried to use traditional analysis techniques while treating this *Sequenza*, trying to find the keys to a form similar to traditional ones. Some clues have been discovered; three examples will be given.

1) At the halfway point of the work, the word "truth" is clearly sung. Might this be of symbolic importance? 2) Before this, just after the two minute mark (see the first page of the Universal Edition score below), the word "woman" is sung in the style of the American Indians with the hand beating against the performer's mouth. Might this represent the repression of woman and Indian? 3) The last word of the work is "sing". Might this be significant in terms of the composer's taste? Is it to seen anecdotally (i.e. a singer sings normally, but vocalizes in this work)?

To be honest, this writer is hardly interested in the solutions to these cute puzzles, for the listener could hardly catch many of such signals anyway. They are reminiscent of the hidden information (i.e. musical elements that are not directly perceivable, but are composed under the surface of a work and are discovered by interested scholars at some point through a composer's letters, or just by minute analysis of a score) found in a number of Alban Berg's works.

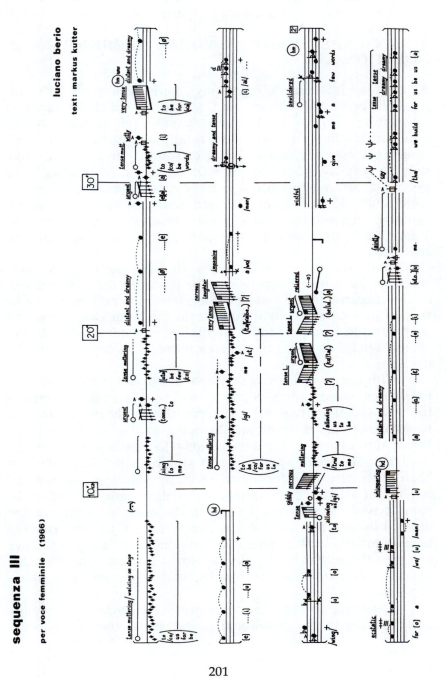

201

Now that we know where not to look and listen in *Sequenza III*, the following sections will attempt to identify a few relevant points in terms of the three-way experiment mentioned above.

## 3. AN EXPERIMENT IN VOCAL TECHNIQUES, IN NOTATION, ETC.

As early as 1959 (see bibliography), Berio was involved in the research he called "Poetry and Music" in which he spoke of attempting to create a continuum (parameter?) between speech and music. In this way new relationships between word (bearing a meaning or consisting of sounds) and syntaxes (not only of language, but also of sounds) could be created using poetry, according to Berio a literary time-based art, as well as techniques derived from his own sonic art. His tape works centered around the voice, *Tema: Omaggio a Joyce* 1958 and *Visage* 1961, are excellent examples of concrete results of this research.

But the live work *Sequenza III* belongs to this same research. Here any given word's (or phrase's) meaning may be in the foreground, or just one sound within the word may be treated in a more phonetic context. In the latter case the sound may be used in a percussive or timbral manner (intelligibly or unintelligibly) or even just to add a bit of chaos after a period of clarity.

This brings us back to that idea of the data bank: of sounds, utterances, words, phrases *plus* as will be discussed in section 4 (below), visual expressions. However, this might be problematic to someone analyzing or just listening to the work. To begin Berio announces in the instructions to the score that: "the borderline between speaking and singing voice will often be blurred in actual performance". Still, by "reading backwards" one might attempt to reconstruct this data bank by taking the sum of notational symbols used in the piece plus all musical notated events. But this work is hardly useful, for one assumes that as many *objets sonores* were not used or simply thrown away as those that finally do appear in *Sequenza III*. In other words, this data bank is finally solely of interest to Berio himself.

Listening to the work, elements like tonality, rhythm, even melody in the traditional sense are all absent. They are nevertheless all there, be it in an experimental modernized form. Central tones are indeed locally present as well as throughout the piece, but they do not have the function of the tonic and dominant of traditional works and do not invite the listener to think in this way. They are there more as references to the vocalist than to the listener. Rhythm is not treated metrically anywhere, but speed and density of information are the new interpretation of the time axis. As the work is indeed for a single voice, the Hauptstimme is all we have. The fact that it changes gestalt every "x" seconds is precisely the heart of Berio's sequence of vocal utterings.

Markus Kutter's text (see section 4 below) is hardly treated in the order in which his words are written. In what David Osmond-Smith calls "word-music", Berio takes each sound, word and phrase as "givens" and treats them in his own way while creating his own musical translation of the poem using its words as elements, fusing poem with sound. This is also the work of many a text-sound poet, but in the case of Berio a larger accent is given to the music of sounds than is the case with most sound poets who often do respect poetry traditions more delicately (e.g. through treating their own sound poetry texts from beginning to end).

Looking at the action notation used on the first page of the score, one notices several things. First of all several sorts of new, unusual, challenging, virtuosic techniques are called for. For example, the rapid repetition in random order of a small number of syllables (words/phones in parentheses) or the vocalization of tense laughter on a number of distinct pitches in rapid ascent. The three- and five-line staves - for relative, exact pitch - do not help much in lessening the (intended) blurring of speech and singing voice. Symbols have been created for example for coughing or beating the mouth with the hand which represents information which cannot be found in the poem. And all those evocative emotions listed above the score staff are enough to make anyone schizoid (there are forty-two different ones in all, 138 occurrences). Such expressive notational devices lead to a literally gestural presentation, a true performance, something made even more evident after reading the last request in the instructions where it is stated that the vocalist is expected to use her own "dramaturgy", given her own emotional code, to create not only the audio part of this work, but the visual performance as well. (The very first activity of this piece is the performer's muttering while entering the stage – here any recording really only tells half the story!)

With all these possibilities, new techniques, with a text which will never be heard in its entirety, what are those things to hold onto during its execution?

First of all Berio is a great craftsman in building up and sawing off tension in his compositions. Ligeti does this through his cluster harmonies; Berio has more discrete methods. The performer literally can take the listener along a voyage of (often nervous) emotions. Although the score looks to be highly fragmented, a performance flows like a stream of sound events. The pairs sung – vocalized, intelligible words – unintelligible sounds give frames of (parametric) reference.

Second of all Berio does reuse several of his vocal devices throughout the piece, often in a slightly different version or combination in repetition. This is similar to tunes with variations and variants. A good deal of contemporary music sounds like a ball of yarn unrolling, going somewhere, but most listeners have trouble guessing in which direction as repetition is taboo. Through Berio's quasi-repetitions, points of reference are built into the work which are most useful to the listener. He has found a most clever solution, given the lack of support of tonality or rhythm.

In other words there are new tools for the listener to use which essentially replace almost everything we have been brought up to use during a musical performance. The almost theatrical live aspects add an extra dimension of familiarity, as the work might be seen to have cabaret-like aspects.

## 4. THE TEXT AND THE "PERFORMANCE"

In conversations Berio has provided us two points of reference as to where this piece comes from. In the first place a memory of his youth: the clown Grock (see Dreßler: 100) played an important role in the work's creation, for it is here where the vocalist can derive inspiration for the articulation of varied emotions and inspiration for turning into an actress using a (musical) body language derived from mime. (In *Sequenza V* for trombone solo, also written in 1966, two props, a chair and a music stand are used; a bewildered "why?" is also uttered early on in the work.) In other words musical and physical gestures work hand in hand for this composer. His childhood memories of the circus are one of his sources of inspiration.

Then there is the poem by Markus Kutter which we have done our best to postpone for so long. The text reads:

| give me | a few words | for a woman |
| to sing | a truth | allowing us |
| to build a house | without worrying | before night comes |

The reason for postponement is no gesture against Mr. Kutter but instead an attempt to avoid misleading the reader into exaggerating the text's importance, at least as the text is read above.

Clearly *Sequenza III* is not a programatic work in the traditional sense. There is no invitation to someone's coughing upon the first reading of these three lines. There is equally no direct reason to reduce any phrase or word to the minimal unit of the phoneme. But then again, as said, Berio's intention was to use the text as a source for a musical translation. His choice of the sounds and emotions for the data bank followed by the generation of the work's structural development is the sequential translation of the three groups of three words above. The text plus the memory of the clown Grock led to Berio's *objets musicaux* (and *objets dramatiques*) which in turn led to the piece. They are all in themselves not important. The performance of the entire score is the experience of the work. In this way, there is a program open to various interpretations, not one the likes of a Janequin madrigal full of bird songs.

## 5. THE ROLE OF TRADITIONAL ANALYSIS TECHNIQUES

It must be clear by now that a traditional analysis of the work can only lead to partial results. What is important is Berio's application of that methodology which calls for what we have named the data bank as composition generator taken from the *modes de travail* typical of electronic music composition and already tested in his works including *Tema: Omaggio a Joyce*. How does one tackle analysis in such a case? How deep should one go?

These answers depend on the goal/application of the analysis. For our own descriptive purposes, we now know enough about this work, at least in terms of the central questions posed in this book's first five parts. For those taking an inventory of new vocal techniques or those studying Berio's *Sequenza* series, perhaps a more intense look at the minutiae of the score is useful. What we know is that Berio was interested in fusing language and poetry on the one hand with vocalizing and music on the other. It is here where his experiment included the search for new syntaxes. It is believed that he was most successful in this research and, like Ligeti, never allowed his now famous musicality to fade into the background at any moment in this piece.

## 6. WHAT TO LISTEN FOR

What kinds of images do we get when we listen to/see this work? How important is it to know the text beforehand? Or the Grock background of the piece?

*Sequenza III* does indeed stimulate the forming of images, obviously including literal visual ones, in rapid succession. This is done as a consequence of his translation of the givens, the text, the various sounds and the dramatic instructions. Still, the background hardly seems important here. The fact is that the listener has those pairs (tension and release, words and utterances, highly dense activity and relative calmness) to assist in forming his or her own succession of images.

We hypothesized at the beginning of the present discussion that the sequence or series referred to in the title might have something to do with the Darmstadt augmentation to serial (atonal) music. The parameter at the heart of this piece is speech/singing. It is coupled with expression as its partner. Many new techniques have been called for to create this parameter, several of which are unquestionably highly difficult. In this way Berio expands horizons for musicians as well as for listeners (not to mention in term of notation) simultaneously. Therefore the work is important historically and, furthermore, is an excellent example as far as our discussions of new techniques, extended vocalizing, new virtuosity and the fuse box are concerned.

On many occasions it has been mentioned that vocal music has been combined with electroacoustic music to form one category of sonic art. There are many who believe this *Sequenza* to be Berio's most radical of the series. In this work, more than in any of the others (with the possible exception of the trombone *Sequenza*), the technique derived from *musique concrète* has been applied. The voice is proven yet again to be capable of creating highly diverse textures. *Sequenza III* is a sound piece and a note piece in equal doses. Here Berio, one of today's most famous composers, is able to remain evolutionary, while composing with revolutionary materials. That is one of his greatest gifts to contemporary music.

1) Recording used: Wergo 60021 with Cathy Berberian performing.

monumental importance of this discovery. Still, the sound of twelve tone music is fortunately not a single one. Schönberg does not sound like Webern who does not sound like Berg who does not sound like Eisler ... Therefore it is not (only) our being able to follow rows and their permutations that is currently at issue.

Carter's inclusion here, therefore, has less to do with his composition techniques and much more to do with what was discussed in chapters VII and XI. He was named along with the younger British composer Brian Ferneyhough as makers of highly complex music – music so complex that one listens to a totality, and not so much the ingredients. This is analogous to the difference between Italian and Chinese cooking – in the former a sauce's taste is derived from a mixture of its various elements; in the latter each ingredient retains a certain amount of autonomy, especially when eaten bit by bit with chopsticks. Carter's music might in this sense be called the diametric opposite of Steve Reich's (XVIe) where similar sounds are combined to such an extent that one can almost crawl into them.

Christian Wolff (1987, 134) has written: "Some scores, in the density of their scoring, the extreme detail of prescriptive notation seem (and, I take it, intend to be) self-enclosed (e.g. Elliott Carter's work), and sound it." Wolff continues: "And yet others, just as dense and detailed, by a kind of refusal of integration or homogenizing, or by their conspicuous excess, sound open (e.g. Ives or Xenakis)." This thought is most valuable to the current discussion because Wolff is speaking from the listener's standpoint. Many a work of both Ives and Xenakis seems to be built on several almost independent sounding layers that simply coexist. A composition from Carter's pen on the other hand tends to give the impression of a system of such complexity – he is ironically a less formal composer than Xenakis(!) – that no listener can penetrate his "self-enclosed" system. Of course dozens of composers and musicologists have taken on the challenge of discovering more and less formalized detail of Carter's work. Hardly any number of the well-known American periodical *Perspectives of New Music* has appeared without Carter going in for another check-up. For those interested in these details, there are loads of highly decent musicological contributions to be found. Still it is

Christian Wolff's remark which brings us to the heart of the subject matter at hand.

## 2. FOUR MEASURES FROM CARTER'S *CONCERTO FOR ORCHESTRA*

The introduction to this work (1969 – published by Associated Music Publishers)[1] is but fifteen measures long. According to the composer in the score's introduction, it "brings into focus kernels of all four movements simultaneously". This includes the high notes of the piccolos, flute, violins and metallic instruments, the middle register notes of a number of instruments including the clarinets, piano and harp, and the low register of the tuba, bass drum, etc. A single register is the germ cell of each movement; all of them appear in this brief introduction.

These registers, and the instruments themselves are introduced and built up in the first eight measures on pages 1-3. Carter has made special requests concerning instrument placement (not a formal parameter here, but a major factor, nevertheless); therefore, the acoustical space is created immediately. Between bars 8 and 9 the harp plays a double glissando coming to the center from its outer registers. At this point we arrive at the pages of our example (see score, measures 9-12).

If one listens to the introduction several times, each and every register, texture, even instrument can be heard here. That is to say, when one is looking for those individual tastes – like in Chinese food – they are in fact all potentially separately heard, *but*, given the enormous amount of information present in these four measures, there is a reduction which one most likely hears in one or two listenings: the extreme high and low registers, the clarinet gestures in measure 9, the crescendo in the same measure announcing the full crescendo in measures 11 and 12. (This high dynamic level is continued into measure 13 at which point the orchestration thins out preparing the bridge into the first movement [there is no rest here] which begins with a texture specifically emphasizing the piano and the currently absent marimba.) The strings, at least as far as measures 9-11 are concerned, hardly seem to be present. The

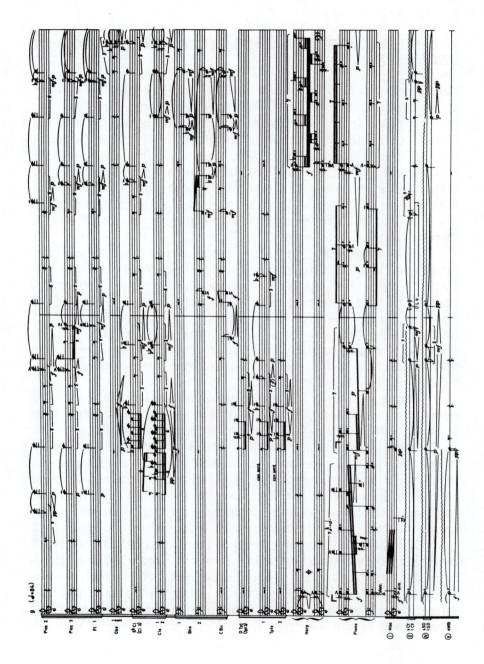

212

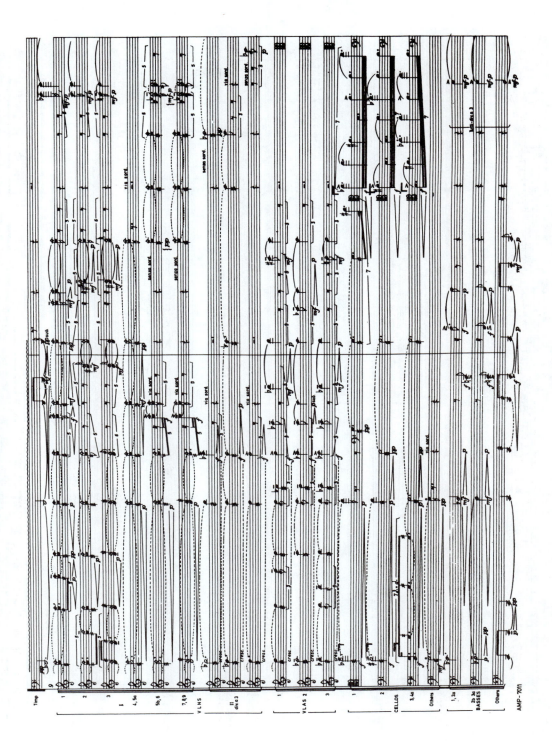

AMP - 7011

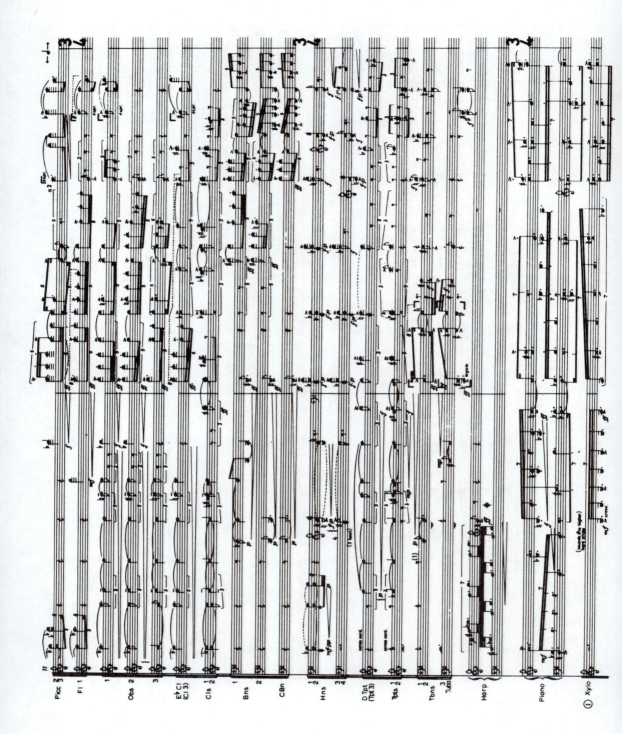

214

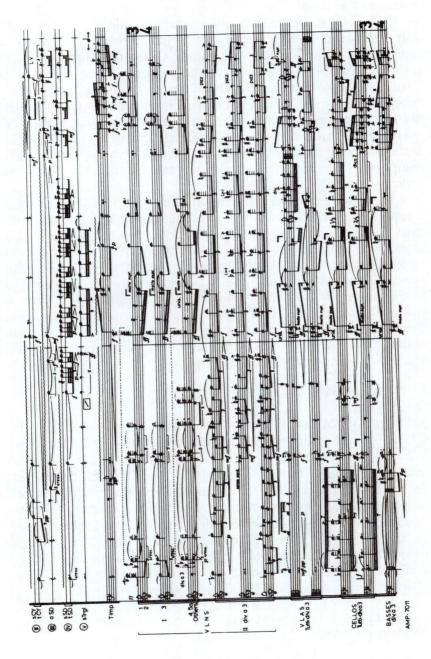

215

piano is supportive as well as the percussion. One might speak of hearing waves of sound profiling registers, textures, instrument classes.

This last sentence may sound quite poetic. But what about that serialism? What about our other parameters? Here a comparison may be made with Ligeti. Given the high density of activity and the dispersion of attack points here the beat is hardly of any relevance to the listener; even the pitches are subordinate to the textures. Where Ligeti reaches this through his subtle micro-polyphony, Carter uses more sophisticated, complex techniques freely derived from serial thought. Serialism and parametric thinking may have influenced this composer, but they are not a given the listener has to or can reckon with.

Let's look at bar 11, the measure in which all present reach a loud dynamic, the trumpets and trombones somewhat louder than the rest with their syncopated, hocketing rising motives. A Ligeti-like situation is created with movement ranging from two eighths to the beat up to septuplets with all other subdivisions in between present. But where Ligeti looks for homogeneity in his static movement and textures, Carter is quite the opposite. Only dynamic is homogeneous here. Texture, pitch and inner-rhythmic relations create a total sound, obviously the sum of its parts, but too complex and self-enclosed to be perceived as such by the listener.

## 3. WHAT (NOT) TO LISTEN FOR

Admittedly not every moment of this work (as well as other Carter compositions) is as complex as these four measures. Whatever the case may be, his music fortunately does not invite the listener to follow "academic" serial dots, but instead to grab onto that occasional main voice, dynamic swell, combination of timbres, moment of rhythmic clarity, changing density and a large number of other components that come and go in that highly esoteric, totally Carter sound. The listener's fuse box is often at the point of blowing, but somehow Carter's craftsmanship cleverly avoids our perception's shutting down.

1) Recording used: Columbia M30112 - New York Philharmonic with Leonard Bernstein conducting.

# XVId. Sophisticated formal structures in experimental music which you <u>can</u> hear if you try – Xenakis' *Nomos* α

## 1. MUSIC OUTSIDE-TIME

As is well known, Iannis Xenakis is the composer of music by number. His numbers do not usually stop at twelve (tones) à la Schönberg nor sixty-four (I Ching hexagrams) à la Cage. The *numéro du jour* is dependent on the musical question of the day.

Many who have tried to learn to understand his means of composing have had the misfortune to give up after studying one or two chapters of his well-known book, *Formalized Music*. Only those with a background in probability, statistics and calculus continue to plow through the numbers.

The goal of this brief discussion is to show that with a wee bit of help, the seemingly impenetrable can be highly understood. Only tables and figures from the composer himself will be used. We will try to understand how the general form of the first page of the score of his first cello solo work *Nomos* α (1966)[1] might be clearly heard by the listener.

Let's begin with Xenakis' main parameters here. (see *illustration XVId/1*; Xenakis: 211) "Pitches" speaks for itself. The only remark of note is that Xenakis uses quarter tones in the work and, as can be expected, all sorts of glissandi. "Instants" refers to starting points of sounds (or rests). "Intensities" are dynamic levels. "Densities" is a typical Xenakis parameter as is the case with Ligeti and calls for x sounds/unit time. "Disorder", a parameter first used by Xenakis can best be illustrated by the composer. (see ***illustration XVId/2*** ; Xenakis: 214)

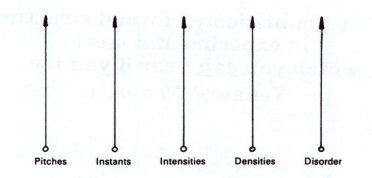

**Illustration XVId/1:** Xenakis' main parameters used in *Nomos α*

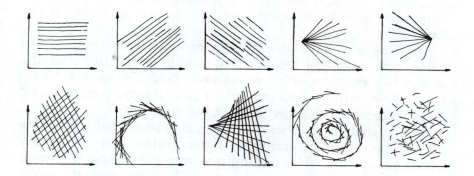

**Illustration XVId/2:** His parameter ranging from order to disorder

In his discussion of the work in *Formalized Music*, only the parameters order, density, duration and dynamic are treated (pitch has therefore been excluded). He creates eight "S" types for sonic order (four based on pizzicato, four on arco) and eight

"K" types which combine density, intensity, and duration. (see *illustration XVId/3*; Xenakis: 232/233)

This paragraph may be skipped by those scared by digits. Xenakis defines twenty-four groups of the numbers 1 to 8 in different orders and furthermore defines an operation between any two of the series. He also provides a table with the outcomes of that operation between any two of the series. (see *illustrations XVId/4, XVId/5*; Xenakis: 221)

| | | |
|---|---|---|
| $S_1 = $ | $K_1 = 1$ | *mf* |
| $S_2 = $ | $K_2 = 2.25$ | *fff* |
| $S_3 = $ | $K_3 = 22.5$ | *fff* |
| $S_4 = $ | $K_4 = 10$ | *mf* |
| $S_5 = $ | $K_5 = 2.83$ | *f* |
| $S_6 = $ | $K_6 = 3.72$ | *ff* |
| $S_7 = $ | $K_7 = 7.98$ | *ff* |
| $S_8 = $ | $K_8 = 6.08$ | *f* |

**Illustration XVId/3:** The eight sonic complexes ($S_n$) and density/ intensity/duration combinations ($K_n$)

| | | | | | |
|---|---|---|---|---|---|
| *I* | 12345678 | *G* | 32417685 | $Q_5$ | 68572413 |
| *A* | 21436587 | $G^2$ | 42138657 | $Q_6$ | 65782134 |
| *B* | 34127856 | *L* | 13425786 | $Q_7$ | 87564312 |
| *C* | 43218765 | $L^2$ | 14235867 | $Q_8$ | 75863142 |
| *D* | 23146758 | $Q_1$ | 78653421 | $Q_9$ | 58761432 |
| $D^2$ | 31247568 | $Q_2$ | 76583214 | $Q_{10}$ | 57681324 |
| *E* | 24316875 | $Q_3$ | 86754231 | $Q_{11}$ | 85674123 |
| $E^2$ | 41328576 | $Q_4$ | 67852341 | $Q_{12}$ | 56871243 |

**Illustration XVId/4:** The twenty-four groups of different orderings of the numbers 1 to 8

| ↓ | $I$ | $A$ | $B$ | $C$ | $D$ | $D^2$ | $E$ | $E^2$ | $G$ | $G^2$ | $L$ | $L^2$ | $Q_1$ | $Q_2$ | $Q_3$ | $Q_4$ | $Q_5$ | $Q_6$ | $Q_7$ | $Q_8$ | $Q_9$ | $Q_{10}$ | $Q_{11}$ | $Q_{12}$ |
|---|---|---|---|---|---|---|---|---|---|---|---|---|---|---|---|---|---|---|---|---|---|---|---|---|
| $I$ | $I$ | $A$ | $B$ | $C$ | $D$ | $D^2$ | $E$ | $E^2$ | $G$ | $G^2$ | $L$ | $L^2$ | $Q_1$ | $Q_2$ | $Q_3$ | $Q_4$ | $Q_5$ | $Q_6$ | $Q_7$ | $Q_8$ | $Q_9$ | $Q_{10}$ | $Q_{11}$ | $Q_{12}$ |
| $A$ | $A$ | $I$ | $C$ | $B$ | $G$ | $L$ | $G^2$ | $L^2$ | $D$ | $E$ | $D^2$ | $E^2$ | $Q_7$ | $Q_4$ | $Q_5$ | $Q_2$ | $Q_3$ | $Q_{12}$ | $Q_1$ | $Q_{10}$ | $Q_{11}$ | $Q_8$ | $Q_9$ | $Q_6$ |
| $B$ | $B$ | $C$ | $I$ | $A$ | $L^2$ | $E$ | $D^2$ | $G$ | $E^2$ | $L$ | $G^2$ | $D$ | $Q_6$ | $Q_9$ | $Q_8$ | $Q_{11}$ | $Q_{10}$ | $Q_1$ | $Q_{12}$ | $Q_3$ | $Q_2$ | $Q_5$ | $Q_4$ | $Q_7$ |
| $C$ | $C$ | $B$ | $A$ | $I$ | $E^2$ | $G^2$ | $L$ | $D$ | $L^2$ | $D^2$ | $E$ | $G$ | $Q_{12}$ | $Q_{11}$ | $Q_{10}$ | $Q_9$ | $Q_8$ | $Q_7$ | $Q_6$ | $Q_5$ | $Q_4$ | $Q_3$ | $Q_2$ | $Q_1$ |
| $D$ | $D$ | $L^2$ | $E^2$ | $G$ | $D^2$ | $I$ | $C$ | $L$ | $E$ | $A$ | $B$ | $G^2$ | $Q_3$ | $Q_6$ | $Q_4$ | $Q_1$ | $Q_{11}$ | $Q_{10}$ | $Q_8$ | $Q_9$ | $Q_7$ | $Q_2$ | $Q_{12}$ | $Q_5$ |
| $D^2$ | $D^2$ | $G^2$ | $L$ | $E$ | $I$ | $D$ | $G$ | $B$ | $C$ | $L^2$ | $E^2$ | $A$ | $Q_4$ | $Q_{10}$ | $Q_1$ | $Q_3$ | $Q_{12}$ | $Q_2$ | $Q_9$ | $Q_7$ | $Q_8$ | $Q_6$ | $Q_5$ | $Q_{11}$ |
| $E$ | $E$ | $L$ | $G^2$ | $D^2$ | $B$ | $L^2$ | $E^2$ | $I$ | $A$ | $D$ | $G$ | $C$ | $Q_{11}$ | $Q_5$ | $Q_6$ | $Q_8$ | $Q_7$ | $Q_9$ | $Q_2$ | $Q_{12}$ | $Q_3$ | $Q_1$ | $Q_{10}$ | $Q_4$ |
| $E^2$ | $E^2$ | $G$ | $D$ | $L^2$ | $G^2$ | $C$ | $I$ | $E$ | $L$ | $B$ | $A$ | $D^2$ | $Q_{10}$ | $Q_7$ | $Q_9$ | $Q_{12}$ | $Q_2$ | $Q_3$ | $Q_5$ | $Q_4$ | $Q_6$ | $Q_{11}$ | $Q_1$ | $Q_8$ |
| $G$ | $G$ | $E^2$ | $L^2$ | $D$ | $L$ | $A$ | $B$ | $D^2$ | $G^2$ | $I$ | $C$ | $E$ | $Q_5$ | $Q_{12}$ | $Q_2$ | $Q_7$ | $Q_9$ | $Q_8$ | $Q_{10}$ | $Q_{11}$ | $Q_1$ | $Q_4$ | $Q_6$ | $Q_3$ |
| $G^2$ | $G^2$ | $D^2$ | $E$ | $L$ | $C$ | $E^2$ | $L^2$ | $A$ | $I$ | $G$ | $D$ | $B$ | $Q_9$ | $Q_3$ | $Q_{12}$ | $Q_{10}$ | $Q_1$ | $Q_{11}$ | $Q_4$ | $Q_6$ | $Q_5$ | $Q_3$ | $Q_8$ | $Q_2$ |
| $L$ | $L$ | $E$ | $D^2$ | $G^2$ | $A$ | $G$ | $D$ | $C$ | $B$ | $E^2$ | $L^2$ | $I$ | $Q_2$ | $Q_8$ | $Q_7$ | $Q_5$ | $Q_6$ | $Q_4$ | $Q_{11}$ | $Q_1$ | $Q_{10}$ | $Q_{12}$ | $Q_3$ | $Q_9$ |
| $L^2$ | $L^2$ | $D$ | $G$ | $E^2$ | $E$ | $B$ | $A$ | $G^2$ | $D^2$ | $C$ | $I$ | $L$ | $Q_8$ | $Q_1$ | $Q_{11}$ | $Q_6$ | $Q_4$ | $Q_5$ | $Q_3$ | $Q_2$ | $Q_{12}$ | $Q_9$ | $Q_7$ | $Q_{10}$ |
| $Q_1$ | $Q_1$ | $Q_7$ | $Q_{12}$ | $Q_6$ | $Q_9$ | $Q_5$ | $Q_8$ | $Q_2$ | $Q_{11}$ | $Q_{10}$ | $Q_3$ | $Q_4$ | $A$ | $L^2$ | $D^2$ | $E^2$ | $L$ | $B$ | $I$ | $G^2$ | $G$ | $E$ | $D$ | $C$ |
| $Q_2$ | $Q_2$ | $Q_{11}$ | $Q_9$ | $Q_4$ | $Q_{10}$ | $Q_6$ | $Q_1$ | $Q_8$ | $Q_3$ | $Q_{12}$ | $Q_7$ | $Q_5$ | $E$ | $I$ | $G$ | $C$ | $L^2$ | $D^2$ | $L$ | $E^2$ | $B$ | $D$ | $A$ | $G^2$ |
| $Q_3$ | $Q_3$ | $Q_8$ | $Q_5$ | $Q_{10}$ | $Q_7$ | $Q_{11}$ | $Q_9$ | $Q_6$ | $Q_2$ | $Q_2$ | $Q_4$ | $Q_1$ | $L^2$ | $G^2$ | $I$ | $L$ | $B$ | $E^2$ | $D$ | $A$ | $E$ | $C$ | $D^2$ | $G$ |
| $Q_4$ | $Q_4$ | $Q_9$ | $Q_{11}$ | $Q_2$ | $Q_8$ | $Q_{12}$ | $Q_7$ | $Q_{10}$ | $Q_5$ | $Q_6$ | $Q_1$ | $Q_3$ | $G^2$ | $A$ | $D$ | $B$ | $E^2$ | $L$ | $D^2$ | $L^2$ | $C$ | $G$ | $I$ | $E$ |
| $Q_5$ | $Q_5$ | $Q_{10}$ | $Q_3$ | $Q_8$ | $Q_1$ | $Q_9$ | $Q_{11}$ | $Q_{12}$ | $Q_6$ | $Q_4$ | $Q_2$ | $Q_7$ | $E^2$ | $E$ | $A$ | $D^2$ | $C$ | $L^2$ | $G$ | $I$ | $G^2$ | $B$ | $L$ | $D$ |
| $Q_6$ | $Q_6$ | $Q_2$ | $Q_7$ | $Q_1$ | $Q_2$ | $Q_{10}$ | $Q_3$ | $Q_9$ | $Q_4$ | $Q_5$ | $Q_8$ | $Q_{11}$ | $C$ | $D$ | $E$ | $G$ | $G^2$ | $I$ | $B$ | $L$ | $E^2$ | $D^2$ | $L^2$ | $A$ |
| $Q_7$ | $Q_7$ | $Q_1$ | $Q_6$ | $Q_{12}$ | $Q_{11}$ | $Q_3$ | $Q_{10}$ | $Q_4$ | $Q_9$ | $Q_8$ | $Q_5$ | $Q_2$ | $I$ | $E^2$ | $L$ | $L^2$ | $D^2$ | $C$ | $A$ | $E$ | $D$ | $G^2$ | $G$ | $B$ |
| $Q_8$ | $Q_8$ | $Q_3$ | $Q_{10}$ | $Q_5$ | $Q_{12}$ | $Q_4$ | $Q_2$ | $Q_1$ | $Q_7$ | $Q_9$ | $Q_{11}$ | $Q_6$ | $D$ | $L$ | $B$ | $G^2$ | $I$ | $G$ | $L^2$ | $C$ | $D^2$ | $A$ | $E$ | $E^2$ |
| $Q_9$ | $Q_9$ | $Q_4$ | $Q_2$ | $Q_{11}$ | $Q_5$ | $Q_1$ | $Q_6$ | $Q_3$ | $Q_8$ | $Q_7$ | $Q_{12}$ | $Q_{10}$ | $D^2$ | $B$ | $E^2$ | $A$ | $D$ | $E$ | $G^2$ | $G$ | $I$ | $L^2$ | $C$ | $L$ |
| $Q_{10}$ | $Q_{10}$ | $Q_5$ | $Q_8$ | $Q_3$ | $Q_6$ | $Q_2$ | $Q_4$ | $Q_3$ | $Q_1$ | $Q_{11}$ | $Q_9$ | $Q_{12}$ | $G$ | $D^2$ | $C$ | $E$ | $A$ | $D$ | $E^2$ | $B$ | $L$ | $I$ | $G^2$ | $L^2$ |
| $Q_{11}$ | $Q_{11}$ | $Q_2$ | $Q_4$ | $Q_9$ | $Q_3$ | $Q_7$ | $Q_{12}$ | $Q_5$ | $Q_{10}$ | $Q_1$ | $Q_6$ | $Q_8$ | $L$ | $C$ | $L^2$ | $I$ | $G$ | $G^2$ | $E$ | $D$ | $A$ | $E^2$ | $B$ | $D^2$ |
| $Q_{12}$ | $Q_{12}$ | $Q_6$ | $Q_1$ | $Q_7$ | $Q_4$ | $Q_8$ | $Q_5$ | $Q_{11}$ | $Q_2$ | $Q_3$ | $Q_{10}$ | $Q_9$ | $B$ | $G$ | $G^2$ | $D$ | $E$ | $A$ | $C$ | $D^2$ | $L^2$ | $L$ | $E^2$ | $I$ |

**Illustration XVId/5:** The table providing the results of Xenakis' operation on all twenty-four sets

For example A = 21436587 and E = 24316875. The operation is: from the second series (E), reading left to right, take the first number's (2) entry from the first series (the second number of A = 1; this is the first number of the result), then the second's entry (the second number of E = 4; the fourth number of A = 3), etc. If we continue in this manner, we get the series: 13425786, which turns out to be series L. On the table the first series (A) is listed above and the second (E) to the left: AE= L.

Xenakis uses this operation to determine the order of events he calls "paths" in *Nomos* α. The precise how and when is for the connoisseur. We just need to know that this number 8 is of great importance.

These paths are created still without an exact music-notational equivalent. This is what Xenakis calls composing *outside-time*; the values present in these paths will be used for splitting up the K values which as stated include three parameters in one. We will not further describe this process here. (see *illustration XVId/6*; Xenakis: 226)

**Illustration XVId/6:** Information relevant to one of Xenakis' paths

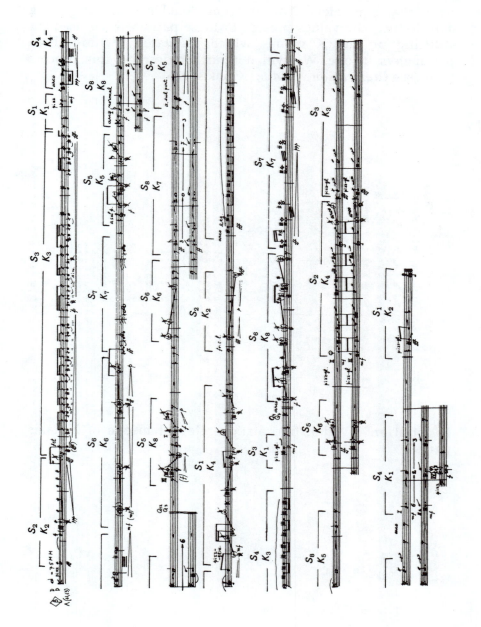

222

## 2. NOMOS α INSIDE-TIME

In fact the series: D/D, Q12/Q3, Q4/Q7 were the first three paired outcomes of the work as can be seen on the first page of the score as reprinted in *Formalized Music* (see score page – Xenakis: 235, the score is published by Boosey & Hawkes). The first eight suffixes of the S's and K's are equivalent as the first pair consists of D/D. The second group beginning shortly after the start of the third system no longer is "synchronous" as the second pair consists of Q12/Q3, two different series. If one were to look up all the values of the K's and S's here, and were then to read the entire Xenakis discussion in detail, many minor points of detail on the score would become clearer. But that is not our goal here. The translation of the numeric *outside-time* information into music notatable form is the point where music *inside-time* takes over.

What can be clearly seen and heard is that at every S/K break, the music gets treated highly differently. S2 is a rising glissando, S3 is "disordered" (arco). S1 is "ordered", but as K1 is so short, this order lasts but one tone. S4 is sustained sounds with aberrations, etc. Now when one listens to the first few moments of the work, this fragmentation is crystal clear. This continues consistently throughout the piece. That there is a modulus of eight textures before they restart in another order can actually be heard after getting to know the work better. The treatment of the K's is a bit more difficult to follow, but the dynamic/density/duration changes do not offer any difficulty to the listener in general. Finally the pitch parameter has been treated separately as Xenakis explains in his text. A complete study of his book does provide tips as to how this was approached, but unfortunately not in as much detail as the building blocks described here.

In other words, by just making a mild acquaintance with these two by eight building blocks (the S's and K's) and having a knowledge of the concept of "paths" and a familiarity with the Xenakis sound at the time (glissandi, sharp dynamic changes, no interest at all in the (a)tonality war), one can see how a work like *Nomos* α is put together. With this in mind, it must be said that only about four of his works were constructed in this particular way. Another story must be told to better understand his stochastic, strategy, and Markovian works with their other *numéros du jour*. The discovery that a Xenakis work can be followed at all, appreciated in a way we follow sonatas and fugues, was the modest goal here.


## 3. WHAT TO LISTEN FOR

The experience of *Nomos* α especially given what we now know is the intersection of the appreciation of the Xenakis sound and the discovery of his building blocks for this piece. Obviously it is not necessary for the listener to *understand* what this mathematical composer is doing at any given moment, just as in the case with Carter's atonal techniques. Nevertheless, obtaining a feeling for his architecture is an excellent companion to the easier acquisition of a taste for his sound. Repeated listening to his music is the best way to do this, first through recognizing his particular timbres and dynamics and then by looking at the musical houses this architect (he is the writer of the book entitled *Musique architecture* and has indeed two separate careers) has built for us.


1) Recording used: Angel S-36560 - Pierre Panassou, cello.

# XVIe. Music as process – Reich's *Piano Phase*

## 1. 'THE GOAL IS TO HAVE NO GOAL.'
### – (Lao Tze as paraphrased by John Cage)

Process music is non-teleological music. Perhaps the only goal to a process composer, besides extra-musical goals, is the proof of the applicability of the process itself. In chapters VI and VII the liberation of formal structure as well as of notation were the focus, along with the need to couple this with that something to hold onto.

In Steve Reich's early, more experimental works, both process and that something to hold onto (the motives) are handed to the listener on a golden platter. The perceptual experience of these works is quite an extraordinary one. Through the process's almost mechanical simplicity and the overtly announced major motives in the phase works, both process and motive become taken for granted and a special sound experience is open to all. Reich's *Piano Phase* (1967 for two pianos, or alternatively for two marimbas[1]) illustrates this excellently.

## 2. THE SCORE

The score presents no challenge to the reader, but a most challenging one to the performer. Here follows a description of the entire work. A pentatonic theme is introduced by player 1 in measure one and repeated four to eight times. (see Universal Edition score fragment) In the second measure the second player fades in and joins and the theme is played tutti another twelve to eighteen times. Then the phase effect begins. The second player, the one with the most challenging part, is asked to accelerate very slightly during four to sixteen repetitions, continuing to the point that he or she has advanced exactly one sixteenth note of this twelve sixteenth note motive. Player 2 is then exactly one sixteenth "out of phase with" (ahead of) the first player. This slight derailment is repeated sixteen to twenty-four times before player 2 again accelerates until this difference has become two sixteenths. Each acceleration and each bar are to last between a minimum and maximum number of repeats. At bar 14, the two players are again "in phase" and play their tutti measure between four and eight times. Thus ends the first phase of the work.

Bars 15 and 16 are a solo bridge for player 1 as the old motive is heard four to eight times before the motive is shrunk to eight sixteenths in bar 16 and played six to eight times. Player 2 fades in in bar 17, this time playing another motive in contrasting motion. Here player 1 has retained the old pentatonic scale of (E-F sharp-B-C sharp-D) and player 2 plays a different motive (E-A-B-D) of four notes which includes the addition of a sixth pitch to the five already known from the first motive, the A. Once this new counterpoint has been established, a second, shorter – the measures have been reduced by four sixteenth note – and dissimilar – the motives are no longer the same – phase round takes place ending in bar 25. It is now player 1 who tacets and player 2 who has a second bridge, this time retaining the same material. In bar 26 player 2 loses first two of the eight sixteenth notes, and in bar 27 the next two leaving four sixteenths per bar. In measure 28 a new tutti is played after player 1 fades in, a last phase round is executed lasting just four more bars, and after the called for tutti in bar 32 has been repeated between twenty-four and forty-eight times, the players cue one another and stop on the following down beat. A performance lasts approximately twenty minutes.

## 3. THE LISTENER'S EXPERIENCE (THE PROCESS OF LISTENING)

Granted this lengthy description of the entire work is a bit superfluous, but the fact is that there are few works in music history which can be so fully described in so few words. But as stated, this simple process design of Reich's is something which fades into the background as the listener becomes accustomed to the material and the work's development (with the exception of the two unexpected changes in bars 17 and 28).

When the music is out of phase, either in the repeated measures "x" sixteenths removed or between the measures when the second player is accelerating, most unusual, often fascinating sonic things can happen which depend on the instruments used, the dynamics played, the acoustics of the performance space and, last but not least, the manner in which the listener is focused on the work. For example it is conceivable at many points not to hear piano (or marimba) sounds at all, but instead to hear new timbres made by the combinations of harmonics which are literally out of phase. In fact there are four basic types of sounds to be perceived: the most uninteresting perhaps is to be found in the solo and tutti passages where one clearly follows the motive. The most consonant non-tutti moments occur in the measures that are an even number of eighth notes (i.e. one, two or three quarters) out of phase as the interval combinations all tend to be consonant creating simple harmonic sounds. The last two types contain more complex harmonic structures. In the case of the uneven number of eights out of phase, dissonant textures are heard. When player 2 is "in between" measures the beat is weakened, made vague, and one hears clouds of ever-changing harmonic textures. As the number of repetitions often changes, no one really consciously tries to follow the overly evident process, but is instead carried away by these four types of musical situations. Again, here the music of notes and sounds merges elegantly.

The work is somewhat meditative due to the listener's taking of the process as well as of the motives for granted. Repetition and meditation have of course often been combined musically. As a matter of fact other minimal composers, LaMonte Young and Terry Riley are quite overt about the meditative qualities of their works and announce them as such. Therefore the different ways of listening: active listening, passive listening and even almost "tuning out" all take place due to the huge amount of repetition. Each listener does this at his or her own pace.

Admittedly the process aspect of this work is hardly sophisticated in comparison with techniques employed by other composers discussed in this book; nevertheless, this elementary example does show the potential of goalless music in raising our perception to deal with sounds in a more liberated fashion.

1) Recording used: Hungaraton CD 12855 – performed by the Amadinda Percussion Ensemble.

# XVIf. Available (open) forms – Brown's *Available Forms I*

## 1. BROWN ON OPEN FORM

The tale of open form has been told many many times in many ways, a few of which were treated at length in chapters VI and VII. For once let's have the composer tell the story as he saw it at the time. The following remarks have been taken from Earle Brown's contribution to the form number of the *Darmstädter Beiträge zur neuen Musik* (1966) as well as from the introduction of the Associated Music Publishers score ("score" written after quotations) of *Available Forms I*.

In the introduction to his article, Brown states that he is less interested in "the liberation of sound" (the cause of many) than in the "liberation of Time" (p. 58 – his own capital T). This thought is most relevant for it means that Brown has not chosen the expansion of musical material as one of his particular goals. He prefers new architectures with existent materials. Brown often uses the word "synergy" to describe his type of architecture: "cooperative action of discrete agencies such that the total effect is greater than the sum of the two effects taken independently (e.g. actions taken by the body's organs)" (p. 59).

To achieve this, Brown states that "a work, and any one performance of it [should be] seen as 'process' rather than as stative and conclusive" (p. 60). It "intentionally transforms the disparate independent entities into one particular integral entity ... which is the particular work performed by this

229

particular conductor and orchestra at this particular moment" (score). Two basic approaches are mentioned by the composer:

> "1) a 'mobile' score subject to physical manipulation of its components, resulting in an unknown number of different, integral and 'valid' realizations.
>
> 2) *a conceptually* 'mobile' approach to basically fixed graphic elements; subject to an infinite number of performance realizations through the involvement of the performer's immediate responses to the intentionally ambiguous graphic stimuli relative to the conditions of performance involvement" (p. 60).

Clearly our case at hand belongs (primarily) to the first category. What is important here is how Brown sees the developments that led to graphic notation and to open form as overlapping with one another. In this way "a performance is composed rather than a composition is performed" (p. 61). He adds that his concern is "*per*-forming rather than *pre*-forming" (p. 63). It goes without saying that for the players, the conductor and the listeners, hearing the work on several occasions brings one closer to the piece; otherwise any performance becomes "the work" (think of the discussion of *the* recording in chapter II) which is in the case of Earle Brown most unfortunate.

His greatest source of inspiration when speaking of open form can be found in the mobiles of Alexander Calder as well as the assemblages William Seitz collected for his exhibitions. An assemblage's elements do not have to be performed in order to be experienced. Using Calder as inspiration Brown speaks of open form works as works containing "condition(s) of mobility" (p. 62). In his 1959 notebooks he writes:

> "The *recognition* of these conditions (relations) and their contextual use is not based on function but on their un-conformed existence. (Not used for rhetorical effect.) A unique independent existence for the work... keeping myself and performers at a distance (ambiguous) ... the work to be its own definition. (Revelatory rather than

declamatory.)" (p. 67 – the odd punctuation and overdose of parentheses are from the composer's pen.)

## 2. BROWN ON AVAILABLE FORMS

In the same article Brown looks back at some of his notes concerning *Available Forms I* for orchestra written in 1961. He writes:

"*Time* is the structural element (as space in visual arts).
The *Events* have flexible *time* orientation but each basically different.
The *Events* have flexible *loudness* potential.
The *Events* have flexible sequence and over-lap potential.
The *Events* have fixed frequency fields (shaped, notated).
The *Events* have fixed timbre distributions.
When time (rhythm, tempo, continuity; stops, holds, starts,) and loudness and sequence and juxtaposition are flexible, *Form* must be left open for the potentials to operate. (Feedback between the events as flexible objects, infinitely combinatorial, and conductor/performer ... Mallarmé's 'operator').
Not re-creating a pre-conceived form (reading through a *thing*) but creating, in the moment of hearing, a form arising from those unique circumstances of composing, rehearsing, working and responding as one does *only* at that moment' (p. 64).

In a remark in the performance notes in his score he adds:

"There is intentionally not too much material in this piece in order for the musicians to *hear* their position in context. It has proven to be practical in that the performers have enough time in rehearsals to become familiar with the sound of the event and of their relationship within it. It is, of course, ambiguous and never the same twice. The ambiguity does not distress the performers; it involves them creatively and creates a feeling of intensity and engagement in the performance felt by the musicians, the conductor, the audience, and me. What I have tried to achieve with this score – the composed events as 'plastic' material and the given conditions of control, ambiguity, and uncontrol – is an intensification of the sense of being *involved* in the uncertain but urgent process of the work defining itself from moment to moment during performance" (score).

This is an almost manifesto-like statement which brings us to the heart of *Available Forms I*. It is here that Earle Brown most clearly states the experience aspect of his mobile, "ambiguous" works. He requests his players to learn to handle not only the musical material, but their circumstances as well. This is the creativity sharing so often referred to in this book. Below in chapter XVIg we will see how Christian Wolff approaches similar questions through the eyes of a political philosopher.

The sound of Earle Brown's music is hard to place in terms of the major schools of thought of the 50s and 60s. He was clearly a member of the Cage-Wolff-Feldman-Brown quartet as far as musical innovation is concerned, but their individual manners of putting notes/sounds together was extremely diverse. Brown's sound is perhaps the least tangible of all four. His aleatory is to be found in the mobiles and in freer notation, not in the notes he has chosen. He is less subjective than Feldman in his compositional approach given his number-based study of music theory and composition with Joseph Schillinger. His jazz background also plays a role as far as his search for "feeling" on the part of all players is concerned. Furthermore Brown's works are generally fairly difficult. The relative difficulty of some of his scores has been created to get rid of that "free for all" attitude so often wrongly applied to Cage's music. Those that play a work of Brown's run little risk of misunderstanding as far as this question is concerned.

## 3. THE PIECE [1]

This Brown mix of views has led to one of the most successful and better known open form works, *Available Forms I* (his term for open form) for orchestra. How does he create such circumstances that call for a special engagement on the part of the performers? The score consists of six pages, three of which are divided into four "events", the other three contain five. The conductor, who is only responsible for start/stop cueing (and giving dynamic/tempo hints as well through the "speed" and "largeness" of downbeats), has a placard on a music stand with an arrow pointing to a number between one and six which tells the players which page number is to be called for next. The event number is given by the fingers of one hand while the other hand is used for conducting. Length, order, and nuance are all decided by the conductor. Interpretation is a personal and collective experience. Brown tells the players what alternatives they have if they have finished an event and the conductor has not yet stopped them. Other than duration, most of the notation is pretty much straightforward for those a bit acquainted with contemporary action notation. The most ambiguous graphic reaction notation is only present on page 4, our example here.

In event 1 (see score page - Associated Music Publishers), the notation is most simple; the greatest freedom of choice is in duration. In event 2 the players play until stopped by the conductor. This, too, is fairly straightforward. Still getting a true balance is the challenge here. Event 3 calls for all sorts of arpeggios at varying speeds to be chosen by the performers. Event 4 – and remember these events do not necessarily have to be played in this particular order, or *at all* – has the texture left open. Brown does request that repeats not be taken simultaneously by these three players. Event 5 uses the most radical notation of the piece. Still this notation is infinitely less radical than the Cage page taken from the Concert for Piano and Orchestra. The squiggles indicate very clear areas of pitch. The arrows for the timpani parts are for glissandi after attacks.

This page contains five highly diverse textures, similar to five differently colored surfaces in one section of a Calder mobile. A study of pitch demonstrates a preference for the dissonant, but there are no Palestrinian nor Webernian taboos here. Rhythmic analysis is impossible. It can only be made of interpretations. Timbral qualities can best be grouped into classes given the limited freedom of dynamic and tempo.

Flöte
Oboe
Eb Clar.
Bb clar.
Bass clar.
Bassoon
Horn
Trumpet
Trombone
Harpe
Piano

234

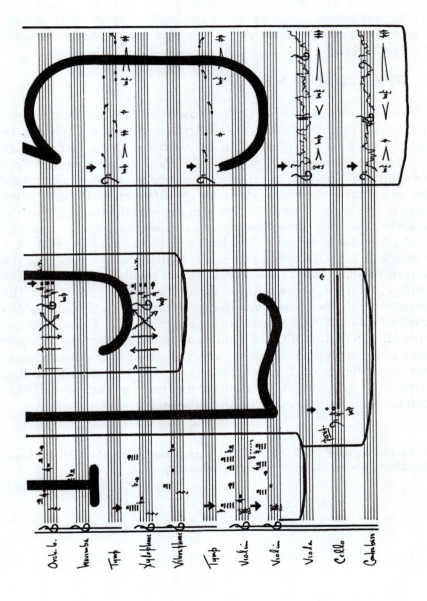

235

As the African drummer says (and the jazz musician as well), the stricter the model, the greater the freedom of improvisation or interpretation. This is Earle Brown's credo as far as his open form works are concerned. As these events are never played the same way twice, as the order of events (twenty-seven in all) are not to be repeated, Brown's "synergy" is sought; his score is his "assemblage".

## 4. WHAT TO LISTEN FOR

Of all the composers, both Brown and Wolff with their particular esoteric sounds are difficult to describe. It should be clear that this has nothing to do with the open form, which invites the listener to experience different musical panels, each of which is also free in terms of interpretation, moving around in different sequences at every performance. What Brown wants the listener to listen for can be found in several of the quotations listed here. His open form works present a model and offer the musicians the chance to participate in creating a variety of musical circumstances in which group creation is the call of the day. Where the scores are not totally graphic – Brown wrote most of these works early on – his choice for the dissonant, the beatless, ever-changing timbral combinations can easily be heard. The music is less complex than Carter's, more complex than Ligeti's and Feldman's, less random than Cage's and more esoteric than most. The challenge to the musician is the experience of constant creation. The experience to the listener is the sound version of the mobile and assemblage combined with that esoteric Brown sound.

1) Recording used: RCA VICS-1234 – performed by members of the Rome Symphony Orchestra, Bruno Maderna, conducting.

# XVIg. Politically influenced music-making – Wolff's *In Between Pieces*

## 1. CHRISTIAN WOLFF'S MUSICAL COMMUNITY

Back in chapter V, a great deal of attention was given to various political ideals as formulated by a number of composers. This discussion led to the subject of the "musical community", one of the most important proposals of the second part of this book. In the late 60s and early 70s Cornelius Cardew tried to create a new musical community by collectively making new music along with the members of the Scratch Orchestra, which consisted primarily of amateurs, many of whom were dealing with the new sounds of contemporary music for the first time. The famed examples of music played in alternative spaces, for example around a lake, call for yet another sort of temporary community to come to life. What kind of communities might exist in terms of the music of this politically engaged composer?

Christian Wolff's politically oriented music has two traditional components: his music most often uses conventional (i.e. instrumental and vocal) materials to create new sound experiences in time. Therefore like Earle Brown he is not primarily interested in the "liberation of sound" as will become clear presently. Secondly, Wolff notates scores which act as models for all those interested in his type of engagement music. In contrast Cardew's music was performed exclusively by the Scratch Orchestra. Wolff's music is thus similar to

238 Whats the Matter with Today's Experimental Music?

almost all music historically with respect to its being written for any and all musicians. So far the community remains vague.

Before focusing more specifically on the engagement aspect of his work, the question of "openness" must again be briefly treated. In 1987 he wrote the following (Wolff: 133):

> "'Open' [should be seen] as a fluid notion which includes social and political meanings. It is not so much a technical issue (indeterminate techniques, whether applied to composing or performing) as a matter of how the music sounds ... It is the content, whose meaning changes with the history of the listeners, that allows the music to maintain and define its openness."

Continuing this argument about openness, he states:

> "More specifically, musically, practically, one can ask: if openness is in the scoring (form) – by way of composing procedures (e.g. random means, computerized programming) or elements variable and indeterminate with regard to performance – can you hear it? At this point I believe I can only speak for myself as listener, at any given, particular occasion." (Wolff: 134)

As already pointed out in chapter VI, Wolff searches for openness in how the music sounds and is played. This is more important to him than the look of the score. One is reminded of his comment mentioned in the Carter discussion in which he considered the complex scores of Carter as "self-enclosed" and those of Ives and Xenakis as "open". This comment was also made from the listener's standpoint as can be demonstrated by the fact that neither ever wrote an open form composition. To complete this discussion of openness, Wolff makes a minor attack on McLuhan and Cage:

> "Form suggests the question of content. What or where is the content in open form work? It's often said that form *is* content, or the medium's the message. But that's insufficient. Even in the case where one says that sounds [and silences] are just sounds, with a life of their own, the sum, so to speak, of form and content. I agree with

Cornelius Cardew when he points out that only we who
hear, score and produce them can attribute to and in this
sense cause them to have such a life." (Wolff: 135)

In other words, the "cause" of most experimentalists, the freeing
of sound and expansion of musical material is not enough. It
can only work when integrated with content/formal questions
as far as Wolff is concerned, for the autonomy of sounds is not
in itself open. Instead the dialectical nature of content (that we
give to sounds) insures the openness of form.

His article, *Open to Whom and to What* is one of the few
retrospective texts of its sort, written after more than thirty
years experience. The separation of social and political openness
from other non-social methods of musical control deserves a
chapter of its own; what is of interest here is that open form as
was assumed by many is not the main road to openness
according to Wolff, but instead the treatment of content from
the listeners' viewpoint. That is Christian Wolff's main thesis.

Coming back to the question of the musical communities,
two aspects of Wolff's reputation as composer are relevant. First
his music sounds fairly enigmatic to most listeners. Secondly
the "playing together" aspect of his work is highly developed
and corresponds truly to his political ideals. These two points
are surprisingly contradictory, for if a musical community arises
between musicians as will be illustrated below, why does the
music seem intangible to many a listener? Is it Wolff's
intellectual character? His taste? His personal version of
openness?

The author has had the opportunity both to perform and
to have been present at several Wolff concerts. Looking back at
the formula raised in part 2: A player "X" from society "Y1"
interprets a piece of music from a composer "Z" from society
"Y2" in a way that it communicates to an audience in society
"Y3", it might be said that the communicative aspect based on
local values is not Christian Wolff's cup of tea. His interest is in
setting up situations which are treated musically by his musical
community, which is first and foremost the performers. The
public witnesses a communal process.

How this takes place can be demonstrated through two
final citations from Christian Wolff as taken from an interview
with Walter Zimmermann. When asked whether Wolff could

describe his process of revealing musicians' energy resources, Wolff replies:

> "I think it has to do with two things. One is the fact that my music is often just material. But not raw material exactly. It's set up in such a way as to require anyone who wants to seriously deal with it to exert themselves in a particular way. Not just technically, to learn how to play it, but also imaginatively ... how to fill out what's to be filled out, how to use the material. And so that's just the individual in relation to the score. But most of the scores have to do with groups of people. And it then turns out that a lot of the music making, and this comes out of the score too, has to do with how the individuals relate to each other as they play. And that in turn opens up a whole other set of circumstances, which of course take on a special character, but which is focused by the music."
>
> (Zimmermann: 268)

This is an excellent description of the engagement principle which is present in a large number of Wolff's compositions. The music is the focus, the musicians collective musicality and musical relations create the circumstances which are presented in performance. In the same interview, Zimmermann asks Wolff whether a "tribal feeling" is thus created among the musicians (Zimmermann: 272). Wolff replied:

> "Something like that ... communicate a sense of cooperation, and above all the pleasure that it gives. In other words to satisfy yourself you don't need to be a winner ... a whole group of people, first the musicians, and eventually presuming musicians and audience, ... makes a community that enjoys itself together."

This is then the Wolff credo. It is honestly difficult to speak of pure old-fashioned "enjoyment" after listening to some of the more enigmatic works. Performing many of these same works on the other hand can give a special kind of musical, "tribal" pleasure. It is not that Wolff has failed; perhaps despite his ideal of the community's including the public, these works' scores tend to inspire the creation of unusual performances where that thing to grasp onto is more related to the circumstances than to the sounds themselves. As Wolff has plead for openness from the point of view of the listener, one must have a sophisticated appreciation of these circumstances before feeling a part of that musical community. In sum, many musicians have truly experienced Wolff's communal ideal. Fans of the New York Action School, Cage-Feldman-Brown-Wolff, form the only true community of listeners.

## 2. A WORK BY THE COMPOSER OF *CHANGING THE SYSTEM*

Christian Wolff is different from Earle Brown in a sense other than the questions of form illustrated above; Wolff also does not discuss his (political) desires in his scores. *In Between Pieces* (1963)[1] for three musicians (any instruments) is an excellent example of his music. The instructions before the work discuss solely the notation and the form. In this case the work consists of seven pages. The first five are to be played in their normal order. The last two contain five rehearsal numbers which can be played in any order, with two requirements: section four is to be played once, section three is to be the closing section. The work, using reaction notation contains both "closed" and "open" form.

Looking at page 3 of this work, we can get a very good impression of how Wolff attempts to change the system of music-making (see score page – C. F. Peters Edition).

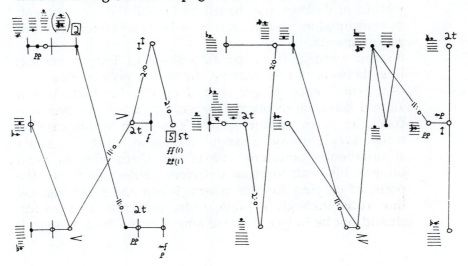

A quick look at the page shows that a good deal of coordination among the players is called for and that a performance can easily lead to an enigmatic organization of sounds. In any event, the following information is taken directly from the introduction of the score. All symbols on page 3 (which contain most used in the first five pages) are discussed.

"Black notes are variously short, up to one second. White notes are of any length, sometimes determined by the requirements of coordination (below). Diagonal lines from one player's note to anothers = second player plays immediately after the first stops.

If the diagonal line is broken by a number followed, after a colon by a zero (_____2:0_____), the second player plays that number of seconds after the first has stopped.

Vertical lines between notes = play simultaneously (both attack and release of the notes are all black or all white, otherwise attack only).

Horizontal lines from one note to the next within a player's part = legato.

Each note, by itself, represents one sound in one timbre and pitch. A number followed by a 't', under or over a note = the number of timbres to be played.

A number in a box = the number of pitches to be played, simultaneously, overlapping or one after another.

When a note is accompanied by one of these numbers, i.e. represents more than the pitch or timbre, any one of the pitches or timbres may be used to fulfill the requirements of coordination, and the rest may be independent of these requirements.

Shorter vertical lines, or extensions of longer vertical lines between notes, passing through a note = play on a beat which each player should choose for himself and should continue to observe wherever called for, unless it coincides with another player's beat, in which case he must straightway change it. Note that in some simultaneous notations one of the three players must observe his beat: he must therefore be the one to cue the point of playing for the others. When the short vertical line runs through a black note, that note's duration should not be longer than the length of the beat, though it may be shorter (unless another note follows, legato, on the next beat).

A white note with a vertical line through it must fall on the beat but may then be of any duration.

Pitches are given, sometimes with a choice, next to the note to which they apply. Read either treble or bass clef (only); sound at pitch. If no pitch falls within your range, transpose at least two octaves.

Short lines off a pitch at an angle = fraction of a tone less than half sharp, if angle is up, flat, if down.

Where no pitch is given, choose any.

[Upward arrow] = highest pitch in a given situations (on a string, highest overblown on a fundamental, etc.)

[Downward arrow] = lowest

* [not present on page 3 - LL] = a noise."

Not only can the music sound enigmatic, some of the notation can be (deliberately) confusing as well. In the second half of the page, player 3 has a simultaneous crescendo/decrescendo on one (?!) note. Shortly before that there is also a simultaneous m*f*, p.

The general movement is quite slow; between some "cues" eleven seconds lapse. This gives an excellent chance to absorb and react to the previous sound. Assuming that every performance does lead to highly differing results – one could completely write out a part, but this is not exactly the composer's intention – the experience of watching the three performers make sounds based on what they hear and what they collectively create – what they feel sounds right – can be a most unusual and rewarding one.

*In Between Pieces* is, in contrast to Brown's work, not particularly virtuoso in terms of material. Wolff's experimental technique is to be found in the redefinition of the musician's listening and participating. One can not have a clear expectation of how this page 3 is to sound by just looking at the score. That is part of the work's openness. (Remember, the entire orchestration is free.) The finishing touch by Christian Wolff is his offering of communal circumstances for any and all musicians to participate in finding their personal *and* collective solution to the (in between) pieces of this politically based musical puzzle.

## 3. WHAT TO LISTEN FOR

As in the case of Earle Brown, this question is almost impossible to answer as far as Wolff's most open works are concerned. The title "What to be aware of" is perhaps more correctly formulated. Personal experience has shown that his music is most effective when seen. Watching the performers working together can be quite fascinating. For as often is the case, one watches the players working and thinking, trying to find the right pitches and gestures throughout a given performance. Listening to a recording of that same performance misses an essential element. In fact a recording of an open Wolff work is perhaps but a sonorous snapshot in the life of that work.

More important is the fact that these open works are eternal works in progress. The more you see them performed, the more intimate you become with them. What to look for is the opportunity to experience a work's performance more than once performed by the same players as well as others. Given the current situation of concerts offered, this will be challenging to say the least.

Last but not least, performing his works are true learning experiences. First of all one learns that kind of thinking involved in finding the right sounds. Second of all one learns more about the other players in preparing and performing the work. As Wolff and Brown have said, their music is not written for great soloists, but instead for people willing to work together to create collective, ensemble music. Perhaps this is the most important tip that can be given in the case of Christian Wolff: play his music, for in so doing you will be forced to experience new kinds of listening and reacting to the sounds you hear.

1) Recording used: Odeon C165-28954/7Y performed by members of the Ensemble Musica Negativa.

# XVIh. Music as organized notes and sounds – de Leeuw's *Mountains*

## 1. PREAMBLE: IMPORTANT DE LEEUW THEMES

Despite the fact that he is primarily known for his vocal and instrumental works, Ton de Leeuw is a composer who has never really considered composers' being forced into categories as having any relevance. De Leeuw attempts to transcend all such boundaries (of being an instrumental or computer or audio-visual or installation or whatever composer) by possessing a more universal sense of music as a phenomenon based on organized notes *and* sounds. In the case at hand, the blend of notes and sounds of the live bass clarinet and recorded synthesizer was the composer's experiment.

As it is feared that this Dutch composer may be less known than others discussed here a short introduction will be given presenting three often recurring themes which can be found in de Leeuw's work. These themes are highly interrelated: one is idea-oriented, one is oriented to general practice and the last is more specifically articulation-oriented. For simplicity they have been called: The East, Fusion and Clarity/Unity.[1]

a) **The East:** In any given review or critical discussion of de Leeuw's work, a mention of his interest in non-Western music, specifically of Eastern cultures, acculturation and/or his well-known extra-musical, often political, opinions seems inevitable.

De Leeuw's Eastern theme includes goals such as the reduction of individualistic expression in performance, transcending dualisms of movement/rest, dynamic/static and confronting Mother Nature with human nature. He calls for individual acculturation to take place within our "ecology of sounds". De Leeuw develops musical elements reminiscent of various cultures' folk musics. He has been known to have musicians improvise in ways influenced by Eastern practices (see for example his voice and tape composition, *Magic of Music II*). Finally many of his works since 1980 have been inspired by numerous aspects of Eastern modality. In other words, this theme is a guide in terms of musical content, musical thinking and even extra-musical ethics.

b) **Fusion:** If one composer today deserved the *E Pluribus Unum* award (with no USA-pun intended), de Leeuw would be a likely candidate. Throughout his entire career he has continually brought together into his compositions seemingly dissimilar techniques, be they ancient, "exotic" or experimental. For example, de Leeuw is the only composer the current writer has run into who has claimed to have had Japanese notions of sobriety on his mind while writing his serial works. He searches for a new unity from these amalgamations and speaks of composition being a sounding box "reacting on all sources coming from outside". One notices archaic elements (as in his electronic work, *Chronos*, which uses a recording of ancient Bulgarian women's choral music as one of its main layers of sound) and non-Western language materials in tape compositions, isorhythmic procedures in experimental instrumental works, and personal applications of almost every innovation known to post-World War II music: multi-parameter serialism, microtonality, his own version of "automatic writing" (derived from the surrealists - de Leeuw learns his newly developed technique and then puts the rules aside and composes intuitively in the relevant works), aleatoric techniques, new forms of improvisation, new notations and performance practices, flexible instrumentation, spatial music, use of new technologies, parametric applications of numeric relationships, search for new sound colors, syntactic approaches to sound, and finally his own interpretation of "centricity". It has been said that he adopts and adapts new procedures to the needs of his own style, needs that vary from one composition to another.

c) **Clarity/Unity:** Most critical discussions of de Leeuw's compositions include complimentary remarks concerning the comprehensibility of his works. This aspect derives from de Leeuw's approach to form and what he calls "transitions" within a given form (through repetition, variation, static or non-evolutionary form and centricity). Critics often remark on how one is able to perceive all of the elements of a given de Leeuw composition at all times as the number of employed timbres or layers are finite.

Although this third theme is the most abstract, it is one of great consistency in his works. To come full circle, many of the notions de Leeuw applies to achieve his unity are derived from Eastern thought.

Let's now look how these three themes are applied in his work of sound integration, *Mountains* (for bass clarinet and stereo tape: 1977 – 18'15, score published by Donemus).[4]

## 2.   THE FIRST TWO REHEARSAL NUMBERS OF *MOUNTAINS*

A good deal of de Leeuw's musical training took place in Paris. It is therefore no wonder that both *musique concrète* concepts and serial techniques found their way into his early tape works (not to mention the use of modern modal scales influenced by his teacher, Olivier Messiaen). Yet the work chosen here dates from the later era of voltage-controlled electronic music which began in the mid-60s. It was at that time that de Leeuw installed a modest synthesizer studio at his home, developed what one might call his personal tape-style and suddenly increased his output of electroacoustic compositions.

A brief analysis of the beginning of the work (see the score pages 2-3, rehearsal numbers **A** and **B**) is useful before briefly returning to the three themes. Preceding the score the composer has also notated an overview of the work in terms of its macro-structure (see score, page 1 below).

# Page 1 of *Mountains* –
## A macro-structural overview of the entire piece

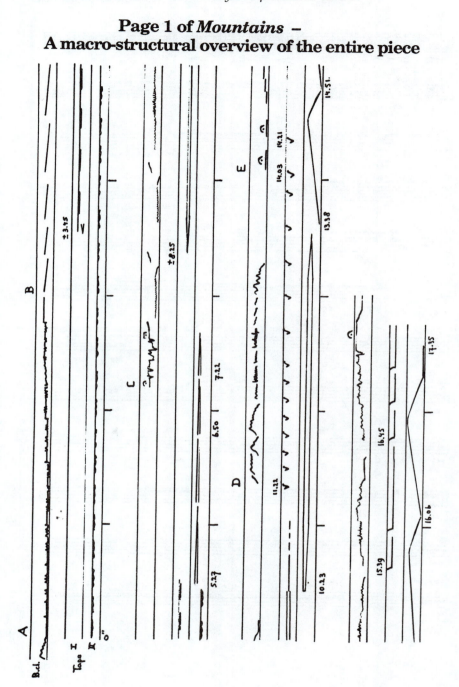

This overview page emphasizes general pitch development – register and upward and downward movement are placed in time for each voice – and interplay of the tape and the live instrument. It also gives a clear impression of the work's general structure including the special overlapping of thematic material: the transitions, most of which occur at the borderlines between rehearsal numbers, see for example the introductory gestures of the bass clarinet before rehearsal number **A** and the bass clarinet transition at the beginning of **C**.

De Leeuw has described the work as follows: "The slowly ascending and falling lines, the high plateaus on which the music seems to stand still, readily provided me with the title. This work is an integration of instrumental and electronic sounds [both bass clarinet and electronic sounds possess a central square wave-like timbre-LL] rather than one of opposition. Echos of folk music can be heard throughout... mingled with the contemporary idiom and the electronic means that are used." (Composers' Voice recording: CV 7801)

**Descriptive analysis**: Although *Mountains* contains non-pitched material, the entire work revolves around the minor third interval. This becomes quite clear early on:

*Bass clarinet part:* Looking at the macro-form diagram, one might say that there is a descending line in the brief introduction followed by a slowly ascending line in **A** leading again to descending materials in **B**. The score shows that the chromatic introduction leads the player to two main pitches a and c. In the beginning the a seems to play the role of the tonic, yet later on it could equally well be the c. In other words one can speak of a dual center of pitch which is true for most of the clarinet part in the entire work. The tremolo repetitions grow and diminish in duration and rise in pitch through the inversion c/a. Apart from one b-flat in the eighth system, the first new notes are to be found in the last measure of page 2, the beginning of the clarinet's transition to **B**, which, despite its chromatic alterations, also centers on the minor third, this time c/e-flat. **B** is focused on small-interval tremolos, but retains the two original central notes, leading finally to the original tonic a. As far as the time dimension is concerned, in **A** and to an extent in **B** the long-held notes tend to give the listener a feeling (yet again) of beatlessness as no listener follows the tempo during the tenuto "drones" which are accompanied by the tape moving along at its own independent pace.

*The Tape:* Slightly after the beginning of **A**, the tape is started and will run until shortly before the end of the work. On the second channel a seemingly repetitive, yet continuously changing motive is heard containing the tones c/d/e-flat, the first and third pitches are most prominent leading to a diminished triad with the bass clarinet. Specific to these unpredictable, yet recognizable variations is the floating of the inner tuning of the motive, which is thus not always in tune with the non-varying clarinet. Rhythmically so much is happening that any given simultaneity with the live part is happenstance. When the clarinetist plays the transition, he essentially emphasizes the outer pitches of the tape's motive, realizing the first unison and concurrently the first integration between both parts.[3] The tape motive continues in **B**, being joined at approximately the beginning of the sixth system of page three by the first channel which contains less pitch-oriented drones (due to its contrasting dissonant diads). At one point an echo effect is heard with the original second channel motive in stereo; this leads to a third tape element during the clarinet's tacet at the end of **B** which first consists of a drone minor third a/c – the clarinet's tone centers – and later separates in tremolo form.

This sense of interchange of material along with dynamic exchange of foreground and background modes between the two "voices" is typical throughout the entire piece. The later sections, which can similarly be described parametrically, add new motives and motivic variations. It is during the last two rehearsal numbers that the minor third is shifted away from a/c to its final e/g, while the clarinetist's earlier narrow register is broadened to a more virtuoso conclusion.

Now we can briefly revisit the three de Leeuw themes.

The East: Summarizing the above: while considering the de Leeuw quotation pertaining to the work, one must first look at the treatment of the time dimension of *Mountains,* specifically with regard to its flowing form, its ambiguous tone centers and then at its motivic material for Eastern and folk influences.

Fusion: This same quotation coupled with the short description above indicates in what ways fusion has taken place. Eastern drones, modern modal textures, sawtooth timbres, beatless and highly rhythmic passages are just a few elements fused into this work and have all been employed in one or more of the various points of integration among both parts.

Clarity/Unity: A quick run through the score is adequate proof of how overly important this theme is. The listener can hold onto tone centers, drones, returning motivic materials, the swell and flow of dynamic and (restricted) timbral movement, contrasting movement between the concentration on the minor third and the more dissonant, rapidly changing motivic passages throughout the work. In reaction to the success of *Mountains,* the critic Ernst Vermeulen once wrote: "In the genre of the combination of instrument and tape, not as contrasting figures, but instead in osmosis, this work is a milestone."

## 3. WHAT TO LISTEN FOR

The most important reason for the inclusion of this work is that de Leeuw seems to enjoy narrowing the gap between instrumental and electroacoustic traditions with this work. Almost all sounds of the tape part could be written out on a five-line staff. Only new symbols would be necessary to handle the gentle timbral flow of the synthesized sounds. A modest version of action notation used for the bass clarinetist where time lengths are mildly flexible could also be used for note patterns on tape that do not follow a constant beat.

The fact that de Leeuw is interested in integration means that the bass clarinet player must not only listen to the tape for cues, but also mix his or her part timbrally with the tape during performance. To do this the wall between electronic and instrumental music must be broken down.

In the instrumental part there are passages which clearly are influenced by a simple technique he often uses in his electronic works, namely the use of what is known as a sample-and-hold module (this will be the only technique mentioned here). In de Leeuw's case he gives one input of his sample-and-hold unit the choice of all pitches of a given motive and the other input an independent signal which essentially chooses which motivic note is available at a given time without the composer's intervening. A clock or a touch of a keyboard determines how often the motive's note is to be changed. This approach can often be heard on the tape with its quasi-repetitive sequences of notes of its various motives. De Leeuw has treated a number of motives similarly in the bass clarinet part, but here the "sample-and-hold" effect has been written out. Again in this case experience in one branch of music can be used in the other. (The motives heard on the tape are clearly taken from de Leeuw's experiences in the vocal-instrumental world.)

Ton de Leeuw is no radical. His experimentation is mild; his ear highly musical. In *Mountains* the goal was to utilize techniques from his experiences in instrumental music and from his tape works and combine them with inspirations derived from folk music and Eastern philosophy. What the listener can follow is a great deal due to the music's clarity. His motivic materials are hardly revolutionary. His light breaking up of the beat could only become harmful at the moment a ballet were to be made for the piece. The timbres are not so numerous that someone could get lost during the piece. The piece has a clear chain structure, including its transitions and calling for a number of motives along with the tone centers and the work's main interval to be  brought back from time to time for perceptual reference. Sound and note are blended in a work whose program reminds one of a certain Debussy symphonic work. The impression of nature, despite de Leeuw's use of the highly synthetic sawtooth wave, in both is equally strong.

1) For further reading, see de Leeuw's own texts plus those by Dominick, de Groot and Helm in the Dutch journal *Key Notes*.

2) Recording used: Composers Voice CV 7801 – Harry Sparnaay, bass clarinet.

3) Of course a unison between both parts is but one way to create de Leeuw's integration. Other interesting points of integration in the score that fall outside of the current description are: rehearsal number **D** (page 5 of the score: beginning at the second half of the second system) – as the clarinet suddenly begins to play after a five second tacet similar thematic and timbral materials can be heard in both voices; rehearsal number **E** (page 7 first system) – here the tape has the most movement, the clarinet is playing drones at the common tone center; also the last few clarinet notes on the last system of page 7 is a brief point of intersection between the two voices; finally the high minor third motive on page 8 provides the last truly integrated texture.

# XVIi. Recent electroacoustic music – Risset's *Sud*

## 1. INTRODUCTION

Jean-Claude Risset realized this young, but already relatively well-known work in 1984-1985 at the *Groupe de recherches musicales* (GRM) studio in Paris, the studio where *musique concrète* was born. The work lasts twenty-four minutes; the Wergo CD recording (WER 2013-50) was used for the enclosed score.[1] Risset, after his studies in France, worked for a period in the United States at the Bell Laboratories where, under the direction of Max Mathews, computer music synthesis was born. Risset later became the first director of IRCAM's computer music department in Paris. He is currently director of the computer music studio in Marseille.

## 2. A COMPUTER WORK PROFITING BY ANALOG AND INSTRUMENTAL EXPERIENCES

In the text included with the Wergo recording, "Computer Music: Why?", Risset has written that in his early compositional experiences he had discovered that *musique concrète* provided the composer with a large variety of sounds, sounds which unfortunately could only be transformed in rudimentary ways. In contrast, in electronic music (i.e. the "competitor" born at the WDR studios in Cologne) there was greater control of sounds, but here the electronically generated tones themselves were simple and rather dull. As Risset had already written a number of instrumental pieces in his early years, he decided at one point that he had no desire to compromise either richness of texture or refinement of control over them in his future compositions.

Risset has spent about twenty-five years doing research, development and composing computer music. It is here that he feels that he has command over expanded materials and control. *Sud* exemplifies this feeling as a number of "concrete" sounds are used. Of these sounds instrumental textures can be found in percussion and keyboard instruments some of which have been modified by the computer. There are also computer-generated sounds employed. It is interesting that the work has been realized at GRM, for there still seems to be expertise in *concrète* techniques today, but now the composers use the more modern medium of the computer instead of doing the work with a microphone, tape recorder and a few machines for limited sound transformation referred to above.

## 3.  *SUD*'S PROGRAM AND ITS SOUND SOURCES

The immediate program in this work is its homage to Risset's new home, the south of France, the Midi (not to be confused with that other musical one which most likely has not been used here). Local sounds, especially that of the Mediterranean, of various birds and insects, are used. All three movements are centered around the sea. Other sound sources include wooden and metal percussion instruments as well as a (synthesized?) harpsichord. Furthermore, synthesized sounds are used including a number resembling the concrete ones (for example an electronically generated bird song). A special technique known as "cross synthesis" where one sound can effect another is also present. Examples of cross synthesis are where the loudness of an electronic sound is influenced by the dynamic of water; or where the "pitch" of water is centered around and thus determined by one electronically controlled.

As in instrumental music there are pitched sounds and noise-like textures. One extra subdivision is necessary in this work: most pitched sounds can be notated on our musical staff, but a few are microtonal and move so quickly (see for example time fifty-eight seconds below) that only general directional movement can be perceived and transcribed.

As the third, final movement is the only one to be presented in detail here, a short description of the first two will now be given. In the first movement Risset introduces his cast of characters sequentially so that the listener can become accustomed to what sorts of sound will be used. Risset call this "soundscape photographs". He has described the movement programmatically as "the sea in the morning". What is noticeable in all three movements is the almost organic dynamic curve derived from waves. The instrumental sounds are used only for "gestures" according to the composer. Already in the first movement a great number of "hybrid" sounds (the result of the above-mentioned cross synthesis) can be heard as well as the sound of real and synthesized birds and insects. In this movement Risset introduces a "major-minor pitch scale" (G-B-E-F#-G#) which is used in different ways in the outer movements. Here the scale is used to construct what he calls "harmonic clouds". In this way references to tonality in the sense used in chapter VII coexist with sonorous textures which seem quite foreign to the tonal world.

The second, the most aggressive movement has been named "call – a bell animated by the sea". The textures here, though using some of the same sound sources of the longer first movement, are more restricted, using more abstract textures than the outer movements. One might say that Risset has used and A-B-A' form in terms of content in the three movements.

Very few textures of the first movement do not appear in the third: only the glissando electronic texture at 3'45", the piano at 4'30", the synthesized bird texture at 6', the storm at 7'15" and the sound of individual insects (flies?) shortly before the end of the movement are unique here. The atonal harpsichord passages in the third movement as well as the "cascade" texture and the chimes are not present in the first movement.

The texture of water (in its natural and hybrid forms), the electronic drone and the chime (plus a buoy's bell?) sounds are the only ones in common between the second and final movements.

It must be mentioned here that other than the very brief remarks about the work's program and the list of *classes* of sound sources, the listener generally does not need to know any of the details listed above. For herein lies the difference between listening to demonstrations of how sounds are made and just listening to the work.

## 4. A SCORE FOR THE THIRD MOVEMENT

Two post-scriptive scores of this eight minute long final movement made for this book have been included here. The first, the more detailed score has been produced during several listening sessions with the recording. It shows where all textures start and stop and gives (relative) pitch and loudness information in a detailed as well as evocative manner where possible. The "rehearsal numbers" have been created for the further analysis of the work as well as for the second score which shows the structural development of the movement on a single page. A key has been provided for those interested in known which sound abjects have been used and where (a sort of cross-reference). One detail of importance is that the major-minor scale here is used as a "harmonic grid". Its tones are sometimes heard simultaneously, sometimes one or more of them are more accented. Risset uses various filter techniques to arrive at these varying  textures, but here again we enter the kitchen of electroacoustic music and that is not our intention here. This grid is the third movement's equivalent of those "harmonic clouds" in the first movement.

The scores have been made as an attempt to show how the music has been structured by Risset. They also show that some of his sound sources help to generate such structures (the Berio discussion mentioned this technique as well). The mixture of electronic, instrumental and nature sounds is one of Risset's great achievements in the work. But greater still is that a musical work of importance has been created using contemporary technological know-how without compromising the composer's own talent.

# Key – Sources used in *Sud 's* third movement

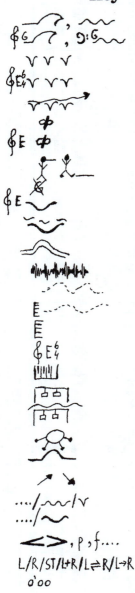

Water (sea waves, rustic: under a dock) – natural timbres

Water – interaction with electronic sounds at given pitch(es)

Birds – natural timbre

Birds – interaction with electronic sounds at given pitch(es)

"Electronic birds" with general pitch direction notated

Insects – natural timbre

Insects – interaction with electronic sounds at given pitch(es)

Human voice (in background) and human footsteps

Pitch previously announced ends here

Electronically generated continuous sound at given pitch(es)

Electronically generat. cont. sound with pronounced harmonics

Electronic flute-like sound including glissando directions

Noise effect

Short electronic sound-"cascades" + direction of movement *

Idem + direction of movement at given pitches

"Harmonic grid" = G-B-E-F#-G#

E major triad in second inversion = B-E-G#

(Ring modulated-harpsichord texture) piano – atonal passage

Metal chimes and/or buoy bell(s) and/or triangle(s)

Metal chimes, etc. – electronically modified

Wooden chimes

Variable (moving) band-pass filter

Pitch direction of the variable filter ... or of pitch itself

Amplitude of this sound "follows" that of water/birds

Pitch of this sound "follows" the continuous electronic sound

Crescendo, decrescendo; dynamic symbols are traditional

Left/Right/Stereo/L and R (separate layers)/Movement

Time is given in minutes-seconds.

* This sound is reminiscent of the moving microtonal sounds used in John Chowning's *Turenas* (see chapter IX). The pitch here is unimportant, impossible to notate.

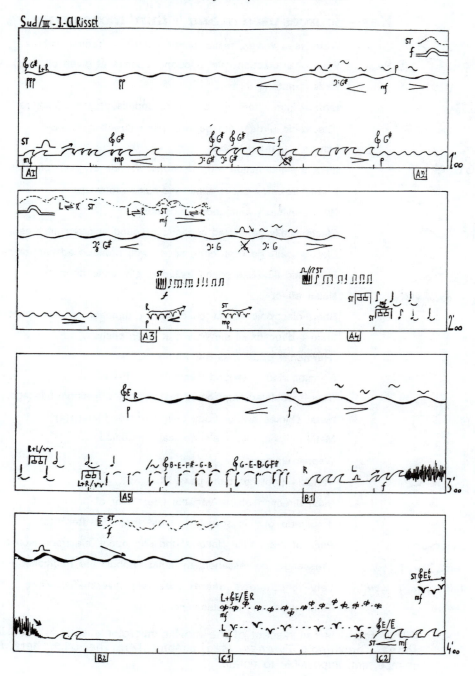

Sud/III - J.-Cl.Risset

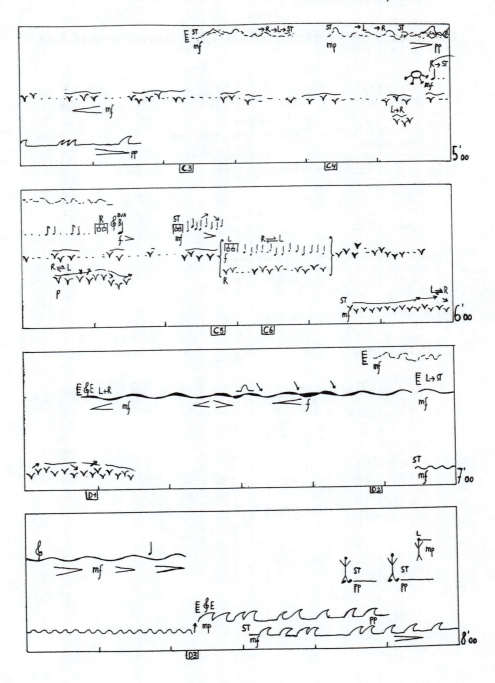

## Structural development of the third movement of *Sud*

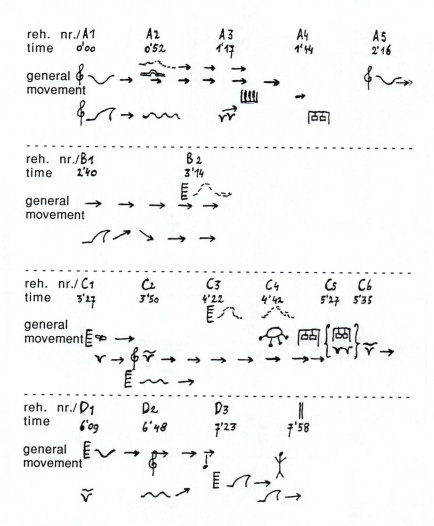

## 5. A FEW CLOSING REMARKS (WHAT TO LISTEN FOR)

A few traditional compositional devices are worthy of mention. In the early stages of the work, one notices that the general direction of pitch as well as of dynamic is rising. (Locally though the sea sounds rise in A1, descends in the electronic sound, to rise again at the reprise B2 – one might think of the motion of a wave here.) The general trend is a descending one at the end of the movement (there is also a thinning out of sound during the last eighty seconds of the work) giving it a mild symmetric character.

At any given moment there are never more that four textures present. This gives the work a quality of clarity and makes it relatively easy to follow. Morton Feldman always claimed he was more inspired by a Gustav Mahler with his subtle use of few textures at all times than of an Elliott Carter with his overt application of complex textures. Apparently Risset subscribes to the Mahler and de Leeuw low level texture school. Often when the full four are present, two are based on the same source (e.g. natural and hybrid water sounds simultaneously heard).

The short gestures are never heard at the beginning of the rehearsal numbers. Between A2 and A5 several are heard. In B2, the cascade is present. In C3 to C5 the cascade is heard again as well as percussive textures. In D2 the cascade is treated for the last time.

The parts themselves, as can be seen on the general structure page, are characterized as follows: 1) introduction of materials (as in the first movement), 2) the sea (reprise from 1), 3) birds and insects and 4) the sea (finale). The movement begins clearly with G# as its tone center in various octaves. After the "atonal" harpsichord interruptions, the E becomes the tone center at the beginning of A5. It will be prominent as a single tone and as the tonic of the triad (in C2 – this replaces the "tonic" electronic drone of A, B and D) and is the main tone of the major-minor scale (the grid) from this moment onward until the end where it is the last tone heard at 7'52".

Returning to Risset's remarks in the second section above it may be concluded that his backgrounds in instrumental music, *musique concrète* and electronic music and two dozen years of musical computing have been most influential here. As far as the listener is concerned, Risset's choice for known, identifiable, programatic textures assists in one's following the unfolding of the work. Despite the fact that the sea and forests are heard, this never detracts the attention of the listener to the point that one thinks he or she is listening to an "environments" recording. The use of abstract textures in no way competes with the concrete ones. There are of course several composers who employ concrete sounds but try to make them as unidentifiable as possible. In this way distraction is made impossible and the sounds are perceived immediately within a musical context. Risset leaves the sounds more or less as is and still is able to present the listener with a rewarding musical, that is to say, music of sounds experience.

1) An INA/GRM CD recording of *Sud*, INA C1003 is also available.

# XVIj. An analysis of Shinohara's *Tayutai* for koto (1972) – a three-dimensional approach of assimilation in experimental music

## 1. *TAYUTAI*

This work[1] was written by the Japanese composer, Makoto Shinohara (born in 1931, currently residing in Utrecht, The Netherlands) for koto, voice, and various percussion instruments: Chinese shell chimes, Japanese bamboo chimes, urchin chimes from The Philippines, two high-pitched wooden boards or boxes and two stone plates (various pitches). The koto player, who plays the percussion part and is equipped with two sets of koto plectra, a pair of rubber, wooden and plastic sticks and one cembalom stick, is expected to perform the vocal part as well, although this work may also be performed as a duo. The duration, due to the use of visual notation, has no fixed length. A sum of the called-for time lengths is 6'20", yet performances have lasted up to 7'20".

The piece has been chosen for analysis, not only due to its experimental nature, but also due to its binds with specific traditions. It is in fact this meeting of the experimental with the traditional that will be focused upon. The published score (Zen-On Music, Tokyo) and two recordings of the work have been consulted for analysis: first, the solo version as recorded by Akiko Nishigata[2] and an unpublished recording of a concert at the San Francisco Museum of Modern Art (1978) at which the composer performed together with the vocalist, John Duykers.

*Tayutai* means fluctuation. As Shinohara has written in the program for the San Francisco concert, "The piece represents the psychological fluctuation between hope and despair and has an introspective character." This confrontation of hope and despair is most evident in the vocal part consisting of isolated single words vocalized (sung, spoken and using techniques approaching *Sprechgesang*); yet this conflict can be found in the instrumental parts as well as will be discussed below.

The work will be presented as follows: first the three dimensions implied by this chapter's title will be introduced in section 2; the three "voices" will then be analyzed, first separately, and then as a whole. After these analyses, the three dimensions will be discussed separately as a re-analysis of the work. Finally, a concluding section will briefly compare *Tayutai* with other Shinohara compositions which might be looked into similarly.

## 2. THE HYPOTHESIS – A THREE-DIMENSIONAL ANALYSIS

It is the opinion here that *Tayutai* can be viewed as a work synthesizing three different compositional ways of thinking: 1) that which can be found in Japanese music (and in fact in other distinctively different traditions as well!), 2) that of post-World War II Europe, i.e., techniques developed in Darmstadt, and 3) that of the experimental music which involves laboratory work, be it aleatoric or, alternatively, large-scale pre-compositional experimental development.

The choice of these three "dimensions" is in essence an obvious one. Shinohara is learned in koto techniques and is thus able to use and experimentally "abuse" this instrument musically. The addition of percussive sounds is, according to the composer, hardly revolutionary. In a conversation in June 1984, he spoke of a *noise factor* inherent to much traditional Japanese music. As there are no specific pitches called for in the percussion parts, as many of these sounds are unpitched, as many koto sounds are percussive in nature in the work, this *noise factor* can be said to be highly present. Further the combination of voice and koto is a common one, although we will see that the employed vocal techniques are not traditional ones.

The Darmstadt element is particularly understandable when regarding the fact that the composer studied in the 1950s with Messiaen, worked as Stockhausen's assistant in 1965 and has moved around "Darmstadt circles" for more than two decades. Although the accent on diverse timbral changes in this work may be influenced by a Japanese heritage, the research of the 1950s and 60s in Darmstadt in structuring timbre is nevertheless shadowed in a great deal of Shinohara's compositions.

Finally the experimental is most likely the germ-cell from which *Tayutai* has grown. The large research leading to the collection of possible timbres and sound combinations in this very colorful work shall form the basis of proof that experimentation played a major role in the piece's conception and in its architecture. Although it is premature to make a comparison, one of the reasons which brought this writer to look closely at this composition was the playful hypothesis that *Tayutai* was actually the yet unwritten *Sequenza Jū-ichi* (eleven, in Japanese; Berio has composed ten so far) for koto.

Before it can be proven how evident this three-dimensional hypothesis is, the piece will first be analyzed in descriptive terms.

## 3. A DESCRIPTIVE ANALYSIS

### a. The Score
While following this descriptive analysis, the reader is requested to consult the score and the two charts printed below as the following texts will only complete that which is notated on the charts. Rehearsal numbers have been added onto the published version of *Tayutai* for convenience. Charts #1A and #1B correspond to parts b, c, and d of this section; chart #2 belongs to part e.

Before embarking on the koto part, a few words from the composer might be of relevance. Shinohara mentioned in the 1984 conversation that, when composing this work, he began by collecting his materials, building what might be considered to be a data bank from which he did not need to use all collected possibilities. Once this was completed, the architectural phase of the work began. Shinohara claims to be less strictly formalistic than his colleague, Stockhausen, in his work and advised not to try to find a non-implied superstructure in the piece. Instead, he spoke of almost independent links of a chain. Interestingly, the koto part was written completely before the percussion and vocal parts were added. This sort of independent construction is not unique to *Tayutai* as will be discovered in the conclusion. Still, the latter parts can by no means be seen as an accompaniment to a koto solo, for the analysis of the vocal part will show that Shinohara is almost constantly involved in a modern form of word painting – the koto is but one element of this.

Key to chart #1A: For the first three columns see the score.

Density:  0 – Tacet
         1 – Very few notes (less than one/second)
         .....
         5 – Very many notes (ca. ten/second)
         6 – Sound continuum

Descr:  K:1 –  Koto: one specific tone-center (or at most two); each note has a different color; several dynamic changes; tone repetition.

K:2 –  Koto: chordal passage with a tonal basis.

K:3 –  Koto: chordal passages lacking influence by one or two central tones – approaching atonality.

K:4 –  Koto: combination of K:2, K:3 – chordal (may be arpeggiated), somewhat atonal, but repeating a constant lowest pitch.

K:5 –  Koto: atonal passage.

K:6 –  Koto: continuity of sound with free choice of pitches.

KP:1–  Percussive koto technique: an extra timbre is added through the use of (a) stick(s).

KP:2–  Percussive koto technique: Bartók pizzicato.

KP:3– Percussive koto technique: atonal passage.

KP:4– Percussive koto technique: unpitched – *suri-zume*.

KP:5– Percussive koto technique: other unpitched percussive continuity, including use of plectrum.

KP:6– Percussive koto technique: clusters (atonal, aggregate effect).


P:wo– Percussion: wooden board(s) or box(es).

P:st– Percussion: stone plate(s).

P:sh.ch, b.ch, u.ch – Percussion: respectively shell chimes, bamboo chimes and urchin chimes.

Key to chart #1B: For the first three columns, see score.

Fourth column: p= pitched, rp=relatively pitched.

Fifth column: 0=no glissando, 1=rising, 2=falling and 3= both rising and falling motion.

Description: "–" (hyphen) means that at least two rehearsal numbers form a group as far as text treatment is concerned.

## b. The Koto Part

– **Tuning:** One of the most unusual characteristics of the koto part is its tuning (see the prose descriptive page of the score). At reh. num. A not all twelve pitches are present; the IVth string is temporarily tuned to D sharp so that the first truly important tone-center, E, can be approached from close by. At reh. num. B, the IVth string is tuned via B-flat to its permanent pitch, A. At this point all twelve tones are present with only one doubling (triple octave), G-sharp, on strings III and XIII. Here the tuning is vaguely Bergian (thinking of his Violin Concerto), following the four-interval pattern m2, P4, m2, P5... In this way these intervals plus the tritone and m6 are quite present, yielding intervallic contrast between consonant and dissonant adjacent and alternating string. In any event this tuning is a major deviation from traditional koto tunings.

– **Techniques:** It is here that East meets West most frequently. The koto notation list (point 5 of the descriptive page of the score) names a few traditional koto techniques as well as a number of "new fashioned" notational symbols (Bartók pizz., quarter-tone symbols, clusters, etc.).

As far as the Japanese techniques are concerned, for the sake of completeness Willem Adriaansz's well-known reference, *The Kumiuta and Danmoto: Traditions of Japanese Koto Music,* has been consulted. Only four traditional left hand techniques were found that had not been specified by the composer:

> – *En*; e.g., reh. num., A –
> second note: pitch is raised to next higher tone in the scale after being plucked.
> *Kasaneoshi*; e.g., reh. num. A –
> third note: pitch after being plucked is pressed down, released and pressed down again.
> *Oshihanashi*; e.g., reh. num. B –
> second note: pitch is raised and let loose before following tone.
> *Ichijū oshi*; found relatively often – here a string is raised a m2 before being played.

There were no non-notated right hand techniques found that were apparently derived from traditional koto literature.

### c. The Percussion Part + Percussive Koto Effects

As mentioned above, "noise effects", although a relatively unimportant part of traditional koto music, are seen by the composer to be a "natural extension" of pitched, highly timbral material in Japanese music in general. In *Tayutai*, this extension can be found in the form of extended koto techniques and in the fact that the koto player is occasionally requested to utilize a modest assortment of percussion instruments. A quick inspection of chart #1A shows the following: in the description, percussive koto effects (KP) are more common than purely percussive sounds (P). In the former case, half of the extensions are pitched and can be seen as coloristic augmentations to koto techniques. The non-pitched, or highly atonal koto-percussive sounds (KP:4–6, KP:3) are, with exception of a drum-like approach to the instrument (reh. nums. E, O and Q), also coloristic extensions which can be easily related to the traditional sound of the koto. Only the tapping of the underside of the instrument may be seen as one of the less present percussive sounds. This is in fact the longest percussive sound, the chimes being of middle length and the wooden and stone sounds most staccato-like. The extra instruments are almost entirely used for punctuation, termination, contrast, amplification, in short, typical traditional Japanese percussive elements. In this sense, the percussive part is an extension to the koto part and by no means a second instrumental voice.

### d. The Vocal Part

An acquaintance with koto music and a second look at Adriaansz's book for confirmation show that Shinohara has pretty much ignored what might be called standard vocal techniques for koto music. A sole exception is his occasional use of slow-moving vocal glissandi. The text, consisting of twenty-seven single words (only one of which is repeated a second time), is itself a break with koto tradition; it most likely has no link at all with any kind of singing tradition.

The fact is that the vocal part is where the composer's confrontation of hope and despair becomes lyrical, almost literal. Chart #1B illustrates that almost every other word in the text is treated as an example of word painting of one sort or another. The voice, like the instruments, presents a large spectrum of timbres. Fourteen of the words are notated on relative pitches, which adds an element of freedom, comparable to that of the visual notation used throughout. The combination of the vocal colors plus the interrelationships between the words sung and the corresponding musical ambience makes the work quite unique regardless of the application of the traditional approach of word painting.

One can conclude that the composer spent a great deal of effort in finding the correct timbre for each sound/word, an experiment of its own right.

## e. The Three Parts as a Whole: a Few Form Elements

A surprising consistency which arises in the study of *Tayutai* is the presence of diverse symmetries, one of the few relatively tangible architectural devices in the work. Symmetry will be treated empirically to illustrate its variety.

– The koto part at reh. nums. A and BB shows a similar timbral treatment of a central tone with restrained dynamics.

– The voice part begins and terminates with what may be called a poetic treatment of the text: five words at reh. nums. A–C and four words at reh. nums. AA–BB.

– A three-part symmetry can be found at reh. nums. D, N (middle of the work) and Z. The koto part is very dynamic, avoiding any central tone. The voice in the early and middle fragments is treated in hocket fashion with the koto. At reh. num. Z, the vocal part is involved in another symmetry described below.

– Glissandi in the vocal part: reh. nums. I and W contain a rising fifth, reh. nums. K and L rise and fall successively. Only reh. num. Z is exceptional, due to its being the climax of the work in terms of register and dynamics..

– There are two symmetric points of interest in the vocal part in the middle of the work. First reh. nums. K and L form a dynamic pair via the glissandi; this is followed at reh. num. M at which *naze* is twice spoken. Reh. nums. O and Q (with their percussive neighbors P and R) might be considered the symmetric partner of K and L, making more dynamic the two "why's" at reh. num. M.

– Although time-wise the following is not symmetric with respect to the middle-point, reh. nums. K and S are the only two examples of concretely notated atonal chordal movement, with K rising and S descending in direction.

– The amount of relative pitch vocalization of the text is more present in the beginning and at the end of the work and less so in the middle.

– Finally a special local-symmetry of interest can be found between reh. nums. O and Z with reh. num X as turning-point. The first words are all negative in nature (with the possible exception of the word "heart'), the last all positive, with the work's title, "fluctuation", as the balancing point. Provocatively, the instrumental part does not follow this change literally, but more so in terms of musical energy.

Furthermore one could inspect many details of exchange between koto and voice parts in terms of prominence, exchange and so on. However, in chart #2 one finds rather little pitched interchange between the two voices; at points where one would expect symmetric coordination, this is most lacking (e.g., the pitches at the end of the work, the seventh interval at reh. num. BB after the ninth at Y). Also one can hardly speak of nuclear tones in the work, although the double fifth in the koto part A-E-B often comes to prominence along with the ambiguity of the neighboring tritones E-A sharp, F-B.

In fact, when studying *Tayutai* using the rehearsal numbers as links of a twenty-eight part chain (twenty-seven words + one repetition, twenty-eight reh. nums.), one cannot find a superstructure, but instead many handles to grab onto and then drop later on. Symmetry analysis, timbral analysis (including the presence and absence of pitched material) are useful tools, but do not provide *the* key to the work, a key which, due to the work's block-structure, probably does not exist. A word painting analysis is most successful, but implies a very linear structure; *Tayutai* is not so linear.

The reason this writer is not disconcerted by the avoidance of over-definition of the work's form can be found in its notation, that is spatial or visual notation within well-defined boundaries. Shinohara knows at any given moment precisely what he is searching for, but that small amount of freedom in time relationships, in sound-color possibilities, in vocal techniques given to the performer(s) is a reflection of the element of subjectivity, or perhaps better said, the careful avoidance of total-structural thinking that makes formalism only a partial factor of *Tayutai*'s coherence. Do keep in mind that, with the exception of the climax at reh. num. Z where the low D is played every 2", there is a total lack of rhythmical pulse throughout this entire work.

As stated in the hypothesis, descriptive analysis is but one approach to the composition. The following section will try to identify three major influences ("stimuli" may be a more proper word) which led to this work.

## CHART #1A
## KOTO & PERCUSSION PARTS
### Descriptive Typology / Rehearsal Number

| REH NUM | SUM TIME | TIME LEN. | DEN-SITY | Description* |
|---|---|---|---|---|
| A | 0'00 | 34" | 1 | K:1 - accent on timbre. |
| B | 0'34 | 30" | 1 - 4 - 1 | K:1 - retune IV D sharp-B flat-A; KP:4 - at the end. |
| C | 1'04 | 21" | 1 - 4 | K:2 - establishment of three of the primary tones, A, E, F; then P:wo - *gagaku*-like accelerando percussive effect [with less traditional mirror rit. and unexpected $f$ > pp decresc.]; change of ambience; percussion cues *utsuro*. |
| D | 1'25 | 7" | 5 | KP:1,3 - irregular rhythm; grace notes = double fifth A-E-B; rubber sticks used. |
| E | 1'32 | 14" | 6 | KP:5 - rub strings with plastic stick handle + tremolo underside koto -> continuity and exchange with vocal part. |
| F | 1'46 | 5" | 6 - 0 | KP:5 - rub strings to the right of the bridge with wo. stick edge [answer to *osore*]; the first tacet. |
| G | 1'51 | 12" | 1 - 0 | P:wo, b.ch - two loose sounds; an interruption in the tension derived from this first silence; answered by *kanashi* and further silence. |
| H | 2'03 | 15" | 1 | K:2 - tonal fluctuation, ambiguity (fifths above D sharp, E). |
| I | 2'18 | 12" | 1 | K:1 - voice departs on the same note. |
| J | 2'30 | 4" | 5 | KP:6 - fluctuation via clusters (use of rubber stick handle); similar to reh. nums. D, K, S. |
| K | 2'34 | 12" | 2 - 6 | K:1,3 - Two hands, two playing techniques: single note tremolo, chords of 5,6,5,6,7,8,9 notes (fluctuating). |
| L | 2'46 | 17" | 6 | K:1 - contin. of reh. num K (voice departs on this note); and KP:4 - on three different strings. |

| | | | | |
|---|---|---|---|---|
| M | 3'03 | 12" | 1 | P:u.ch - punctuation of end of tremolo; radical change of atmosphere -> 2 x *naze*. |
| N | 3'15 | 7" | 5 | K:5 - first non-chordal atonal fragment. |
| O | 3'22 | 9" | 6 | KP:5 - similar to reh. num. E; plastic stick rubs strings violently; other hand strikes underside of koto quickly, irregularly (here similarity to reh. num. K - two hands, two parts). |
| P | 3'31 | 2" | 1 | P:st - shortest segment = one note interruption of continuity between reh. nums. O, Q; announcement of *midare*; extremely Japanese form of interruption: a discrete, dynamic unpitched sound for breaking up a continuum. |
| Q | 3'33 | 6" | 6 | KP:5 - continuation of reh. num. O. |
| R | 3'39 | 3" | 4 | KP:4 - functions with respect to reh. num. Q as reh. num. F is to reh. num. E; note unusual use of plastic stick handle, and P:st - similar to reh. num. P (i.e. end of disorder); also very short - here not as interruption, but instead as bridge. |
| S | 3'42 | 6" | 2 | K:3 - see also reh. nums. J, K; quasi-cluster all six notes wide; fluctuating lowest note (two chords descend, one ascends, and then three descend); as reh. nums. J, K *ff*. |
| T | 3'48 | 7" | 1 | P:wo x 2, st x 1 - three loose notes - influenced by *Ikari*, percussive objects are struck at their loudest; breaking up of continuity. |
| U | 3'55 | 7" | 5 - 0 | KP:1,3 - use of freely bouncing plastic stick; similar to the six note chords at reh. num. S - here arpeggiated. |
| V | 4'02 | 8" | 5 - 0 | K:1, P:st - single note accelerando with Japanese closing punctuation via percussive strike (although the expected dynamics are reversed!); unique segment surrounded by silence - preparation for reh. num. W. |

| | | | | |
|---|---|---|---|---|
| W | 4'10 | 13" | 6 | K:6 - two hands, two techniques; (see also reh. nums. K, O, and Q); nervous equivalent of vocal part. |
| X | 4'23 | 23" | 1 | K:1 - on note where voice has arrived at reh. num. W; and KP:2 - for timbral variation; the longest segment after the introduction (reh. nums. B, C); point of reflection between textual negative and positive; beginning of dynamic rest. |
| Y | 4'46 | 16" | 1 | K:2, 1 + final glissando - first moment of tonal ambiguity and fluctuation since reh. num. H; resolution on the unexpected note G, although the voice takes over the F at this point; and dynamic rest; only reh. num. which could be divided into two separate parts. |
| Z | 5'02 | 34" | 2 - 3 | K:4, KP:2 - ostinato note is first note in vocal part; segment with the largest register (instrument and voice) and widest dynamic range of the entire work; arrival at dynamic climax of work (end of reh. num. Z); only point of piece defying any form of symmetry. |
| AA | 5'36 | 22" | 6 - 0 - 6 - 0 | KP:5 - similar to reh. num. F; and P: all three ch's - inevitable explosion after reh. num. Z; only use of all three chimes at once; return to tranquillity as in the introduction of the work. |
| BB | 5'58 | 20" | 1 | K:1 - see beginning; koto tacets before final word. |
| end | 6'18 | | | |

*) For the key,: see text; for pitches and dynamics, see chart #2.

# CHART #1B
# VOCAL PART
## Descriptive Typology / Word + Interpretation

| REH NUM | JAPANESE WORD | ENGLISH TRANSL. | PITCHED/ REL.PITCH | GLISS- ANDOS | DESCRIPTION* |
|---------|---------------|-----------------|--------------------|--------------|--------------|
| A | *hitori* | alone | rp | 0 | - First five words = introduction; |
| +A | *iru* | being | rp | 0 | - word painting minimal; |
| B | *yūbe* | evening | rp | 1 | - continuity is suggestive of Japanese *haiku,* with yube being a special concrete word; |
| C | *urei* | anxiety | rp | 0 | - ambiguous, calm atmosphere; first evidence of "psychological fluctuation..."; |
| +C | *utsuro* | emptiness | rp | 0 | - this word staccato with light separation of syllables; solo followed by silence -> emptiness. |
| D | *tanomi* | hope | rp | 0 | staccato; great separation of syllables; first real exchange with koto; hope confronts first dissonant, disordered fragment. |
| E | *osore* | fear | p | 3 | quasi-hocket with koto with repetition of syllable sounds (oso-o-re-e). A sonorous fear in both parts - counterpart of previous hope. |
| (F) | | | | | |
| G | *kanashi* | sad | rp | 0 | half-whisper, introverted (solo) sadness. |
| (H) | | | | | |
| I | *omoi* | thought | p | 1 | - voice prominent above constant koto tone; a rising thought leading to... |
| +I | *kirameki* | sparkle | p | 0 | - ...sparkling in acceleration answered (psychological contrast) even more dynamically be koto clusters. |
| (J) | | | | | |
| K | *nozomi* | wish | p | 1 | - again a psychological coupling with nervous koto playing with addition of drone; here the wish is accompanied by a similar atonal disorder/dissonance -> tension, leading to... |

L    *munashi*    vain          p          2      - ...a descending
                  "in vain" accompanied only by the tremolo
                  drone.

M    *naze* x 2   why           rp         0      twice
                  articulated at approximately the halfway
                  point of the piece. An allusion to Berio's
                  *why?* in "Sequenza V"? First *naze* arrives
                  after first truly percussive explosion;
                  second gains impact due to a koto tacet;
                  symmetry point-1.

N    *mayoi*      hesitation    rp         0      staccato with
                  separated syllables; hocket-like hesitations
                  with the koto.

O    *kurushimi*  suffer        p          (3)    - tremolo
                  nervous suffering, amplified arhythmically
                  by koto; followed, after a sharp   percussive
                  explosion, by...

(P)
Q    *midare*     disorder      P          (3)    -...an equally
                  nervous *midare,* (an important term in koto
                  literature) in the same ambience; the
                  inevitable end to the disorder is the noise-
                  amplifying *suri-zume* along the low strings;
                  symmetry point-2.

(R)
S    *ikari*      anger         rp         0      continuity
                  followed by discreteness; similar atonal
                  ambience as can be found at reh. num. K
                  (wish); local dynamic climax.

(T)
U    *kokoro*     heart         rp         0      three isolated
                  heart beats between two nervous areas (reh.
                  nums. O-S, W); also placed between non-
                  rhythmical isolated koto fragments; second
                  concrete word in piece -> most poetic moment
                  since reh. num. C.

(V)
W    *nayumi*     trouble       p          2(,3)  literal
                  trembling in all parts.

X    *tayutai*    fluctuation   p          0(!) - ironically
                  stable fluctuation; only the koto F sharps
                  fluctuate; turning point between several
                  negative and positive words in text; music
                  reminiscent of beginning of piece.

Y    *akogare*    yearning      p          0      two single tones
                  (voice - F, koto - primarily G) striving for
                  consonance.

Z  *yorokobi*  joy             p          1      - as joy leads
                to radiance, the largest glissando, widest
                vocal and koto ranges are presented...

+Z  *kagayaki*  radiance        p          1      - ...leading to
                the dynamic climax of the work - confirmed
                by percussive chime explosion at
                the beginning of the following reh. num. AA.

AA  *tomoshibi*  light          rp         0      - conclusion
                (four words) similar to introduction; relative
                calm; isolated sounds, each of
                great coloristic importance;

+AA  *furusato*  home           rp         0      - home = third
                concrete word -> more poetic influence -
                made clear through delivery in silence;

BB  *negai*      desire         p          0      - interval
                between voice and koto is inversion of reh.
                num. Y; half-whisper = sound of desire;

+BB  *ai*        love           rp         0      - as "h o m e", in
                total silence; possible happy ending left to
                the discretion of the listener.


*) For the key: see text; for pitches and dynamics, see chart #2.

## CHART #2
## Weighted Transcription of Most Prominent
## Pitched Material and Dynamics
## Including Pitch Correspondences

dynamics: **ppp** & **pp** - 1, **p** - 2, **mp** - 3, **m*f*** - 4, ***f*** - 5, ***ff*** - 6,

**A** = atonal;  no  weighting  possible.

## 4. *TAYUTAI*'S THREE DIMENSIONS

Sometimes when traveling one spends more time on the road than at certain destinations. To arrive at this section *Tayutai* had to be looked at in detail. Charts will not be necessary in discussing influence. The aim here is to see where *Tayutai* came from, at which points Shinohara broke loose from the various "traditions", and finally to pose the question of the great importance of innovation, that is experimentation in this work.

### a. Japanese Music Tradition, among others
Makoto Shinohara is a Japanese composer who has lived in Europe since the 1950s. yet he is seen by several musicians of his own country as one of the most Japanese (i.e., not as an internationalist) of today's composers. Certainly one can find works by Shinohara which pose great problems when looked upon from the Japanese perspective only; *Tayutai*, on the other hand, is one of the most explicitly Japan-influenced of the works.

The instrument in question leads to such extreme associations with Japanese tradition, that it is hard to disconnect the instrument from its own literature. (A majority of the few attempts that have been recorded seem to have led to inferior pop-like studies.) Nevertheless, the koto offers great potential to the modern composer. As Japanese tradition and contemporary music both concentrate on sound color to a great extent, alternative rhythms and rhythmical structures, the liberation of the note, or the sound, the choice of the instrument with its percussive extension is a logical one. Shinohara, fortunately, has honored the instrument while exploring its sound potential simultaneously.

Although the vocal part to *Tayutai* is not Japanese in terms of its techniques, the approach is seemingly influenced by Japanese poetry which easier relates non-associated words like "being" with "evening" than one is accustomed to in the West. The introverted ambience of the entire work is quite possibly influenced by Japanese poetic tradition as well. Also the fact that the koto player is requested to perform the vocal part conforms to tradition.

The punctuating role of the percussion instruments has deep Japanese (or Eastern) roots. It fits so naturally into the continuity of the piece that one wonders why this trio was not discovered earlier in traditional music. Shinohara's use of visual notation may seem ultra-modern at first view, yet it would be virtually impossible to capture the essence of Japanese musical color, time expression and emotion otherwise.

Yet tradition does not limit itself to Japan. Word painting is an international phenomenon. Shinohara may very well find himself on a list with Janequin, Monteverdi and Schumann in future music history surveys. His approach to word painting may differ from the known Western models, but diachronically, word-sonorous associations have changed radically. Shinohara's associations are obviously contemporary ones.

Even the recent past has created certain traditions for today's composers. Shonohara's French and German years coincided with a period in which a new tradition was evolving in and around Darmstadt. His Darmstadt influence is the subject of the second dimension.

## b. Die Darmstadt Schule und ein Japaner

When one thinks of Darmstadt, one thinks of works like Messiaen's *Mode de valeurs et d'intensités*, Boulez's *Structures I & II*, and the Stockhausen *Klavierstücke*. Of course non-neoserialists were present at this famous crossroads; yet, the main subject of early Darmstadt was *Die Reihe* and everything that had to do with it, its parameters, its combinatorial potential, its subharmonic series, and so on.

Shinohara has always been an independent composer, never a true-blue member of any school of composition; still, Darmstadt and especially Stockhausen had their influence on him. Shinohara has not written a truly serial piece here, but has, by the nature of this totally new koto tuning, allowed himself to try out some Darmstadt techniques in this work. He has also written the piece parametrically, if only in the sense that one entire part was completed before the other was begun!

His studies with Messiaen are evident in the use of a block-structure in the piece. Although Varèse was probably the composer who brought this sort of approach to the fore, Messiaen applied it in his own way from the 1940s onward. It is unimaginable that Messiaen would ever take the approach to the extreme of *Tayutai*; on the other hand, Japanese tradition has nothing comparable to offer. In this sense, Shinohara is assimilating the old traditions with the new in this work.

Obviously the great presence of tone-color study has been slightly influence by the Darmstadt years. It was in Darmstadt that tone color was liberated to a full-time partner of pitch, rhythm and dynamics as far as parametric thinking is concerned in composed Western music.

A Darmstadt composer, whose way of innovation was, in those years, a very personal one was Luciano Berio, translating *Die Reihe* into his native tongue for use in a very special series of works known as *Sequenze*. In these works Darmstadt is only half present. Berio is busy rediscovering the possibility of rows (which became less and less present in his later pieces); at the same time, he was busy discovering experimentally and *musically* the sound potential of various instruments. In other words, his experiment was not only one of sound parameters.

Shinohara has definitely appreciated the *Sequenze* by writing one of his own. The source of the ultimate sound search on a given instrument can be found in Berio. yet the coupling of this research with tradition is his own. It is in fact this association which makes *Tayutai* so experimental.

## c. Experimental Music for Koto

*Tayutai* has been inspired by a great deal of musical sources and in so doing is totally unique. It is a large-scale experiment of assimilation incorporating various traditions, old and new, techniques of contemporaries and even older techniques of the composer, himself. "Where is there breathing room for creation with all these influences?", one may ask. In fact bringing these highly different approaches, sounds, words, emotions, and techniques together leaves the composer with a great deal of freedom, and an even greater challenge to:

1) not overly abuse or make overly present one of the influences,
2) combine dissimilar elements,
3) add something new, and
4) find proportions that have never existed before (i.e., to assimilate the dissimilar).

Herein lies the challenge of *Tayutai*, a truly modern, experimental composition exploiting accessible information which in principle does not belong together. This combination projected onto the musical field of composition yields and experiment *pur sang*, an experiment in which the dose of innovation, despite the number of influential sources, is by definition high.

Many have said that experimental music has been losing energy since the 1960s; yet one wonders whether those who support such claims have not been keeping track of this sort of assimilation-music. In fact an important part of today's experimental is based on this very principle. Shinohara is an overt case; he has demonstrated that assimilation deserves evaluation and reaction and a greater evolution.

## 5.  SOME CONCLUSIONS AND COMPARISONS

It has often been said that all first, and possibly all second world inhabitants are members of an enormous consumer society. One can purchase products fabricated throughout the world; one can also listen to music of all ages and all cultures. It comes as no surprise with the omnipresence of information in these cultures that an artist turn to assimilation as a source of inspiration.

*Tayutai* is an excellent example of the combination of various traditions with various contemporary elements as the basis of a music composition. This chapter has been an attempt to locate some important points of assimilation through the use of traditional, descriptive empirical analysis.

Shinohara's *Tayutai* is not his only work which deserves this sort of attention. Other clearly Japan-influenced works are worthy of mention: *Kyūdō A* and *B* (In Quest of Enlightenment) is a particularly interesting case. The "A" version (1974) is for a solo shakuhachi player. The "B" version, written a year earlier, is for shakuhachi and harp (East meets West yet again). The "A" version is simply the extraction of the shakuhachi part from the "B" version. Is the "A" version emptier, incomplete? Is the harp unnecessary? Other works of interest are his *Nagare* (Flow–1981) for shamisen and bells, *Juhichigen-No-Umare* (Birth of the Bass Koto – 1981) for bass koto solo, and *Turns* (1983) for violinist and koto player or violinist alone. Equally interesting are his electronic works, such as his *Mémoires* (1966) and *Broadcasting* (1974), which deserve a similar treatment, be it through the looking-glass of modern technology.

In future discussions and analyses of today's music, especially that which fits into the experimental category, it is hoped that one add the questions of the sources of the employed musical material and of assimilation to the list of planned topics. In this way one might better understand how, to use a contemporary term, information is processed in recent compositions.

The author would like to thank the composer without whom it would have been impossible to accumulate and arrange this chapter's materials. Also thanks are due to Zen-on Music, Tokyo, for permission to print the entire score along with this text.

1) This text is a slightly modified version of an article that appeared in *Interface* 16/1–2 (1987): 75–96.
2) Recorded on: JVC-Victor (Japan])KVX-1102.

1. 13 strings (indicated by I to XIII in the score) are tuned at first as follows:

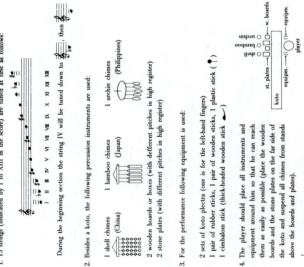

I  II  III  IV  V  VI  VII  VIII  IX  X  XI  XII  XIII

During the beginning section the string IV will be tuned down to [notation], then [notation].

2. Besides a koto, the following percussion instruments are used:

1 shell chimes (China)    1 bamboo chimes (Japan)    1 urchin chimes (Philippines)

2 wooden boards or boxes (with defferent pitches in high register)

2 stone plates (with different pitches in high register)

3. For the performance following equipment is used:

2 sets of koto plectra (one is for the left-hand fingers)

1 pair of rubber sticks, 1 pair of wooden sticks, 1 plastic stick ( )

1 cimbalom stick (thick-headed wooden stick )

4. The player should place all instruments and equipment around him so that he can reach them as easily as possible (place the wooden boards and the stone plates on the far side of the koto and suspend all chimes from stands above the boards and plates).

5.
x — damp the resonance of the string

● — let the string resonate

ord — ordinary

NR — near the ryūkaku (ryūkaku is the name of the string-holder at the right end of the koto)

OFFR — off the ryūkaku

L — left hand

R — right hand

∿ — yuri-iro (vibrato)

— tsuki-iro (quick fluctuation to a higher pitch after the attack)

— hiki-iro (quick fluctuation to a lower pitch after the attack)

— suri-zume (rub along the string with the plectrum to left or right)

— sukui-zume (pluck the string with the back of the plectrum)

— with the finger tip

— keshi-zume (a fingernail of the left hand lightly touches the end of the string before the attack. The string gives a twanging sound with a buzzing vibration.) in one movement the plectrum plucks the string 1 vigorously and immediately afterwards strikes the wooden body.

— mute (a finger-tip of the left hand touches the end of the string before the attack. The sound becomes damped and loses the resonance.)

■ — strike the ryūgaku (ryūgaku is the name of the wooden surface at the extreme right end of the koto.)

— cluster

— 1 quarter tone higher than # ♮

— accelerando

— ritardando

— fluctuating rhythm

● — normal (for the voice)

○ — whisper (for the voice)

— between normal and whisper (for the voice)

6. In the vocal part of the score pitches are indicated sometimes absolutely by traditional notation and sometimes relatively by visual notation.

The vocal part is written for a male voice with the range [notation]. For the female voice all notes must be transposed an octave higher.

7. The vocal part and the instrumental part are intended to be executed by a single performer, but a duet performance by a singer and a koto-player is possible.

8. The indication of duration in seconds, given for each passage, is approximate. The duration of each sound is relatively determined by the visual notation.

9. The duration of the whole piece is about 7 minutes.

288

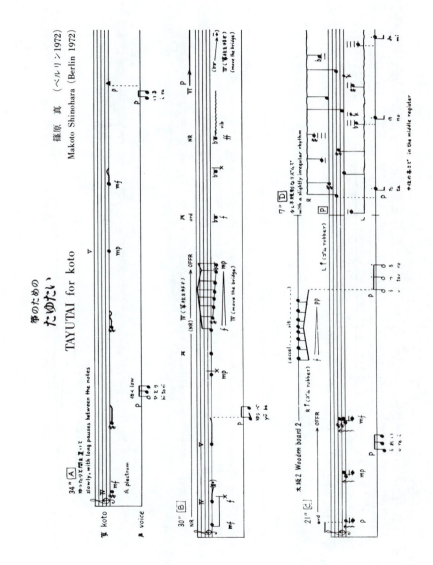

箏のための
たゆたい
TAYUTAI for koto

篠原 真 （ベルリン1972）
Makoto Shinohara (Berlin 1972)

289

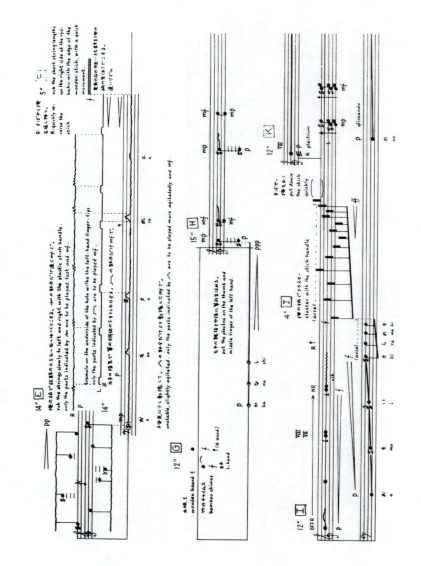

290

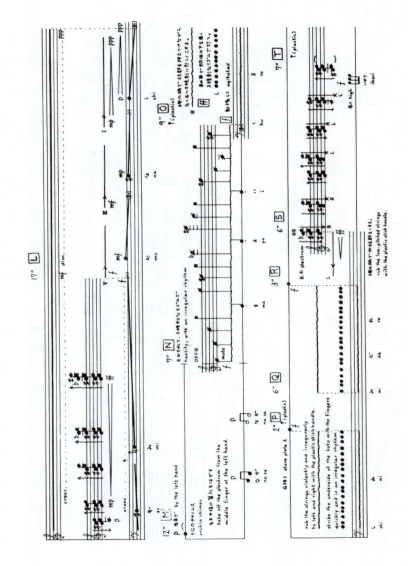

291

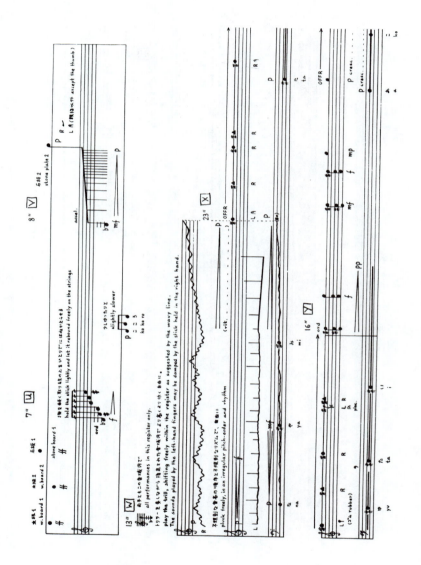

292

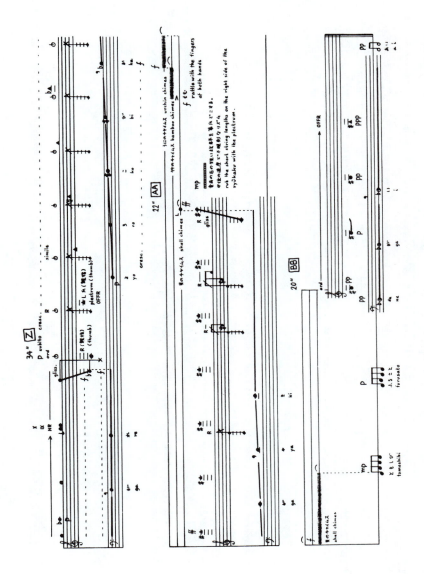

# Bibliography

Adriaansz, Willem
  1973  The Kumiuta and Danmoto: Traditions of Japanese
        Koto Music. Berkeley: University of California
        Press.

Attali, Jacques
  1977  Bruits. Paris: Presses Universitaires de France.
        (English ed. Noise – The Political Economy of Music.
        Manchester: Manchester University Press [Vol. 16 –
        *Theory and History of Literature* series] – 1985)

Barlow, Clarence
  1980  *Busreise nach Parametron...*, Neuland Jahrbuch
        1:114–118.

Behrman, David
  1965  *What Indeterminate Notation Determines*,
        Perspectives of New Music Spring/Summer 1965
        3/1:58–73.

Benitez, Joaquim M.
  1978  *Avant-garde or Experimental? Classifying
        Contemporary Music*, International Review of
        Aesthetics and Sociology in Music IX/1:53–77.

Berio, Luciano
  1987  *Poésie et Musique – Une Expérience*, Contrechamps
        No. 1:24–35 (original Italian version – 1959).

295

Blumröder, Christoph von
1982a   *Parameter*, in Hans Heinrich Eggebrecht, ed.
        Handwörterbuch der Musikalischen Terminologie.
        Wiesbaden: Franz Steiner (first printing-1972):8pp.
1982b   *Formel-Komposition, Minimal Music, Neue
        Einfachkeit. Musikalische Konzeptionen der
        Siebziger Jahre,* Neuland Jahrbuch Band 2, 1981/82:
        183–205.


Boehmer, Konrad
1967    Zur Theorie der offenen Form in der neuen Musik.
        Darmstadt: Ed. Tonos.
1970    *Experimentelle Musik,* Musik in Geschichte und
        Gegenwart, Supplement E–Z. Basel, 155–161.


Bookchin, Murray
1974    Post-Scarcity Anarchism. London: Wildwood House.


Brown, Earle
1966    *On Form,* Darmstädter Beiträge zur neuen Musik
        10:57–69.


Cage, John
1961    Silence. Middletown, CT: Wesleyan University
        Press.
1968    A Year from Monday. Middletown, CT: Wesleyan
        University Press.
1969    Notations. West Glovar, VT: Something Else Press.
1981    For the Birds. In Conversation with Daniel Charles.
        London, Salem, NH: Marian Boyars   (orig. French
        version: Pour les Oiseaux. Paris: Belfond, 1976).


Cardew, Cornelius
1961    *Notation – Interpretation,* Tempo 58:21–33.


Cardew, Cornelius, ed.
1972    Scratch Music. Cambridge, Mass.: M.I.T. Press.

Charles, Daniel
1978  Gloses sur John Cage. Paris: 10-18.
1979  John Cage oder Die Musik ist los. Berlin: Merwe
(similar, but not identical to "Gloses").

Chion, Michel
1983  Guide des Objets Sonores: Pierre Schaeffer et la
Recherche Musicale. Paris: Eds. Buchet/Chastel &
INA.

Chopin, Henri
1979  Poésie Sonore International. Paris: Jean-Michel
Place.

Clarke, Eric F.
1987  *Levels of Structure in the Organization of Musical
Time*, Contemporary Music Review 2/1:211–238.

De Lio, Thomas
1981a *Sound, Gesture and Symbol: The Relation between
Notation and Structure in American Experimental
Music*, Interface 10:199–219.
1981b *Structural Pluralism: Some Observations on the
Nature of Open Structure in the Music and Visual
Arts of the Twentieth Century*, Musical Quarterly
LXVII/4 10/81:527–543.
1983  *Toward an Art of Imminence: Morton Feldman's
"Durations 3, III"*, Interface 12:465–480.

Dickson, David
1978  Alternative Technology and the Politics of Change.
Glasgow: Fontana Collins.

Dominick, Lisa
1983  *Mode and Movement in Recent Works of Ton de
Leeuw*, Key Notes 17:15–23.

Dreßen, Norbert
1982  Sprache und Musik bei Luciano Berio:
Untersuchungen zu seinen Vokalkompositionen.
Regensburg: Gustav Bosse Verlag.

Eco, Umberto
  1977    Das offene Kunstwerk. Frankfurt/Main: Suhrkamp
          (orig. Opera aperta 1962).

Eimert, Herbert and Hans Ulrich Humpert
  1973    Das Lexicon der elektronischen Musik.
          Regensburg: Gustav Bosse.

Emmerson, Simon, ed.
  1986    The Language of Electroacoustic Music. Hampshire:
          MacMillan Press.
          (Contains articles by Emmerson, Wishart, Smalley,
          Keane, Pennycock, McNabb, Truax, Harvey, Boulez
          and Machover.)

Erickson, Robert
  1975    Sound Structure in Music. Berkeley: University of
          California Press.

Fink, Robert and Robert Ricci
  1975    The Language of 20th Century Music. A Dictionary
          of Terms. New York: Schirmer.

Griffiths, Paul
  1980    *Avant-garde*, The New Grove Dictionary of Music
          and Musicians. London: MacMillan,  742–743.
  1981    Modern Music. The Avant-garde since 1945.
          London: J. M. Dent.
          (NB: Note Griffiths' change of approach in this
          book!)

de Groot, Rokus
  1986    *Aspects of Ton de Leeuw's Musical Universe*, Key
          Notes 23:17–31.

Häusler, Josef
  1969    Musik im 20. Jahrhundert. Bremen: Schünemann.

Haubenstock Ramati, Roman
  1965    *Notation – Material and Form*, Perspectives of New
          Music 4/1:39–44.

Helm, Everett
1979    *The Music of Ton de Leeuw*, Key Notes 9:3–13.

Hiller, Lejaren, jr. and Leonard M. Isaacson
1979    Experimental Music. Composition with an
        Electronic Computer. Westport, CT: Greenwood
        Press (first printing – 1959).

Hofstadter, Douglas R.
1979    Gödel, Escher, Bach: an Eternal Braid. London:
        Harvester Press.

ten Hoopen, Christiane.
1986    De Nauwkeurig Genoteerde Telvervaging bij György
        Ligeti. Amsterdam: "Doktoraal" Thesis (Univerity of
        Amsterdam). A shorter resumé or this thesis can be
        found in: *Statische Musik: Zu Ligetis Befreiung der
        Musik von Taktschlag durch präzise Notation,*
        MusikTexte 28/29 (March, 1989): 68–72.

Karkoschka, Erhard
1966    Das Schriftbild der neuen Musik. Celle: Moeck.

Kostelanetz, Richard, ed.
1970    John Cage. New York: Praeger.

Klüppelholz, Werner and Lothar Prox, ed.
1985    Mauricio Kagel. Das filmische Werk I: 1965–1985.
        Amsterdam: Meulenhoff/Landshoff.

Landy, Leigh
1981    *Music and Politics: A Reply,* EAR Magazine 6/3:3.
1982    *New Music and the Media, or Mr Businessman's
        "Veni, Vendidi, Vici" (I came, I advertised, I
        conquered),* EAR Magazine 7/2:3,4.
1983a   *New? Notation,* EAR Magazine 8/1-2:11–16.
1983b   *Foutloos Musiceren: Techniek vs. Technologie
        (Performance without Errors: Technique vs.
        Technology),* Politiek en Sociale Vorming. 1/3:12–
        14.

(Landy, Leigh)

1984    *At a Fork on the Way*, EAR Magazine 8/5, 9/1, 9/2, 9/3 (ms-87pp).

1985    *Das Studium der experimentellen Musik an der Universität Amsterdam: Befreiung oder Isolierung der neuen Musik?*, Musik und Bildung 10/Okt.:693–694, 703.

1987a   *Comp(exp♪)* ≅ $f_t$ *(Σ "parameters" (∿))*, Avant Garde No. 0 "Presentation":27–40.

1987b   *An Analysis of* Tayutai *for Koto (1972) Composed by* Makoto Shinohara. *A 3-Dimensional Approach*, Interface 16:75–96.

1988    *How Often Have You* Seen *Your Compositions Performed? A Plea for More Audio-visual Collaborations in Experimental Music*, Interface 17:241–249.

1989    *John C* Ⓐ *G E: Anarchist Musician*, Avant Garde No. 3 "Anarchia":67–84.


de Leeuw, Ton

1976    *Composers' Voice*, Key Notes 3:66–74.


Ligeti, György

1973    *Apropos Musik und Politik*, Darmstädter Beiträge zur neuen Musik XIII:42–46.


Loevendie, Theo

1977    *Existing Gaps Can Be Narrowed*, Key Notes 5:32–41.


Marcuse, Herbert

1964    One-Dimensional Man. Boston: Beacon Press.


Mertens, W(im)

1980    De Amerikaanse Repetitieve Muziek. Bierbeek, Belgium: Vergaelen. (There is also an English translation: American Minimal Music. London: Kahn and Averill [1988].)


Meyer-Eppler, Werner

1953    *Elektronische Kompositionstechnik*, Melos 20 1/1953:5–9.

Mion, Philippe, Jean-Jacques Nattiez and Jean-Christophe
    Thomas
    1982    L'envers d'une œuvre: *De Natura Sonorum* de
            Bernard Parmegiani. Paris: Eds. Buchet/Chastel &
            INA. (Recording: *INA/GRM* AM714.0.)

Müller, Heiner
    1986    Gesammelte Irrtümer. Frankfurt: Verlag der
            Autoren.

Nettl, Bruno
    1974    *Thoughts on Improvisation: A Comparative
            Approach,* Musical Quarterly LX/11/74:1–19.

Nono, Luigi
    1960    *The Historical Reality of Music Today,* The Score
            27:41–45.

Nyman, Michael
    1974    Experimental Music. Cage and Beyond. New York:
            Schirmer.

Oliveros, Pauline
    1984    Software for People. Baltimore: Smith Publications.

Pauli, Hansjörg
    1971    Für wen komponieren Sie eigentlich?.
            Frankfurt/Main: Fischer.

Paynter, John
    1982    Music in the Secondary School Curriculum: Trends
            and Developments in Class Music Teaching.
            Cambridge: Cambridge University Press.

Paynter, John and Peter Aston
    1970    Sound and Silence: Classroom Projects in Creative
            Music. Cambridge: Cambridge University Press.

Prigogine, Ilya and Isabelle Stengers
    1985    Order Out of Chaos: Man's New Dialogue with
            Nature. London: Flamingo/Fontana.

Reich, Steve
    1974   Writings about Music. New York: New York
            University Editions and Halifax: The Press of the
            Nova Scotia College of Art and Design.

Reszler, André
    1973   L'esthétique anarchiste. Vendôme: Presses
            universitaires de France.

Sabbe, Herman
    1987   *Das erste der* Zehn Stücke für Bläserquintett,
            Musikkonzepte 53: 48–57.

Schaefer, John
    1987   New Sounds: A Listener's Guide to New Music.
            New York: Harper & Row.

Schaeffer, Pierre
    1966   Traité des Objets Musicaux. Paris: Eds. du Seuil.
    1973   La Musique Concrète. Paris: Presses universitaires
            de France.
    1977   *Vers une Musique Expérimentale,* Revue musicale
            303–305 (first published in no. 246, 1957).

Schafer, R. Murray
    1976   Creative Music Education. NY: Schirmer.
    1977   The Tuning of the World. New York: Knopf.

Schillenger, Joseph
    1941   The Schillenger System of Musical Composition
              (2 vols.) New York: Carl Fisher (1978 repr. NY: Da
            Capo). (+ see also von Blumröder.)

Slawson, Wayne
    1985   Sound Color. Berkeley: Univiversity of California
            Press.

Sohm, Hans, ed.
    1970   Happening and Fluxus: Materialien. Cologne:
            Kölnischer Kunstverein.

Stockhausen, Karlheinz
  1963   Texte I zur elektronischen und instrumentalen
         Musik (1952–1962). Cologne: DuMont.
  1964   Texte 2 zu eigenen Werken – zur Kunst Anderer –
         Aktuelles (1952–1962). Cologne: DuMont.
  1971   Texte 3 zur Musik (1963–1971). Cologne: DuMont.
  1978   Texte 4 zur Musik (1970–1977). Cologne: DuMont.
  1989a  Texte 5 zur Musik (1977–1984) "Komposition",
         Cologne: DuMont.
  1989b  Texte 6 zur Musik (1977–1984) "Interpretation",
         Cologne: DuMont.

Stoianova, Ivanka
  1987   *Heilmittel: Konzerte in Paris mit Xenakis –
         Uraufführungen.* MusikTexte  19 4/1987:53–54.

"Webster"
  1968   *Experiment,*  Webster's New World Dictionary:
         College Edition. New York: Signet.

Wilson, Peter
  1984   Empirische Untersuchungen zur Wahrnehmung
         von Geräuschstrukturen. Hamburg: Schriftenreihe
         zur Musik Bd. 23 – Verlag der Musikalienhandlung
         Karl Dieter Wagner.

Wishart, Trevor
  1985   On Sonic Art. York: Imagineering Press (incl. 2
         cassette tapes).

Wolff, Christian
  1987   *Open to Whom and to What,* Interface 16/3:133–141.

Xenakis, Iannis
  1971   Formalized Music. Bloomington: University of
         Indiana Press.

Zeller, Hans Rudolf, ed.
  1979   Cage Box: John Cage Festival. Bonn.

Zimmermann, Walter
    1981   <u>Insel Musik</u>. Cologne: Beginner's Press (see part 2: *Desert Plants*).

# Index of names